Asset Forfeiture and Insolvency

A Parallel Case Management Guide

Karen M. Gebbia
Honorable Lisa Hill Fenning
EDITORS

Cover design by Catherine Zaccarine.

The materials contained herein represent the opinions of the authors and/or the editors, and should not be construed to be the views or opinions of the law firms or companies with whom such persons are in partnership with, associated with, or employed by, nor of the American Bar Association or the Business Law Section unless adopted pursuant to the bylaws of the Association.

Nothing contained in this book is to be considered as the rendering of legal advice for specific cases, and readers are responsible for obtaining such advice from their own legal counsel. This book is intended for educational and informational purposes only.

© 2019 American Bar Association. All rights reserved.

No part of this publication may be reproduced, stored in a retrieval system, or transmitted in any form or by any means, electronic, mechanical, photocopying, recording, or otherwise, without the prior written permission of the publisher. For permission contact the ABA Copyrights & Contracts Department, copyright@americanbar.org, or complete the online form at http://www.americanbar.org/utility/reprint.html.

Printed in the United States of America.

23 22 21 20 19   5 4 3 2 1

ISBN: 978-1-64105-542-0

Discounts are available for books ordered in bulk. Special consideration is given to state bars, CLE programs, and other bar-related organizations. Inquire at Book Publishing, ABA Publishing, American Bar Association, 321 N. Clark Street, Chicago, Illinois 60654-7598.

www.shopABA.org

Special acknowledgment to: the Subcommittee on Asset Forfeiture and Bankruptcy, whose members contributed substantially to the development of this guidebook. The Subcommittee is an initiative of the American Bar Association, Business Law Section, and serves as a working group of the Bankruptcy Court Structure and Insolvency Process Committee (BCSIP) and the Business Bankruptcy Committee (BBC). The Editors thank the current and recent chairs of BCSIP, namely, Sharon Z. Weiss, Hon. Jean K. FitzSimon, and William H. Schorling, and BBC, namely, Kay S. Kress, Patricia A. Redmond, and Michael St. Patrick Baxter, for their support of this project.

The Subcommittee members include the authors and editors of this guidebook together with Hons. David Coar (ret.), Samuel L. Bufford (ret.), Martin Glenn, Christopher M. Klein, Steven W. Rhodes (ret.); Messrs. Michael St. Patrick Baxter, John W. Kozyak, Lawrence G. McMichael, Gerald F. Munitz, Ronald R. Peterson, Irving H. Picard, William H. Schorling, Gerald K. Smith; and Mmes. Sheila M. Gowan, Sharon Cohen Levin, and Kathy Bazoian Phelps. Professor Gebbia served as Subcommittee Chair, Mr. Leipold as Vice-Chair, and Professors Dodge and Zimmerman and Co-Reporters, at the time this guidebook was written.

The authors and editors thank the following BCSIP attorneys who proofread and updated the final manuscript: Jesús Miguel Palomares, Patricia J. Friesinger, Terry E. Hall, Krista L. Kulp, Shawn A. Etemadi, and Morgan Fashtchi.

This guidebook and the work of the Subcommittee have benefited significantly from clarifications and commentary provided by representatives of the Department of Justice (DOJ), Securities and Exchange Commission (SEC), Executive Office for United States Trustees, and the Executive Office for United States Attorneys. These materials have not been approved or adopted by any governmental agency.

Contents

Introduction 1
Karen M. Gebbia

Chapter 1
   Essential Tensions Between Asset Forfeiture and Insolvency 4
   Karen M. Gebbia

Chapter 2
   Statutory Framework: Bankruptcy Cases and Proceedings 21
   Henry C. Kevane

Chapter 3
   Statutory Framework: Asset Forfeiture Proceedings 51
   Sarah N. Welling & Jane Lyle Hord

Chapter 4
   Coordination of Multiple Proceedings 68
   Adam S. Zimmerman

Chapter 5
   Case Management Orders, Coordination Agreements, and Cooperation Agreements 83
   Jaime L. Dodge

Glossaries:
   I.   Terms, Definitions, and Acronyms 104
   II. Federal Governmental Agencies Involved in Forfeiture and Parallel Proceedings 108
   Miriam Weismann

Appendices:
   A.   American Bar Association House of Delegates Resolution 102A (February 2014) and Report and Recommendation 111
   B.   Brief Summaries of Key Forfeiture Statutes 117

- C. Brief Summaries of Major Cases Involving Both Forfeiture Proceedings and Insolvency Proceedings 126
- D. Standards and Procedures Governing Substitute Property 143
- E. DOJ Guidelines on Minimum Net Equity Levels Prior to Forfeiture 145
- F. Summary of the US Trustees Manual—Treatment of Parallel Proceedings 146
- G. Sample Coordination Agreements and Related Orders 151
- H. Case Management Sample Order 153
- I. Links to Related Materials 157

About the Editors and Co-Authors 158

Introduction

This guidebook is the product of an interdisciplinary and interagency working group that was organized under the auspices of the American Bar Association (ABA). Since 2010, the group has been studying and seeking solutions for recurring tensions between governmental enforcement proceedings involving the forfeiture of a wrongdoer's assets, on the one hand, and insolvency proceedings that assert jurisdiction over the disposition of the same assets, on the other hand. As a result of the working group's report and recommendations, the ABA adopted a resolution in February 2014 encouraging all of the entities, agencies, and courts involved in overlapping forfeiture proceedings and insolvency proceedings to develop protocols and work toward enactment of appropriate legislative and rules changes to address these complex intersections. (The ABA Resolution appears as Appendix A.)

The challenges addressed here have arisen largely as the result of the rapid evolution of forfeiture law and its perceived encroachment on traditional insolvency law. Neither substantive nor procedural law has kept pace with this evolution. This guidebook identifies the regulatory schemes, parties, interests, competing considerations, and policies that are at stake, with the objective of assisting the courts in making fully informed decisions. The purpose of this guidebook is to identify the differences between the forfeiture and insolvency processes, for the courts' and parties' understanding. The descriptions of the different processes and of the potential consequences of those differences are not intended to suggest that one process may be favored over the other, nor to suggest how the courts should rule on any substantive tensions that courts might perceive in those differences, nor to alter in any way current protections for crime victims. It is not the guidebook's purpose to determine whether inequities exist, to recommend how the courts should resolve any perceived inequities, or to consider what congressional action, if any, might be taken. Rather, the guidebook is designed to identify the underlying statutes and rules, articulate the positions and arguments the courts are likely to encounter, and provide courts with resources for managing these cases. These resources include links and references to governmental agency websites and materials, as well as summaries of positions trustees generally assert. A robust understanding of these complexities and competing positions, and access to these resources, will aid the courts in administering these cases and ruling on any settlements, including coordination and cooperation agreements, the parties might propose.

Governmental agencies have the power (indeed, often the duty) to apply forfeiture and disgorgement laws to seize assets involved in a criminal enterprise or garnered by violation of securities or other laws. The forfeiture laws permit seized assets to be distributed to innocent owners or to victims harmed by the underlying wrongful activity, or to be retained by law enforcement agencies under equitable sharing programs. DOJ and SEC policy guidelines elaborate procedures and priorities governing the use and application of seized assets.

Seizure of assets by forfeiture often strips the targeted person or enterprise of essential funds necessary for daily existence. The targeted entity or its creditors may seek the protection of the bankruptcy courts (or, more rarely, other insolvency regimes) either as a proactive measure before the seizure or as a reactive measure after seizure. The entitlement and distributional principles that insolvency law applies to the assets typically differ significantly from the principles forfeiture law applies because insolvency proceedings account for not only innocent owners and victims, but also potentially senior or equal rights of the targeted entity's trade and other creditors.

When these two legal schemes intersect, the government and bankruptcy estate typically both seek control and distribution of the same assets. Unless the government and bankruptcy estate can reach an agreement about how to proceed, a battle may erupt. Such battles involve far more than a mere procedural turf war. The divergent rules and policies governing forfeiture and insolvency may result in the exact same claimants receiving profoundly different distributions, depending on which scheme is applied. Moreover, because there may be only partial, rather than complete, overlap between the claimants and assets subject to each proceeding, some claimants may receive distributions if forfeiture law is applied, but none if insolvency law is applied, and vice versa.

Ultimately, statutory amendments or determinative judicial rulings may be necessary to resolve the substantive conflicts between forfeiture law and insolvency law. Even when (if) substantive legal changes do occur, the judges managing these cases will continue to face complicated procedural coordination issues. The courts overseeing these proceedings today and in the future have significant opportunities to manage these complex intersections in ways that reduce litigation and conflict, and expedite and enhance recoveries to injured persons. As elaborated herein, these judicial management strategies include:

- early and carefully targeted status conferences;
- awareness of the players in the parallel proceedings and of means of encouraging communication among those players, where appropriate;
- case management orders;
- intercourt communication;
- in appropriate cases, joint hearings between bankruptcy court judges and district court judges or other judges overseeing different proceedings in different courts; and
- in appropriate cases, hearing and approval of coordination agreements that settle procedural, evidentiary, and substantive disputes, including with respect to asset allocation and distribution.

Most of the reported cases involve interactions between federal forfeiture law and federal bankruptcy law. The principles addressed, however, are generally applicable to interactions between all types of insolvency proceedings and both forfeiture and disgorgement proceedings, whether they involve multiple federal courts, multiple state courts, federal and state courts, or cross-border implications. This guidebook notes any significant divergences where appropriate.

Additional Background Resources

A general overview of these tensions is available in a Federal Judicial Center (FJC) video titled *Asset Forfeiture and Bankruptcy Case Coordination*, available at Federal Judiciary Channel (Jan. 16, 2014), https://www.youtube.com/watch?v=kQlPZLpg6HE&feature=c4-overview&list=UUIcgGfaeUGYJSo7bLeUr1hw.

Citations and links to governmental agency websites and materials are collected in the appendices to this guidebook.

Other useful background resources include: Symposium, *A Cross-Disciplinary Dialogue: White Collar Fraud, Asset Forfeiture, and Bankruptcy*, 42 Golden Gate L. Rev. 525 (2012) (eight articles); a Business Law Today July 2012 mini-theme series titled *Fraud and the Intersection Between Crime, Bankruptcy and Asset Forfeiture* (five articles); and the Report and Recommendation supporting ABA Resolution 102A (February 2014). Portions of this guidebook are adaptations or excerpts (without line-by-line citation) from the materials cited in this paragraph. They are used with permission of the co-authors of this guidebook who authored the cited materials. Prior versions of a portion of this guidebook appeared in Materials, National Conference of Bankruptcy Judges Annual Meeting 2015 (used with permission).

For a comprehensive summary of forfeiture law in the United States, *see generally* Dee Edgeworth, Asset Forfeiture: Practice and Procedure in State and Federal Courts (3d ed. 2014); Stefan Cassella, Asset Forfeiture Law in the United States (2d ed. 2007).

The reader is cautioned that this is a rapidly developing area of law. In late 2015, for example, the DOJ began reviewing its forfeiture practices. Bills concerning forfeiture have been introduced in several recent Congresses. In April 2017, the United States Supreme Court determined that disgorgement is not merely compensatory but constitutes a penalty for statute of limitations purposes. Kokesh v. SEC, 137 S. Ct. 1635, 1643 (2017). Other cases continue to wind through the courts.

NOTE TO READER regarding defined terms: Key terms and abbreviations are italicized and defined in the text and are capitalized thereafter. These definitions are also collected in Glossary I.

Chapter 1

Essential Tensions Between Asset Forfeiture and Insolvency

1.1 Overview: Tensions Between Forfeiture and Insolvency Legal Regimes
    1.1a Major Points of Conflict
    1.1b Existence and Scope of Stays and Injunctions
    1.1c Evidentiary Rules and Standards of Proof
    1.1d Jurisdictional and Substantive Conflicts Regarding Property
    1.1e Conflicts Regarding Distributions and Priorities
        1.1e.i Court Supervised, Comprehensive, Structured Insolvency Processes Contrast with Forfeiture Processes That Typically Are Discretionary, Narrowly Prescribed, and Not Court Supervised
        1.1e.ii Collective Enforcement in Insolvency Proceedings Contrasts with Discrete Victims' Rights Considerations in Forfeiture Proceedings
        1.1e.iii Comprehensive Priority Schemes in Insolvency Proceedings Contrast with Narrow and Discretionary Distribution in Forfeiture Proceedings
        1.1e.iv Other Important Distributional Tensions: Duplicate Payments, Clawbacks, and Monetization
1.2 Types of Insolvency Proceedings and Forfeiture Proceedings
    1.2a Federal Court Criminal Cases
    1.2b Federal Bankruptcy Cases
    1.2c SEC Enforcement Proceedings and Equity Receiverships
    1.2d SIPA and Federal Regulatory Enforcement Proceedings
    1.2e General Federal Court Civil Cases
    1.2f State Court Criminal Cases
    1.2g State Court Insolvency Cases
    1.2h State Law Regulatory Enforcement Proceedings
    1.2i Other State Court Civil Cases
    1.2j Cross-Border Cases

*****

1.1 Overview: Tensions Between Forfeiture and Insolvency Legal Regimes

Insolvency proceedings and *forfeiture proceedings* share common traits that are rarely found in traditional litigation. In this guidebook, *insolvency proceeding* refers to any domestic or cross-border bankruptcy or Insolvency Proceeding, including liquidation or reorganization under the federal Bankruptcy Code, 11 U.S.C. §§ 101 et seq. (2017), federal or state receivership law, assignment for the benefit of creditors (ABC) under state law, and liquidation under the Securities Investor Protection Act (SIPA), 15 U.S.C. §§ 78aaa–78lll (2017). Forfeiture Proceeding refers to any criminal, civil, or administrative asset forfeiture or disgorgement proceeding by any governmental entity, including the United States Department of Justice (DOJ), Securities and Exchange Commission (SEC), or other federal, state, territorial, or foreign governmental entity. In this guidebook, *forfeiture* is the criminal, civil, or administrative process (including *disgorgement*) by which a governmental entity obtains control over specified property of a targeted entity. Although Forfeiture and Disgorgement are distinct processes that serve different functions, their consequences in terms of intersections with insolvency law are similar. Forfeiture and Disgorgement processes are elaborated in chapter 3 of this work, and their differences are noted where appropriate throughout this guidebook.

Both Insolvency Proceedings and Forfeiture Proceedings affect not only (i) the parties to the cases, but also (ii) the property under the courts' in rem jurisdiction, and (iii) potentially large numbers of persons who claim entitlement to distributions from that property under the complex distributive schemes established by insolvency and forfeiture law. In Forfeiture Proceedings, *property* includes the assets that have been forfeited or disgorged and are under the court's in rem jurisdiction or the control of the enforcement agency. In Insolvency Proceedings, *Property* refers to the assets in which the *debtor*, the individual or entity that is the subject of an Insolvency Proceeding, had an interest on the date the case was commenced, together with other assets recovered under insolvency law that come within the insolvency court's in rem jurisdiction. In essence, each of these proceedings includes a type of collective enforcement scheme under which assets are gathered and may be distributed to persons who are not the principal parties to the litigation.

These characteristics give rise to the principal tension points that the courts managing these cases are likely to encounter.

First, one or more individuals and one or more business entities may simultaneously be: (i) the Debtor(s) in an Insolvency Proceeding, such as a bankruptcy case; (ii) the defendant(s) in a criminal proceeding (under federal and/or state criminal law); (iii) the target(s) of a Forfeiture Proceeding; (iv) the target(s) of a regulatory enforcement proceeding (under federal and/or state law); and (v) the defendant(s) in civil actions seeking to enforce private rights, claims, and causes of action (in federal and/or state court). (The civil actions tend to present the fewest problems in terms of case coordination because the filing of a bankruptcy case typically stays civil litigation.) Convicted fraudsters Bernard Madoff, Thomas Petters, and Marc Dreier are prominent recent examples. (Appendix C provides summaries of these and other recent major cases involving parallel Forfeiture Proceedings and Insolvency Proceedings.) The type of Insolvency Proceeding at issue typically is a Chapter 7 liquidation or a Chapter 11 reorganization under the Bankruptcy Code, but it may be a liquidation under SIPA (as in *Madoff*[1]) or a receivership under federal or state law.

Second, some or all of the Property those persons or businesses own, control, or have an interest in may simultaneously be: (i) subject to Forfeiture; and (ii) within the jurisdiction of the court overseeing the bankruptcy case or other Insolvency Proceeding.

---

1. *See* Appendix C, section 1, for a list of major cases involving Insolvency Proceedings and Forfeiture Proceedings with respect to Bernard Madoff (hereinafter, "*Madoff*").

Third, claimants, including creditors, purported victims, and interest holders, may assert rights in the seized Property or seek distribution from different sources under distinct processes, including bankruptcy or receivership, and legal or equitable principles governing Forfeiture.

A *creditor* is an individual or entity asserting a claim against the Debtor in an Insolvency Proceeding. *Claims* in Insolvency Proceedings include any rights to payment owed by the Debtor. Creditors include secured and unsecured lenders, trade Creditors, contract counterparties, tax authorities, and holders of tort Claims, among others.

A *victim*, as the term is used here, is an individual or entity that is directly and proximately harmed as the result of the commission of an offense providing for Forfeiture, and that either has a statutory right to compensation, as such, or may be allowed compensation at the discretion of the governmental agency at issue.

An *interest holder* is any holder of an equity security of the Debtor, or anyone who asserts an ownership *interest* in the Debtor or the Debtor's Property. *Equity security interests* include shares in a corporation or similar security; interests of limited partners in limited partnerships; or warrants or other rights related to purchasing, selling, or subscribing to either of the foregoing. 11 U.S.C. § 101(16), (17) (2017).

A *claimant* is an individual or entity seeking compensation or reimbursement from Property that is subject to either a Forfeiture Proceeding or an Insolvency Proceeding, or both, whether as Creditor, Interest Holder, or Victim. The categories of interested parties—Creditors, Interest Holders, and Victims—may overlap in whole or in part, as in a Venn diagram. Often, most relevant to courts managing these cases is the fact that Victims may be Creditors, or Interest Holders, or neither. The fact that these categories are not synonymous is the major source of friction between the two systems of remedies.

Fourth, because both types of proceedings determine distributions from a defined pot of money or assets, special effort is required to provide notice to all persons that may hold a Claim against or Interest in the Debtor or the Property, or that may be considered for inclusion in a recovery fund. Issues may arise regarding the scope and content of notices and the means of asserting Claims and Interests.

1.1a Major Points of Conflict

The distinctive enforcement schemes of Forfeiture Proceedings and Insolvency Proceedings evolved independently from each other and peacefully coexisted for many years, primarily because Forfeiture was implemented in a relatively narrow range of cases. Consequently, the intersections between insolvency law and forfeiture law were limited, relatively routine, and rarely controversial. Since the early 2000s, however, two factors have brought these systems into more frequent contact and sharpened the focus upon their divergent enforcement schemes: (i) a dramatic expansion in the statutory authority for, and use of, Forfeiture laws; and (ii) increased law enforcement responsiveness to the victims' rights movement, which has its roots in the 1970s and has amplified the effect of Forfeiture law's expansion.

The earliest incarnations of Forfeiture law were narrowly drawn and limited to Property used as an instrumentality of crime, such as a ship, vehicle, or weapon. Subsequently, Forfeiture expanded to include the proceeds of drug crimes. In 2000 and again in 2006, Congress dramatically expanded federal Forfeiture to include a lengthy list of federal crimes and enforcement actions. This expansion, combined with doctrines such as "substitute property" and "relation back" (discussed at section 1.1d), has dramatically enlarged the universe of Property the government may seize. Today, the government routinely seizes billions of dollars' worth of Property as a mandatory component of many federal sentences and enforcement actions. *See, e.g.,* 18 U.S.C. §§ 981, 982, 1963 (2017); 21 U.S.C. § 853 (2017); 28 U.S.C. § 2461 (2017).

Consequently, the legal regimes involved in Insolvency Proceedings and Forfeiture Proceedings come into tension frequently. These tensions present important judicial case management challenges at three primary intersections: (i) stays and injunctions, including whether the pendency of one case automatically stays action in another case; (ii) coordination and communication, particularly in light of potentially divergent evidentiary and procedural concerns; and (iii) conflicting substantive law regarding fundamental principles, including with respect to the Property, and with respect to the distribution and priorities of Claimants. The absence of definitive legal rules governing these intersections makes the early development of a comprehensive coordination agreement a primary goal. A *coordination agreement* or *cooperation agreement* (collectively, Coordination (Cooperation) Agreements) is a substantive agreement between the governmental agency implementing Forfeiture, on the one hand, and the trustee or receiver overseeing the Insolvency Proceeding, on the other hand, regarding which proceeding will receive what allocation of the designated Property, including any causes of action the defendant/Debtor may hold against third parties under general law or insolvency law's clawback and avoidance powers. Judicial appreciation of the potential parameters of such agreements, and inquiry to the parties regarding the development of such agreements, may play a critical role in case management. Coordination (Cooperation) Agreements are more fully discussed in chapters 4 and 5.

1.1b Existence and Scope of Stays and Injunctions

The courts overseeing parallel Insolvency Proceedings and Forfeiture Proceedings may be asked to consider whether the pendency of any particular proceeding stays any other proceedings. Such stays include the bankruptcy automatic stay, the Securities Investor Protection Corporation (SIPC) automatic stay, receivership stays, and criminal proceeding stays, as described immediately below.

Bankruptcy automatic stay: The filing of a case under the Bankruptcy Code generally stays civil actions, but not criminal cases or governmental regulatory actions, against the Debtor and its Property. 11 U.S.C. § 362(a), (b)(4) (2017). The DOJ/SEC may also posit that the filing of a bankruptcy case does not affect Forfeiture because the DOJ/SEC may assert that the United States' legal title to forfeited Property relates back to the time the underlying offense occurred, as a matter of substantive law, without leave of the bankruptcy court. Courts have considered the extent to which this "relation back" concept applies to various types of forfeited Property, including "substitute property," as discussed at 1.1d, 3.4.

SIPC automatic stay: The filing by SIPC of an application for a protective decree with regard to any securities or commodities broker subject to SIPC oversight halts any pending bankruptcy case until the SIPA liquidation is completed. 15 U.S.C. §§ 78aaa–78lll (2017); 11 U.S.C. § 742 (2017). The SEC may posit that its ability to freeze and obtain control of a Debtor's Property is excepted from the automatic stay and occurs as a matter of substantive law, without leave of the bankruptcy court.

Receivership stays: Unlike Bankruptcy Code and SIPA cases, other federal or state Insolvency Proceedings (such as a receivership or an ABC) do not automatically stay civil actions. Nevertheless, the order appointing a receiver (or an assignee, in jurisdictions in which ABCs are court-based processes) often includes a provision expressly staying other pending civil actions. A Bankruptcy Code or SIPA stay will automatically trump any receivership or ABC stay.

Criminal proceeding stays: The pendency of a criminal prosecution does not automatically stay any other proceeding against the defendant. Nor do any of the other types of proceedings automatically stay criminal or police power regulatory proceedings. To facilitate orderly processes, and protect the defendant's Fifth Amendment rights, the parties may ask one or more of the courts in parallel criminal, civil, or Insolvency Proceedings to impose a temporary stay or equitable injunction with respect to one or more of the proceedings. Principles applicable to other types of parallel proceeding stays, such as those employed in multidistrict litigation, will be instructive in these cases. *See* MANUAL FOR COMPLEX LITIGATION, Fourth, Ch. 20 (2004).

1.1c Evidentiary Rules and Standards of Proof

The courts may be required to consider whether inconsistent evidentiary rules and standards, including with respect to preservation and sharing of evidence and burdens of proof, affect the coordination of the proceedings. Effective case management is often complicated by the absence of definitive procedural rules, the need for communication across courts, and uncertainty regarding whether the timing of the filings and stage of progress in each proceeding may affect substantive results. The desire to establish intercourt communication and address evidentiary and procedural tensions may warrant the entry of coordinated case management orders as early as feasible in the parallel proceedings. These issues are the focus of chapters 4 and 5.

To fashion pragmatic solutions, judges in several large fraud cases pending in multiple federal courts have extrapolated from existing rules to devise interjudicial communication channels and conduct joint hearings to consider case management orders, coordination agreements, or both. *Case management orders* are orders that address procedural, evidentiary, and other matters relating to the coordination of the parallel proceedings, including the mechanics of intercourt communication, joint status and other hearings, and other matters the courts deem necessary and appropriate to facilitate case management.

1.1d Jurisdictional and Substantive Conflicts Regarding Property

The jurisdictional and substantive conflicts between Insolvency Proceedings and Forfeiture Proceedings are readily apparent in their treatment of the Property and Claimants at each stage of the proceedings: gathering Property, determining Claims and entitlements, and making distributions. The courts overseeing these cases often must make substantive determinations in the absence of settled law. The most successful cases in this ill-defined environment often emerge from the courts' skillful implementation of Case Management Orders and their active encouragement of intercourt and interagency Coordination (Cooperation) Agreements.

In a bankruptcy case, the Bankruptcy Code contemplates that all of the Debtor's Property will be gathered under the jurisdiction of the bankruptcy court for equitable distribution. Similarly, ABCs and many receiverships assert control over all of the Debtor's Property for distribution to Creditors and other Claimants generally. Other receiverships seek merely to control specific Property that is subject to particular Claims, for distribution solely to satisfy those Claims, with any remainder reverting to the Debtor. A *receivership* is an equitable state or federal Insolvency Proceeding in which the court appoints a neutral third party as *receiver* to take possession and control of assets or a business, and report directly to the court. The *receivership order* defines the scope and nature of the Receiver's powers. Receivers are most commonly appointed for the benefit of a secured creditor(s) under remedial and enforcement terms of a loan agreement, but may also be appointed in aid of civil law enforcement efforts or where the ownership or control of assets is disputed. An *assignment for the benefit of creditors (ABC)* is an Insolvency Proceeding governed by state law, rather than federal bankruptcy law, in which the business Debtor assigns all of its assets to an *assignee*, who liquidates the assets, gives notice to all Creditors to file Claims, and then distributes the proceeds. Not all states authorize ABCs; of those that do, some require that they be judicially supervised, and others do not.

In contrast, Forfeiture law applies only to Property tied to the particular crime(s) of conviction. Although in theory this may suggest a narrow subset of the defendant's Property, the enlarged definition of crimes and proceedings for which Forfeiture is authorized, combined with broad concepts (defined below in this subsection) such as substitute property, facilitating property, proceeds, and relation back property, may result in broad Forfeitures of virtually all of the assets that otherwise might be administered in an Insolvency Proceeding. This is especially true in a Ponzi scheme where there arguably are few if any "clean" assets. (The *Madoff* case is an example.) From the Forfeiture perspective, the absence of any "clean" assets in Ponzi schemes is precisely the reason that broad Forfeiture authority is appropriate in such cases. From that point of view, non-Victim unsecured Creditors have no legitimate claim to Property that was wrongfully taken from Victims of the offense underlying the Forfeiture, although innocent secured Creditors' interests in property forfeited in substitution for the original property would be recognized over the interests of the government and the Victims.

In short, bankruptcy proceedings and ABCs exercise jurisdiction over all of the Debtor's Property. Receiverships exercise jurisdiction over specific Property (often virtually all). Forfeiture Proceedings exercise control over Property related (directly or remotely, as noted immediately below) to the crimes of conviction.

The implications of Forfeiture may be particularly striking with respect to a business that is seeking to reorganize. In many cases, a business has legitimate Creditors and Interest Holders who were not involved in or aware of impropriety and whose interests might be best protected by reorganization. Depending on the bases for Forfeiture (securities fraud, mail fraud, wire fraud, etc.), however, the court overseeing the Insolvency Proceeding may find that the government has identified (and seized) virtually all of the Property of the (possibly legitimate) business as having been involved in, having facilitated, or constituting proceeds of the crime. (The *Adelphia*, *Dreier*, and *Rothstein* cases are examples.[2])

---

2. *See* Appendix C for lists of major cases involving both Insolvency Proceedings and Forfeiture Proceedings with respect to Adelphia Communications and its founder, John Rigas (hereinafter "*Adelphia*"); Dreier LLP and its sole equity partner, Marc Dreier (hereinafter, "*Dreier*"); and Rothstein, Rosenfeldt, Adler, P.A. and its 50 percent owner, Scott Rothstein (hereinafter, "*Rothstein*").

A *forfeiture order* is an order issued in a Forfeiture Proceeding that authorizes or directs the government to seize identified Property. All Property obtained as part of the criminal enterprise may qualify as *forfeitable property* and may be subject to Forfeiture, including the following:

- *Substitute Property*: A sum of money provided by a defendant and accepted by the relevant agency in lieu of other Forfeitable Property or a forfeitable partial interest in otherwise non-Forfeitable Property.
- *Facilitating Property*: Property used or involved in the commission of the crime.
- *Proceeds*: Any Property of any kind obtained directly or indirectly as the result of the underlying offense, and any Property traceable thereto.
- *Relation Back Property*: Property subject to Forfeiture under the relation back doctrine. The *relation back doctrine* provides that title to any Forfeitable Property vests in the federal government at the time the crime is committed or at the time the Property is used to facilitate the crime. Because title vests in the government at the time of the crime, anything that had been done to the Property thereafter, whether by the defendant or a third party, does not change its character: it is still the government's Property.

In addition to the actual seizure, at least one federal statute allows the government prosecuting certain crimes to freeze assets that might fall into any of the forfeiture categories. 18 U.S.C. § 1345 (2017). Despite the breadth of statutes allowing the government to forfeit and freeze assets, constitutional limits apply. The Supreme Court has held that freezing assets that are neither obtained as a result of the crime, nor traceable to the crime, but that could only be seized as the equivalent of Substitute Property, violates a defendant's Sixth Amendment right to counsel by preventing the defendant from accessing untainted funds. Luis v. United States, 136 S. Ct. 183 (2016). The Court has also held that the Eighth Amendment's excessive fines clause (which the defendant argued prohibited the state from using civil forfeiture to seize a vehicle worth $42,000 to satisfy a maximum statutory penalty of $10,000) applies to the states as well as the federal government. Timbs v. Indiana, 139 S. Ct. 682 (2019).

In a process analogous to obtaining a Forfeiture Order, the SEC routinely requests (in judicial actions) or imposes (in administrative actions) the equitable remedy of Disgorgement. *See* 17 C.F.R. §§ 201.600, 201.601, 201.1100–201.1106 (2017). *Disgorgement* is a judicial or administrative process by which the SEC may seek to aid defrauded investors by divesting a wrongdoer of ill-gotten gains obtained in violation of federal securities laws. In practice, civil Disgorgement and asset Forfeiture are distinct processes that serve different functions. Nevertheless, the SEC and DOJ view both processes as important governmental tools to stop ongoing fraud and provide Victims of crime and fraud with compensation outside of the bankruptcy court. Unless otherwise indicated, this guidebook's discussion of Forfeiture applies equally to Disgorgement.

The breadth of Forfeiture's impact on Insolvency Proceedings is best understood by contrasting Forfeiture to the government's more traditional enforcement powers. Absent Forfeiture, the government's enforcement powers are generally limited to incarceration, restitution, fines, penalties, and sanctions. *Restitution* refers to payments the court orders a defendant to make to the clerk of the court, who then makes distribution to the Victims identified in the order, in the amounts ordered. These enforcement powers, while substantial, primarily impact Insolvency Proceedings in two fairly discrete ways: first, the government is allowed to collect criminal Restitution despite a bankruptcy filing; and second, criminal Restitution obligations are usually not dischargeable in Insolvency Proceedings. See, e.g., United States v. Robinson (*In re* Robinson), 764 F.3d 554, 560 (6th Cir. 2014) ("Though the automatic stay prohibits the enforcement of prepetition judgments against property of the estate, [18 U.S.C.] § 3613 allows the government to collect criminal restitution despite 'any other Federal law.'"). The net effect is that the Debtor/defendant's ability to repay other Creditors may be sharply curtailed by the burden of Restitution payments. Obviously, incarceration may also affect the Debtor/defendant's ability to earn income to repay debts.

Nevertheless, Restitution and fines do not directly affect the Debtor's Property in the way that Forfeiture does. Orders of Restitution and fines typically mandate that the convicted defendant make payments to the clerk of the court, and direct the clerk of the court in the particulars of specific Victim distributions or other use of the payments. Such orders do not actually authorize the government to seize Property; although the government may invoke enforcement mechanisms such as mandatory tax refund transfers and general collection law.

Similarly, Restitution orders do not directly affect the allowance, distributional priority, or payment of Claims in the Insolvency Proceeding. For example, the defendant's *debt* (i.e., any liability on a Claim) to a Creditor is not automatically extinguished simply because the Creditor might receive payment as a crime Victim under a Restitution order. Actual payment under either scheme should reduce payments that might otherwise be due under the other scheme; however, there are no clearly defined mechanisms under current law to prevent duplication of payment. Unlike fines, penalties, and Restitution orders, however, Forfeiture directly divests (or seeks to divest) the insolvency court of control over potentially substantial amounts of the Debtor/defendant's Property, which otherwise would be available for distribution to Claimants.

Finally, the intersection between Forfeiture and insolvency generally does not create tension with respect to the ultimate bodily treatment of the Debtor/defendant (whose punishment is within the ambit of criminal, not insolvency, laws), or potential criminal or other regulatory sanctions against an individual defendant/Debtor. In that context, the intersections are relatively straightforward: the criminal system takes precedence over the bankruptcy system. If an individual who is under criminal indictment files bankruptcy, the criminal prosecution or regulatory enforcement action against the individual will generally be allowed to proceed. If a monetary obligation results (e.g., for Restitution, fine, or penalty), it becomes a Claim in the bankruptcy case. Bankruptcy law denies discharge of the dishonest Debtor and/or fraudulently incurred debts. See 11 U.S.C. §§ 362(b)(I), 523(a)(2), 523(a)(4), 523(c), 727(a), 727(d), 1141(d) (2017). See, e.g., United States v. Robinson (*In re* Robinson), 764 F.3d 554, 559–560 (6th Cir. 2014).

Although the conflicting legal regimes rarely create tension regarding sanctions imposed upon an individual defendant, they frequently clash directly with respect to the treatment of the Property forfeited and the Claimants seeking distributions.

1.1e Conflicts Regarding Distributions and Priorities

The competing distributional schemes are discussed in more detail in chapters 2 and 3. The following discussion briefly summarizes the principal points of tension. These tensions arise because insolvency law and Forfeiture law arose from different legal regimes to protect different interests. The resulting substantive differences typically lead to significant conflict regarding the treatment of Claimants.

1.1e.i Court Supervised, Comprehensive, Structured Insolvency Processes Contrast with Forfeiture Processes That Typically Are Discretionary, Narrowly Prescribed, and Not Court Supervised

Primary objectives of insolvency law are to bring all Claims and Interests into one forum and ensure equitable distribution of Property, without regard to why the Debtor became insolvent. Under the Bankruptcy Code, distribution follows a precise statutorily prescribed scheme. Under a Receivership, the distribution scheme is defined by judicial order and may be more flexible to achieve equity. In either case, the process is highly transparent, court supervised, and inclusive of all Claims and Interests.

In contrast, distribution under Forfeiture law is secondary to the principal purposes of civil or criminal enforcement against the defendant. The government may retain or distribute Forfeited Property for a variety of purposes other than distributions to Victims injured by criminal activity. Distribution under the Remission process (described in chapter 3) is highly discretionary, not made public, and not subject to court supervision. If the government does distribute the proceeds of Forfeited Property to injured parties, the process accounts only for those Claimants who hold "superior interests" in the Property or who qualify as Victims under the crimes of conviction. In contrast to Insolvency Proceedings, general Creditors of a defendant are not entitled to distributions, unless they can establish that they qualify as Victims under the applicable Forfeiture laws for the specific crimes of conviction.

Moreover, the indicted defendant's own plea agreement may articulate both the crimes of conviction (and, thereby, the eligible Victims) and the Property that the defendant consents to have transferred to the government through Forfeiture. Given the motivations underlying both the government's charging decision (including prosecutorial efficiency) and the defendant's plea bargain decision (possibly including leniency in sentencing), neither the charging decision nor the plea bargain is required to consider the impact of these decisions on the related business's possibly legitimate Creditors and Interest Holders. Thus, the prosecutor's charging decision and the defendant's own plea agreement may define both the Property subject to Forfeiture and the limited pool of Victims who may (but will not necessarily) become entitled to distribution from asset recovery funds.

As a result of the differing objectives of criminal law and insolvency law, their distributive principles may treat specific Claimants very differently. These distributive differences have become particularly apparent in the context of fraudulent financial investment and securities schemes that have spawned parallel criminal prosecutions and bankruptcy cases. (Appendix C summarizes prominent cases in which allegations of financial fraud have given rise to both Insolvency Proceedings and Forfeiture Proceedings. The facts, circumstances, outcomes, and citations to the leading cases referenced informally in the text are set forth in these summaries.) Moreover, because Forfeiture applies in a wide spectrum of circumstances, the potential for conflict arises whenever the law permits Forfeiture, including as a component of virtually any federal criminal prosecution, and not solely in fraud cases. Appendix B summarizes the scope of the principal Forfeiture statutes and rules.

1.1e.ii Collective Enforcement in Insolvency Proceedings Contrasts with Discrete Victims' Rights Considerations in Forfeiture Proceedings

In any bankruptcy case with respect to a Debtor/defendant under criminal indictment, or with respect to a business entity related to the defendant, the Bankruptcy Code will treat the Debtor, the Debtor's Property, and the Claimants the same as in any other case, in accordance with bankruptcy's fundamental objectives. Commonly synthesized as the "twin pillars" of modern bankruptcy law, these objectives are: (i) the right to a "fresh start" for the "honest but unfortunate" individual Debtor, or financial rehabilitation for the business Debtor; and (ii) Creditors' rights to restorative and distributive justice, expressed in terms of collective enforcement, maximization of value, and equitable distribution.

A criminal indictment against an individual defendant often triggers the collapse of the Debtor/defendant's business enterprise. The enterprise might range from a single entity deeply integrated in the crime (such as an investment entity that functioned as a Ponzi scheme) to a network of legitimate businesses, each with its own operations and Creditors. For example, both the *Dreier* and *Rothstein* frauds infiltrated the operations of otherwise legitimate law firms, which had clients, professionals, and employees who were not involved in the fraud, but whose interests were profoundly affected by the Forfeiture of the firm's Property.

The business enterprise might seek bankruptcy law protection in an effort to pay its legitimate Creditors by either liquidating or attempting to salvage and reorganize any remaining viable business. From the Claimants' perspective, Insolvency Proceedings serve as collective enforcement mechanisms. The Bankruptcy Code seeks to gather all of the Debtor's stakeholders in one forum. Claimants generally cannot opt out of the bankruptcy process and typically will be bound by the discharge even if they decline to participate. 11 U.S.C. §§ 524, 1141 (2017). Bankruptcy law embodies comprehensive processes for Property collection (11 U.S.C. §§ 540–549), Claims resolution (11 U.S.C. §§ 501–511), and distribution (11 U.S.C. §§ 727, 1129). These processes address the complex interactions among the diverse interests affected by the collapse of the enterprise, including suppliers, customers, Creditors, Interest Holders, owners, etc. Analogous, comprehensive processes define Insolvency Proceedings under other federal, state, foreign, and international law.

Forfeiture, in contrast, is not designed primarily to be a collective Debt-enforcement proceeding. It does not concern itself with all of the Claimants who may assert Claims against or Interests in the Debtor or its Property. Instead, its primary focus is on removing the Property from the possession or control of a defendant. Third parties generally have no rights to extract any portion of that Property from the Forfeiture unless they can demonstrate a superior legal interest in the Property. Similarly, third-party Claimants generally have no right to participate in distributions from government Victim asset recovery funds (if such funds have been created) unless they are able to demonstrate an injury arising from the crime of which the defendant was convicted. Third parties who do not fall into one of these categories are not accounted for under Forfeiture law. Termination of the criminal activity and punishment of the perpetrator are the goals; compensation of targeted Victims is an important but secondary consequence of Forfeiture laws.

1.1e.iii Comprehensive Priority Schemes in Insolvency Proceedings Contrast with Narrow and Discretionary Distribution in Forfeiture Proceedings

After all of the Property and stakeholders have been brought together in the bankruptcy forum, the Bankruptcy Code mandates distribution according to a carefully constructed and detailed priority scheme. 11 U.S.C. §§ 726, 1129(a)–(b) (2017). In so doing, it creates a policy-laden system of ratable distribution and priorities, including an "absolute priority" scheme under which Debt must be paid in full before Interests take a share (analogous to the familiar notion that an insolvent entity may not distribute dividends to shareholders when it is unable to pay Creditors). Receiverships and ABCs take a similar approach, although the Receiver or Assignee may have greater flexibility in fashioning an equitable distribution.

In contrast, distribution under Forfeiture law is secondary to the principal purpose of civil or criminal enforcement against the defendant. The forfeited or disgorged Property is distributed through a largely discretionary process under which the recovered funds may be retained for governmental purposes other than Victim compensation. Forfeited Property is distributed under flexible statutes that allow (but do not require) the Attorney General (or seizing agency) to distribute recoveries to Victims in whatever fashion the Attorney General deems appropriate, and permit the Attorney General to retain or distribute any remaining funds for official use and governmental agency allocations ("equitable sharing"). See, for example, 18 U.S.C. § 981(e)(6) (2017), 28 C.F.R. §§ 9.1–9.9 (2017) (establishing regulations governing remission), and Asset Forfeiture Policy Manual, Ch. 12, § A.3 (2016). Forfeiture Proceedings generally involve one or more distributional processes: (i) *remission,* a process through which the Attorney General may return assets to owners, lienholders, or Victims who qualify under governmental regulations and file appropriate petitions; (ii) *restitution,* a court-ordered process in which the defendant makes payments to the clerk of the court, who then makes distribution to the identified Victims in amounts that are based on DOJ regulations and policies; and (iii) *restoration,* a process by which the United States Attorney (US Attorney) may ask the Attorney General to use forfeited funds to satisfy a Restitution order, if no other funds are available. The DOJ and the Attorney General have broad discretion to pursue one or more of these remedies in any particular situation.

The government's broad discretion is not unlimited, however. Forfeiture law generally prohibits the government from distributing any recoveries to any Claimant other than an owner, lienholder, or Victim whose injuries relate to the specific crime(s) of conviction. In this sense, Forfeiture law is narrowly proscribed in its goals: i.e., law enforcement, not adjudication of competing Claims or Interests relating to the defendant. The definition of Victim often excludes many legitimate and innocent Claimants who suffered harm from a business collapse, such as suppliers, utilities, trade Creditors, employees, investors, and lenders, who dealt with what they perceived to be a legitimate business, yet who are excluded from recovery under Forfeiture principles. From the Forfeiture viewpoint, this exclusion makes sense because such Creditors are not Victims of the offense underlying the Forfeiture.

Nevertheless, conflict arises because legitimate and illegitimate assets may be commingled or difficult to distinguish. Moreover, Forfeiture may dramatically reduce or eliminate recoveries under civil law and traditional insolvency law regimes, *even though* Creditors and Victims may receive nothing from Forfeiture funds. Creditors that have suffered ordinary business losses and uncompensated Victims often perceive this consequence of Forfeiture laws to be unfair.

In sum, Forfeited Property may be distributed to Victims under priorities (or exclusivities) that differ markedly from the distributions that would have been made in an Insolvency Proceeding. As discussed in chapters 4 and 5, the use of Case Management Orders and Coordination (Cooperation) Agreements can help mitigate the perception of unfairness by ensuring the sharing of information among the proceedings toward a comprehensive identification of all Claimants that may have been injured directly or indirectly by the wrongful conduct or that may have other valid Claims against the Debtor/defendant.

1.1e.iv Other Important Distributional Tensions: Duplicate Payments, Clawbacks, and Monetization

Other distributive challenges that arise when Insolvency Proceedings and Forfeiture Proceedings interact include the need to ensure that systems are implemented to avoid double payment; to address the treatment of Claimants who may be entitled to distribution in one action but are subject to "clawback" recoveries in another action; and to consider whether Claimants who are unable to await resolution of the proceedings may sell or assign their rights to receive distribution (i.e., engage in Claims trading, as discussed in chapter 2).

First, as discussed in chapter 5, Coordination (Cooperation) Agreements may include terms designed to settle a variety of distributive challenges that arise in parallel proceedings, including which Property will be distributed to which groups of Claimants or Victims, and how the courts or agencies overseeing distribution might avoid duplicative payments. To the extent that the court is able to encourage the parties to settle as many distributive conflicts as possible without litigation, the costs of litigation that may reduce recoveries for all Claimants should be minimized, and recoveries should be enhanced and expedited.

Second, as discussed in chapter 2, *clawbacks* are proceedings, generally initiated as part of a bankruptcy case, in which the trustee or other representative seeks to recover, on behalf of the bankruptcy estate, payments made or Property transferred by the Debtor to a third party prior to the bankruptcy filing. The *bankruptcy estate* consists of all the Debtor's interests in Property, wherever located and by whomever held, as of the commencement of the bankruptcy case and during the case. Clawbacks may be asserted on a variety of theories under the Bankruptcy Code or state law. Insolvency adversary proceedings that seek to avoid and recover distributions made prior to the bankruptcy filing may have particularly significant ramifications in case coordination. For example, it is common for the Bankruptcy Estate to seek to recover Clawbacks from some of the very persons who seek distributions in both the bankruptcy case, as Creditors or Interest Holders, and from Victim asset recovery funds, as Victims.

Third, as discussed in chapter 2, Claims trading is a common practice by which Claimants in bankruptcy cases can monetize their uncertain hope of recovery by selling their Claims and Interests to persons, who then become entitled to stand in the Claimants' shoes and receive any distribution to which the Claimant becomes entitled. If, in contrast, Forfeiture law may be interpreted to prohibit the government from making distributions to persons who purchase Victims' Claims, Victims who are unable to await potential distributions from Victim recovery funds may have no way to monetize their expectations of recovery. Courts should be aware of this issue and may wish to press the parties to address Victim Claims trading on an ad hoc basis in Forfeiture Proceedings, possibly through Coordination (Cooperation) Agreements.

1.2 Types of Insolvency Proceedings and Forfeiture Proceedings

Interactions between Insolvency Proceedings and Forfeiture Proceedings present especially complex procedural, evidentiary, and substantive challenges because the variety and breadth of the underlying legal regimes engender the potential for conflict between:

- two comprehensive federal schemes (i.e., the Bankruptcy Code and either federal criminal or civil Forfeiture or Disgorgement);
- one comprehensive federal scheme (i.e., either the Bankruptcy Code or federal Forfeiture) and state law (e.g., state Forfeiture law or a state Insolvency Proceeding such as a Receivership or ABC);
- domestic (federal or state law) insolvency and/or Forfeiture law and cross-border Forfeiture or insolvency law; or
- two potentially conflicting state law schemes (Forfeiture and insolvency) either within or across states.

This section identifies and summarizes the types of cases that may arise in parallel Insolvency Proceedings and Forfeiture Proceedings, and the courts in which these cases might be pending. Proceedings in each of these categories may be pending not only with respect to an individual defendant, but potentially also with respect to related businesses and related individuals. The courts overseeing these cases might use the following list as a guide when questioning the parties at a status conference regarding the potential existence of parallel proceedings, including regarding the individual defendant, related businesses, and related individuals. Following this list is additional information about each type of proceeding:

- Federal Court Criminal Cases
- Federal Bankruptcy Cases
- SEC Enforcement Proceedings and Equity Receiverships
- SIPC and Federal Regulatory Enforcement Proceedings
- General Federal Court Civil Cases
- State Court Criminal Cases
- State Court Insolvency Cases
- State Law Regulatory Enforcement Proceedings
- Other State Court Civil Cases
- Cross-Border Cases

1.2a Federal Court Criminal Cases

Title 18 of the United States Code embodies the Federal Criminal and Penal Code (Criminal Code). Federal criminal cases are governed largely by the Federal Rules of Criminal Procedure. Forfeiture is available for a vast array of federal crimes, the most comprehensive (albeit still not exhaustive) listings of which are set forth in 18 U.S.C. §§ 982, 1467, 1963, 2253 (2017). Appendix B summarizes the overall statutory framework of the principal Forfeiture statutes and rules. The Asset Forfeiture Policy Manual (2014), published by the Asset Forfeiture and Money Laundering Section of the DOJ, Criminal

Division, summarizes federal policies governing all types of Forfeiture. It is available at www.justice.gov/sites/default/files/criminal-afmls/legacy/2014/05/23/policy-manual-2013rev.pdf.

1.2b Federal Bankruptcy Cases

Title 11 of the United States Code embodies the federal Bankruptcy Code. Federal bankruptcy cases are governed largely by the Federal Rules of Bankruptcy Procedure and the Federal Rules of Civil Procedure. Bankruptcy jurisdiction rules are set forth in title 28, United States Code.

Within a bankruptcy case, a variety of adversary proceedings may be filed. *Adversary proceedings* are, in essence, individual lawsuits that arise under the Bankruptcy Code, or arise in or relate to the main bankruptcy case (as elaborated in chapter 2).

The federal district court for the district in which the bankruptcy case is pending has the power to withdraw the entire bankruptcy case, or one or more Adversary Proceedings in the bankruptcy case, to the district court. *See* 28 U.S.C. §§ 157, 1334 (2017). Even if the bankruptcy case or Adversary Proceeding is withdrawn by the district court, however, the district court judge handling any bankruptcy matters may not be the same judge who is handling the criminal case or other civil cases regarding the defendant/Debtor. The related criminal or Forfeiture Proceedings may be pending in different states, may be in different districts within a state, or may be assigned to different judges within the same district.

1.2c SEC Enforcement Proceedings and Equity Receiverships

The SEC has a variety of enforcement mechanisms. Civil Forfeiture for securities law violations is implemented circuitously under the federal Criminal Code, through 18 U.S.C. §§ 981, 983 (2017).

Disgorgement of "ill-gotten gains" is an equitable remedy that may be implemented administratively without judicial intervention unless its effect is determined to be "arbitrary, capricious, an abuse of discretion, or otherwise not in accordance with law." *See* 5 U.S.C. § 706(2)(A) (2017). The SEC increasingly seeks Disgorgement as a judicial remedy, often by means of a federal equity Receivership proceeding in federal district court. Appointment of a Receiver enables the SEC to assure that a neutral administrator retains control over Property pending a court's resolution of the underlying merits of the charges or alleged federal statutory violations.

1.2d SIPA and Federal Regulatory Enforcement Proceedings

Stockbroker liquidations may be commenced in one of two ways: (i) in federal district court under SIPA, usually pursuant to an application for a protective decree brought by the SIPC; or (ii) by a liquidation petition under Chapter 7 subchapter III (Stockbroker Liquidation) of the Bankruptcy Code (11 U.S.C. §§ 741-753 (2017)). Generally, commencement of a SIPA proceeding is more likely, but a bankruptcy filing by the Debtor/broker usually ensues. The SIPA proceeding is usually thereupon transferred (referred) to the federal bankruptcy court as an Adversary Proceeding (i.e., as a separate matter denominated SIPC or SEC vs. Debtor).

In general, a SIPA proceeding follows a path similar to that of a Chapter 7 Bankruptcy Code liquidation (as elaborated in chapter 2). The intersections between a SIPA proceeding and Forfeiture Proceeding parallel the intersections between a Bankruptcy Proceeding and a Forfeiture Proceeding.

When a brokerage firm fails (such as *Madoff*), SIPC will either transfer the brokerage's accounts to a different brokerage firm or liquidate the failed brokerage and distribute the proceeds to the failed brokerage's investors. SIPC liquidations may occur through a protective proceeding under SIPA or under a specialized subchapter of Chapter 7 of the Bankruptcy Code.

The filing of a SIPC application for a SIPA protective decree stays the pendency of any existing SIPA bankruptcy case until the SIPC proceeding is complete, and triggers the automatic stay under Bankruptcy Code section 362 or the parallel stay under Title 15. 15 U.S.C. §§ 78aaa–78111 (2017); 11 U.S.C. § 742 (2017). The district court will issue a SIPA protective decree if the Debtor either consents to or fails to contest the application, or the district court finds that specified conditions warranting investor protection have been satisfied. An interim Receiver may be appointed during the gap period between the filing of the application and the entry of an order granting it. 15 U.S.C. § 78eee(b)(2)(B)(i)–(iv) (2017).

After the court issues a protective decree, the court will appoint a SIPA Trustee. SIPC has sole discretion in the selection of the Trustee and its attorney. 15 U.S.C. § 78eee(b)(3) (2017). Upon the entry of the protective decree and appointment of the Trustee, the district court will order that the entire SIPA liquidation proceeding be removed to the bankruptcy court. 15 U.S.C. § 78eee(b)(4) (2017).

The United States Courts' website contains a succinct summary comparing SIPA liquidation proceedings and bankruptcy liquidations.[3]

1.2e General Federal Court Civil Cases

Other types of federal civil cases that may be affected or interrupted by the filing of Insolvency Proceedings or Forfeiture Proceedings include:

- general civil cases brought under federal diversity jurisdiction (including the full range of state law matters such as breach of contract, tort, etc.);
- Receiverships to enforce Creditor rights under state law, if diversity or other bases for jurisdiction exist; and
- federal question cases, such as copyright, patent, or trademark infringement cases.

1.2f State Court Criminal Cases

The defendant may be subject to pending state law criminal prosecution, either instead of or in addition to federal law criminal prosecution.

---

3. Useful reference materials with respect to SIPA proceedings may be found at:

    (a) http://www.uscourts.gov/FederalCourts/Bankruptcy/BankruptcyBasics/SIPA.aspx, and
    (b) http://www.sipc.org/about-sipc/statute-and-rules/statute.

1.2g State Court Insolvency Cases

Receiverships are generally creatures of state law and are commenced in state court unless diversity jurisdiction exists. The laws governing Receiverships vary significantly from state to state. (In September 2016, however, the National Conference of Commissioners of Uniform State Laws approved a uniform law with respect to one type of Receivership, for consideration by the states. The law, designated the Uniform Commercial Real Estate Receivership Act, had been introduced in or approved by several states as of the writing of this guidebook.) Many Receiverships solely enforce remedies by a lender against a specific Property that constitutes its collateral, such as income-producing real estate. Of primary concern in terms of interaction with Insolvency Proceedings, however, are Receiverships that take over management of operating businesses and substantially all of their assets, as to which many Creditors and Victims may assert Claims.

State laws governing ABCs also vary. Some states permit nonjudicial ABCs, such that no court record of such proceedings would be available.

1.2h State Law Regulatory Enforcement Proceedings

State law may provide enforcement mechanisms, such as for state securities laws violations, civil fraud, or regulatory enforcement, through state attorneys general. These actions would be pending in state court. They may take the form of Receiverships that seek to displace fraudulent managers and take over the entire business while the Receiver determines the nature and extent of the fraudulent conduct and injuries to Victims.

The appointment of a state Receiver does not prevent either the business or the target individual from filing a bankruptcy case. Typically, however, the bankruptcy court will not permit the target of state fraud proceedings to regain control of the enterprise or its assets. It will instead appoint a trustee, sua sponte if necessary. Although the bankruptcy case often displaces the Receivership proceedings, both may proceed and present a clash of federal bankruptcy law and state law. *See* Heyman v. Kemp (*In re* Teletronics), 649 F.2d 1236 (7th Cir. 1981) (presenting a classic clash between a bankruptcy trustee representing Creditors and a state court Receiver representing Victims under the former Bankruptcy Act of 1898).

1.2i Other State Court Civil Cases

Routine state law civil actions (such as breach of contract or tort) may be pending against the individual defendant, related businesses, and related individuals. Absent diversity of citizenship, these actions would be pending in state court.

1.2j Cross-Border Cases

Cross-border cases may exist either when a foreign insolvency proceeding, Forfeiture criminal prosecution, or foreign civil actions are pending with respect to defendants or Debtors who are also subject to domestic proceedings; or when a foreign proceeding is pending ancillary to a domestic proceeding (e.g., to enforce a domestic judgment or to forfeit assets held abroad). 18 U.S.C. § 981(a)(1)(B) (2017) (civil forfeiture); 28 U.S.C. § 2467 (2017) (enforcement of foreign judgments); *see also generally* Bankruptcy Code ch. 15 (ancillary and cross-border insolvency cases).

All of the issues that arise in the judicial management of parallel domestic Insolvency Proceedings and Forfeiture Proceedings (as elaborated in chapter 2) may also arise when a domestic Debtor with foreign assets or operations or a foreign Debtor with domestic assets or operations is the subject of both an Insolvency Proceeding and a Forfeiture Proceeding. These cases might involve either domestic or foreign forfeiture, or both, and either foreign or domestic insolvency, or both. When such cases arise, the domestic courts should seek guidance under general cross-border laws and principles, given the absence of specific laws governing intersections between cross-border Insolvency Proceedings and Forfeiture Proceedings. Chapter 15 of the Bankruptcy Code encourages communication and cooperation and provides general guidance for the judicial management of cross-border insolvency cases, although it does not specifically address interactions between insolvency law and Forfeiture law. Similarly, courts should consider whether any Mutual Legal Assistance Treaties (MLATs) provide general guidance. Finally, courts may find that these extremely complex cases warrant retention of a special counsel, examiner, neutral officer of the court, special master (in federal district court but not federal bankruptcy court), or other expert with specific expertise in the management of cross-border insolvency and Forfeiture cases.

Chapter 2

Statutory Framework: Bankruptcy Cases and Proceedings

2.1 Federal Bankruptcy Law: Overview and Historical Foundations
2.2 Jurisdictional Foundation
    2.2a Jurisdictional Grant to the Bankruptcy Courts
    2.2b Constitutional Limits on Bankruptcy Jurisdiction
2.3 Commencement of the Case
    2.3a Venue
    2.3b Effective Date of Order for Relief
    2.3c Available Types of Relief
        2.3c(i) Chapter 7 Liquidation
        2.3c(ii) Chapter 11 Reorganization
    2.3d Requirements for Voluntary Petitions
    2.3e Requirements for Involuntary Petitions
    2.3f Automatic Stay
2.4 Primary Players
    2.4a Debtors, Debtors in Possession, and Trustees
    2.4b Examiners
    2.4c United States Trustee
    2.4d Ombudsmen
    2.4e Creditors and Interest Holders
    2.4f Committees
        2.4f(i) Creation and Role in the Case
        2.4f(ii) Multiple Official Committees
        2.4f(iii) Unofficial (Ad Hoc) Committees
        2.4f(iv) Significance for Parallel Proceedings
    2.4g Other Parties in Interest
    2.4h The Role of Counsel
        2.4h(i) Fiduciary Responsibilities
        2.4h(ii) Retention and Payment
    2.4i The Role of the Bankruptcy Court
2.5 Property of the Estate
    2.5a State Law Role in Determining Property of the Estate
    2.5b Forfeiture Proceedings and Property of the Estate
        2.5b(i) Constructive or Express Trusts
        2.5b(ii) Forfeiture and the Relation Back Doctrine
    2.5c Turnover of Property to the Trustee
    2.5d. Avoiding Powers (Clawbacks)

2.6 Claims and Interests
    2.6a Creditors and Victims
    2.6b Allowance and Determination

2.7 Distribution
    2.7a Maximization and Equitable Distribution Principles
    2.7b Bankruptcy Priorities
    2.7c Automatic Subordination of Certain Victim Claims
    2.7d Chapter 7 Distributions
    2.7e Chapter 11 Distributions
    2.7f Other Chapters
    2.7g Claims Trading

2.8 Discharge and Its Limits
    2.8a The Fresh Start
    2.8b Non-Dischargeable Obligations of Individual Debtors
    2.8c Entity Discharge

*****

2.1 Federal Bankruptcy Law: Overview and Historical Foundations

Bankruptcy law rests on the authority granted to Congress under Article I, section 8 of the US Constitution to "establish . . . uniform Laws on the subject of Bankruptcies throughout the United States." U.S. Const. art. I, § 8, cl. 4. The Bankruptcy Act of 1898 was the first permanent bankruptcy law. Previously, Congress had enacted short-lived statutes in response to financial panics and other economic conditions, but later either repealed them or allowed them to expire. The Chandler Act of 1938 amended the 1898 Act by adding provisions for consumer bankruptcies. The next major revision came forty years later, when the Bankruptcy Act was overhauled and renamed the Bankruptcy Code pursuant to the Bankruptcy Reform Act of 1978. The Bankruptcy Code has subsequently been amended, most significantly in 1984, 1986, 1994, and 2005. Current bankruptcy law is codified principally in United States Code titles 28 (Judiciary Code) and 11 (Bankruptcy Code), and the accompanying Federal Rules of Bankruptcy Procedure (Bankruptcy Rules) promulgated by the Supreme Court.

    The primary purposes of bankruptcy law are to provide the Debtor with a "breathing spell" to reorganize its affairs (hence, the automatic stay that thwarts a rush to the courthouse by Creditors), to grant a "fresh start" to the honest but unfortunate Debtor (hence, the bankruptcy discharge), to maximize value for the benefit of all (hence, the reorganization option), and to promote equality of distribution among Creditors (hence, the strict ranking of Claims and the existence of avoiding powers under the Bankruptcy Code).

    The bankruptcy system is structured primarily as an in rem process, premised on the instantaneous creation of an "estate" upon the commencement of a bankruptcy case. 11 U.S.C. § 541(a) (2017). The Bankruptcy Estate consists of all the Debtor's interests in Property, wherever located and by whomever held, as of the commencement of the bankruptcy case and acquired during the case.

Consistent with the purposes of the bankruptcy law, the bankruptcy court overseeing the bankruptcy case has "exclusive jurisdiction... of all property, wherever located, of the debtor as of the commencement of such case, and of property of the estate." 28 U.S.C. § 1334(e)(1) (2017); *see also* 28 U.S.C. § 157(a) (2017). (Bankruptcy cases are to be referred to the bankruptcy judges by the district courts.)

The Bankruptcy Estate is managed by a bankruptcy *trustee* or, in a Chapter 11 reorganization case in which a Trustee is not appointed, by the *debtor in possession* (DIP) for eventual distribution to Creditors and Interest Holders. Bankruptcy Code section 1107 provides that a Debtor that remains in possession of its Bankruptcy Estate, as DIP, is given all the rights and powers, and must assume all the functions and duties, that are otherwise vested in a Trustee under applicable provisions of the Bankruptcy Code. The Trustee (or DIP) acts in a fiduciary capacity as the representative of the Bankruptcy Estate and has the capacity to sue and be sued on behalf of the estate. 11 U.S.C. § 323 (2017). Of particular importance to non-bankruptcy judges coordinating parallel proceedings is the fact that, upon the filing of a bankruptcy petition, the bankruptcy court overseeing the bankruptcy case has exclusive in rem jurisdiction over all of the Debtor's Property, wherever located. Competing Forfeiture Proceedings typically assert that some or all of that same Property has been wrongfully obtained by the Debtor/defendant, or improperly transferred by the Debtor/defendant to third parties.

The formation of the Bankruptcy Estate and the federal court's exclusive in rem jurisdiction over the estate's Property serve the essential marshaling purpose of a bankruptcy case. The bankruptcy court provides a centralized forum for: (i) disclosing the Debtor's financial affairs (through the schedules of assets and liabilities and other filings required of the Debtor); (ii) aggregating and maximizing the value of the Bankruptcy Estate (through, among other powers, the ability to shed burdensome contracts and sell or restructure assets); (iii) allowing or disallowing the Claims entitled to share in the estate; (iv) determining actions against third parties to augment the estate through the Trustee's turnover and avoidance powers; and (v) distributing the value among parties in interest according to the distributive rankings set forth in the Bankruptcy Code.

2.2 Jurisdictional Foundation

2.2a Jurisdictional Grant to the Bankruptcy Courts

The district court has original and exclusive jurisdiction of all "cases" under the Bankruptcy Code. 28 U.S.C. § 1334(a) (2017). In addition, a district court has original but not exclusive jurisdiction of three types of civil proceedings that may be components of any particular bankruptcy case: (i) those "arising under" the Bankruptcy Code; (ii) those "arising in" a case under the Bankruptcy Code; and (iii) those "related to" a case under the Bankruptcy Code. 28 U.S.C. § 1334(b) (2017). The last category may include routine civil litigation by or against the Debtor. One implication of "related to" jurisdiction is that civil litigation that otherwise might be resolved in state court might instead be heard in the bankruptcy court or federal district court.

Each district court, in turn, may provide that any or all cases and proceedings "shall be referred to the bankruptcy judges for the district." 28 U.S.C. § 157(a) (2017). In practice, all districts have adopted general orders referring all bankruptcy cases to the bankruptcy courts, provided that the district court may withdraw the reference in its discretion and, in certain instances, for cause shown. 28 U.S.C. § 157(d) (2017).

The bankruptcy court often considers both third-party litigation against the Debtor (under its related to jurisdiction) and litigation by the Bankruptcy Estate to recover Property or proceeds from third parties (under its arising under, arising in, or related to jurisdiction). Forfeiture Proceedings may seek to recover the same assets from third parties and may seek to distribute some of those assets to third parties asserting Claims against the Debtor/defendant. Because parallel Insolvency Proceedings and Forfeiture Proceedings are likely to be targeting the same Property and involving at least some of the same Claimants, early and ongoing intercourt communication, combined with targeted questioning of the parties in status conferences, may be extremely valuable.

2.2b Constitutional Limits on Bankruptcy Jurisdiction

The bankruptcy court's statutory subject matter jurisdiction pursuant to sections 1334 and 157 of the Judiciary Code is, nevertheless, constrained by Article III of the United States Constitution. Article III vests the "judicial Power of the United States" in the Supreme Court and the inferior courts established by Congress under Article III. U.S. Const. art. III, § 1. Article III judges enjoy life tenure and compensation that cannot be reduced. In contrast, bankruptcy judges are appointed to fourteen-year terms. Consequently, bankruptcy judges cannot exercise the judicial power of the United States, even if the district courts purport to refer bankruptcy cases to the bankruptcy courts. The federal district courts unquestionably have the constitutional power to exercise the full scope of bankruptcy jurisdiction, even if the bankruptcy courts do not.

The Judiciary Code attempted to draw a distinction between judicial powers and nonjudicial powers by giving the bankruptcy courts power to enter final orders in "core" matters (which the Judiciary Code attempted to define in a way that would not implicate the judicial power of the United States) and to enter only proposed findings of fact and conclusions of law in "non-core" matters "related to" the bankruptcy case (which might otherwise implicate judicial powers). The Supreme Court concluded, however, that the statutory definition of "core" matters included some disputes that required a court to exercise the judicial power of the United States and therefore were not subject to final determination by a non-Article III court. *See* Stern v. Marshall, 564 U.S. 462, 469 (2011). Consequently, even though bankruptcy courts may have *statutory* authority to hear and determine a particular claim, Article III may limit the bankruptcy court's *constitutional* power to enter a final judgment on certain matters, absent the parties' consent.

The courts are continuing to define the precise contours of the bankruptcy court's statutory jurisdictional power (under the Judiciary Code, 28 U.S.C. §§ 101–5001) versus its constitutional jurisdictional power (under Article III). A series of recent Supreme Court decisions has further refined the scope of bankruptcy judges' authority to hear and decide matters "related to" the bankruptcy case within the meaning of 28 U.S.C. § 157(c) (2017). *See* Wellness Int'l Network, Ltd. v. Sharif, 135 S. Ct. 1932 (2015); Executive Benefits Ins. Agency v. Arkison, 134 S. Ct. 2165 (2014). Collectively, these decisions establish that bankruptcy judges may enter final orders only on matters that do not implicate the exercise of Article III judicial powers and are therefore constitutionally within the core scope of the court's in rem jurisdiction under 28 U.S.C. § 157(b) (2017). In other matters that fall within the bankruptcy court's statutory jurisdiction, bankruptcy judges may enter proposed findings of fact and conclusions of law for de novo consideration by the district court. Nevertheless, in the latter, the parties can consent to the bankruptcy judge's entry of final judgment (Wellness Int'l Network, Ltd. v. Sharif, 135 S. Ct. at 1939). Moreover, the district court, as an Article III court, can exercise the full scope of bankruptcy jurisdiction, including deciding "related to" matters, as provided by 28 U.S.C. § 1334 (2017).

The primary case management implication of this trilogy of bankruptcy jurisdiction cases is that, if the parties have not consented to the entry of final judgment by the bankruptcy court in a matter that is merely "related to" the bankruptcy case, the matter will either be withdrawn to the district court or the bankruptcy court will hear the matter and enter findings and conclusions for de novo review by the district court.

A significant case management implication of parallel Forfeiture Proceedings and a bankruptcy case is that the breadth of bankruptcy jurisdiction may bring into the federal courts related civil cases that otherwise might be heard in state courts. Proceedings arising under, arising in, and related to a bankruptcy case may be pending: (i) in the bankruptcy court for final resolution; (ii) in the bankruptcy court for the entry of findings of fact and conclusions of law for de novo review by the district court; (iii) in the district court in which the bankruptcy case is pending; (iv) in another district court (28 U.S.C. § 1409 (2017)); or (v) in a state court. Consequently, when a parallel bankruptcy case and Forfeiture Proceeding are pending, case management requires a comprehensive means of tracking and coordinating any criminal proceeding and all civil proceedings arising under, arising in, and related to the bankruptcy case.

2.3 Commencement of the Case

2.3a Venue

A bankruptcy case is commenced by the filing of a petition with the clerk of the bankruptcy court. Generally speaking, the petition must be filed in the judicial district in which the residence (in the case of an individual), or domicile, principal place of business or principal assets in the United States (in the case of an entity) of the debtor is located within the 180-day period immediately prior to the commencement of the case. 28 U.S.C. § 1408(1) (2017). For corporations and similar entities, the place of incorporation or organization qualifies as an appropriate venue, which means that a high percentage of business bankruptcy cases are filed in Delaware and, to a lesser degree, New York. Using Delaware or New York as the locus for filing the bankruptcy case may complicate coordination of parallel proceedings that frequently are pending in other federal districts.

Both the Debtor/defendant and the government may view a bankruptcy filing, and the choice of venue, as part of their litigation strategy because they may view circuit-by-circuit variations in bankruptcy law as important. Because an entity may file a bankruptcy case in a district where an affiliate has filed its bankruptcy case, Debtors often have a choice of venue simply by ensuring that the affiliate domiciled in the desired jurisdiction files first. 28 U.S.C. § 1408 (2017).

Venue may be transferred to another appropriate district under usual standards for change of venue. 28 U.S.C. § 1412 (2017). Particularly where Creditors have forced the Debtor into an involuntary bankruptcy case, the Debtor may seek to dismiss the case or transfer venue to a site the Debtor views as more amenable to its objectives.

Chapter 4 elaborates the feasibility of consolidating venue of parallel Forfeiture Proceedings, Insolvency Proceedings, and proceedings arising under, arising in, and related to a bankruptcy case.

2.3b Effective Date of Order for Relief

A bankruptcy case may be commenced either voluntarily (i.e., at the direction of the Debtor) or involuntarily (by Creditors). 11 U.S.C. §§ 301–303 (2017). The commencement of a voluntary case is deemed to constitute the entry of an order for relief (without further court adjudication), whereas an involuntary case requires a judicial determination of eligibility and the judicial entry of an order for relief. 11 U.S.C. §§ 301(b), 303(h) (2017). The automatic stay against Creditor action, however, takes effect immediately upon the filing of the involuntary petition, just as it does upon the filing of a voluntary petition. 11 U.S.C. § 362(a) (2017).

This timing difference between the immediate effectiveness of the order for relief under a voluntary petition versus the delayed effect in an involuntary case creates a "gap" period. In involuntary cases, the Debtor may continue to operate the business or to conduct individual affairs without court oversight until the subsequent entry of the order for relief. 11 U.S.C. § 303(f) (2017). Thus, the filing of an involuntary petition protects the Bankruptcy Estate against Creditor actions but does not automatically impose judicial oversight or independent Trustee monitoring to protect the estate against actions by Debtor's management. If imposing outside controls upon the Debtor was one of the goals of the filing, then the petitioning Creditors must seek immediate appointment of an interim Trustee. 11 U.S.C. § 303(g) (2017).

2.3c Available Types of Relief

Bankruptcy cases may be filed under six different categories for relief: Chapters 7, 9, 11, 12, 13, and 15. The most common are Chapter 7 liquidation cases and Chapter 11 reorganization cases, for which both businesses and individuals are eligible, and Chapter 13 "wage-earner" cases, for which only individuals with regular income and a defined, limited amount of debt are eligible. The Bankruptcy Code limits eligibility for the other chapters: only "municipalities" are eligible for relief under Chapter 9; only "family farmers" or "family fishermen" are eligible for Chapter 12; and only business entities that are already subject to an Insolvency Proceeding in a foreign country are eligible to file under Chapter 15. 11 U.S.C. § 109 (2017). Individuals targeted by a Forfeiture Proceeding frequently seek bankruptcy protection under Chapter 7, 11, or 13 and cause their related business entities to file their own Chapter 7 or 11 bankruptcy cases.[1]

---

1. *See, e.g.,* United States v. Robinson (*In re* Robinson), 764 F.3d 554, 557 (6th Cir. 2014) (following entry of an order for criminal Restitution, defendant filed an individual Chapter 13 case); United States v. Erpenbeck, 682 F.3d 472, 474–475 (6th Cir. 2012) (defendant was placed into an involuntary Chapter 7 case); United States v. Freeman, 741 F.3d 426, 428 (4th Cir. 2014) (false Chapter 13 filings formed basis for indictment and Restitution order); United States v. Rothstein (*In re* Rothstein), 717 F.3d 1205, 1206 (11th Cir. 2013) (defendant's law firm was placed into an involuntary corporate Chapter 11 case). Similar parallel proceedings occurred in the *Dreier, Madoff, Cladek, Wannakuwatte, Slatkin,* and *Adelphia* cases. *See* Appendix C (providing case summaries).

Also, the government may require the defendant to file bankruptcy, individually and on behalf of related business entities, as part of the defendant's plea agreement. In at least one case, the filing of a voluntary bankruptcy case was a condition of the defendant's plea bargain. Plea Agreement at 3, United States v. Wannakuwatte, No. 2:14-cr-067 (E.D. Cal. 2014).

2.3c(i) Chapter 7 Liquidation

Any individual or entity may file for Chapter 7 relief. A Trustee, typically a lawyer or an accountant, is automatically appointed in every Chapter 7 case. The Trustee has the duty to liquidate, i.e., "collect and reduce to money," the nonexempt assets of the Bankruptcy Estate. 11 U.S.C. § 704(a) (2017). (Exemptions apply only in individual Debtor cases, not entity Debtor cases. 11 U.S.C. § 522 (2017).) The Trustee is a fiduciary selected and appointed by the *United States Trustee* (a DOJ official, as explained more fully in section 2.4c), or elected by Creditors to manage and distribute the Property of the Bankruptcy Estate. 11 U.S.C. § 704(a) (2017). The Trustee will usually not administer Property that is overencumbered by secured debt. 11 U.S.C. § 554 (2017). Occasionally, with the court's permission, the Trustee may temporarily operate the Debtor's business in order to accomplish an orderly liquidation or to sell the business as a going concern. 11 U.S.C. § 721 (2017). Any proceeds of the liquidation are distributed to Creditors according to strict statutory priorities; any surplus (extremely rare) is remitted to the Debtor. 11 U.S.C. § 726 (2017).

In approximately 95 percent of Chapter 7 cases, there is no nonexempt, nonencumbered Property to distribute. In these "no-asset" cases, the courts notify Creditors not to bother filing Claims. Creditors or the Trustee may object to the Debtor's discharge on the grounds of fraud or other wrongdoing, but, absent an objection, the court will enter the discharge within a few months. 11 U.S.C. §§ 523, 727 (2017). If assets exist to be administered, the Trustee completes the distributions, then files a final account of the administration of the Bankrutpcy Estate, and the case is closed.

2.3c(ii) Chapter 11 Reorganization

In the typical individual or business Chapter 11 case, the Debtor remains "in possession" and continues to control the business and assets as DIP, subject to the requirements for court approval of out-of-the-ordinary course transactions and any plan of reorganization. 11 U.S.C. § 1107 (2017). A Trustee may be appointed for cause, thereby ousting the Debtor. 11 U.S.C. §§ 1104, 1107 (2017). The existence of parallel criminal or civil fraud proceedings involving the debtor by a governmental agency usually constitutes sufficient cause for appointment of a Trustee.

Chapter 11 cases may result in either reorganization or liquidation. The ultimate goal of the Chapter 11 case (as well as Chapter 12 and 13 cases), and the predicate for distributions to Creditors, is the confirmation of a *plan of reorganization* (*Plan*), usually with the general consensus of Creditors. The Debtor entity may emerge as an operating business under a Plan that either reduces or stretches out debt payments (or both), or the assets may be sold either as a going concern or in a liquidation mode to third parties. Such a sale may occur during the case or at the end of the case as part of the Plan. Fully encumbered assets may be turned over to secured Creditors. The range of Plan alternatives is broad, ultimately limited only by the Debtor's creativity and persuasiveness and by certain requirements of the Bankruptcy Code. 11 U.S.C. §§ 1123, 1129 (2017). A Chapter 11 plan may propose myriad means for the disposition of the estate. For instance, the plan may provide for the retention of all or any part of the estate by the debtor (which, as a reorganized entity, could then carry on its business with its pre-bankruptcy property rights intact). Alternatively, the plan might provide for the distribution of parts of the estate to interested parties (such as the return of collateral to a secured creditor or the establishment of a liquidating trust to hold certain property for the benefit of creditors) or the merger of the debtor with another entity.

2.3d Requirements for Voluntary Petitions

A voluntary case requires a petition signed by the Debtor and counsel. 11 U.S.C. § 301 (2017); Fed. R. Bankr. P. 1002, 1008. The petition must conform to the official forms promulgated by the Judicial Conference of the United States. Official Form 101 (Jud. Conf. of the U.S. 2015). If the Debtor is an entity, the petition requires evidence of proper corporate authorization for such an action under applicable non-bankruptcy law. Fed. R. Bankr. P. 1007(a). The lack of capacity to commence a case may lead to dismissal of the case. Court-appointed Receivers have been held to have standing to file a voluntary petition for a corporate or limited liability entity.

The Bankruptcy Code does not require that a Debtor be insolvent in order to file a bankruptcy case. Solvent companies and individuals can and do sometimes file for bankruptcy protection, usually to address immediate cash constraints, to prevent a lienholder from seizing assets, to unwind avoidable transfers, or to take advantage of the Bankruptcy Code's provisions regarding the rejection of executory contracts. Seizure, or threatened seizure, of assets in a Forfeiture Proceeding often triggers a voluntary bankruptcy filing by creating cash flow constraints or impairing a Debtor's access to equipment, books, and records necessary to operate.

2.3e Requirements for Involuntary Petitions

Unsecured Creditors have the right to force a Debtor into an involuntary bankruptcy case if the Debtor is not generally paying its debts as they come due. Involuntary petitions are rare because the unsecured Claims usually will receive little or nothing in most cases (absent sizeable voidable transfers). Consequently, the effort and expense of an involuntary case often exceed any potential recovery. Nevertheless, involuntary petitions are sometimes triggered by Creditor concerns over potential fraudulent conduct by a Debtor, Creditors' desire for a Trustee, or the threat that the Debtor may transfer assets under dubious circumstances. The threat or pendency of Forfeiture Proceedings may prompt an involuntary filing by Creditors who fear they will not qualify as Victims and who believe their only hope of a distribution arises under the bankruptcy priority scheme, or who recognize that the timing of the bankruptcy filing may significantly reduce the government's ability to reach Substitute Property under the Relation Back Doctrine in a Forfeiture Proceeding.

An involuntary petition against a Debtor may only be filed under Chapter 7 or 11. Involuntary petitions are not permitted under Chapter 9, 12, or 13. Usually, three Creditors holding Claims of at least $16,750 in the aggregate (this number adjusts every three years, by statute) must sign, but a single Creditor may file if the Debtor has fewer than twelve Creditors. 11 U.S.C. §§ 104, 303(b) (2017).

The Debtor may contest the appropriateness of the filing before an order for relief is entered. The bankruptcy court may enter an order for relief only if: (i) the Debtor fails to dispute the petition; or (ii) if the court determines either that the Debtor is generally not paying its debts as they become due, or that a custodian, such as an assignee for the benefit of Creditors, was appointed or took possession of substantially all the Debtor's Property before the filing. 11 U.S.C. § 303(h) (2017). Involuntary petitions sometimes fail, most commonly where the Debtor demonstrates that the petitioning Creditors are ineligible because their Claims are subject to bona fide dispute. 11 U.S.C. § 303 (2017).

2.3f Automatic Stay

The filing of the petition, whether voluntary or involuntary, operates as an automatic stay applicable to all entities, of most acts and proceedings against the Debtor, Property of the Debtor, and Property of the Bankruptcy Estate. 11 U.S.C. § 362(a) (2017). The automatic stay is a cornerstone of the bankruptcy system. It insulates the Debtor from uncontrolled Creditor action that would erode the estate or harm the Debtor's rehabilitation. Creditors may seek to modify or terminate the stay for cause upon motion to the bankruptcy court. 11 U.S.C. § 362(d) (2017). Parties in parallel cases should advise the courts of the pendency of a bankruptcy case immediately so that the courts may determine the scope of the automatic stay and any related discretionary stays.

The bankruptcy court ultimately has exclusive jurisdiction to grant relief from the stay and to determine stay violations, but other courts have jurisdiction to determine whether the stay affects their pending cases.[2] Questions regarding the extent to which the automatic stay in bankruptcy affects parallel civil, criminal, and related Forfeiture Proceedings may confront the courts early in the pendency of the parallel proceedings.

Bankruptcy Code section 362 contains numerous exceptions to the stay, several of which bear upon Forfeiture Proceedings. Most importantly, the stay does not apply to the commencement or continuation of: (i) a "criminal action or proceeding" against the Debtor; or (ii) an action by a governmental unit to enforce its "police or regulatory power." 11 U.S.C. § 362(b)(1), (4) (2017). Many courts have concluded that a Forfeiture Proceeding is either a criminal proceeding (as an in personam Forfeiture action directed against the defendant) or represents the government's exercise of its "police or regulatory power" (as in an in rem civil Forfeiture action) and is thus exempt from the stay.[3] Both criminal actions or proceedings, and governmental actions to enforce police or regulatory powers, may proceed despite the stay.

---

2. *See, e.g.*, Chapman v. Bituminous Ins. Co. (*In re* Coho Res., Inc.), 345 F.3d 338, 344 (5th Cir. 2003) (state courts have jurisdiction to rule on effect of stay; bankruptcy courts have exclusive jurisdiction to modify the stay and to determine effect of stay violations, including providing for retroactive annulments); Gruntz v. County of Los Angeles (*In re* Gruntz), 202 F.3d 1074, 1082 (9th Cir. 2000) (en banc reh'g) (state court modification of stay is unauthorized infringement on bankruptcy court authority; any such ruling is void and not entitled to full faith and credit); McGhan v. Rutz (*In re* McGhan), 288 F. 3d 1172, 1179–1180 (9th Cir. 2002) (state court lacks authority to modify stay or discharge injunction).

3. *See* United States v. Klein (*In re* Chapman), 264 B.R. 565, 572 (B.A.P. 9th Cir. 2001) ("Under § 362(b)(4), the government is not stayed from pursuing the Action to judgment even if the end result is that the proceeds are not property of the estate."); United States v. Erpenbeck, 682 F.3d 472, 480–81 (6th Cir. 2012) ("But the Code exempts from this automatic stay 'the commencement or continuation of a criminal action or proceeding against the debtor.' Because criminal forfeiture is part and parcel of a criminal case, it falls squarely within this exemption.") (citations omitted); Gruntz v. County of Los Angeles (*In re* Gruntz), 202 F.3d 1074, 1087 (9th Cir. 2000) (en banc reh'g) (criminal proceedings are never stayed, even when used to collect a debt).

Generally, a governmental enforcement action is permitted to proceed to judgment despite the automatic stay. The stay nevertheless has generally been held to prevent collection of any money judgment obtained, except through the bankruptcy Claims process. 11 U.S.C. § 362(b)(4). In the case of a Forfeiture Proceeding, however, some courts have held that a judgment for criminal Restitution altogether supervenes the automatic stay and remains enforceable despite the commencement of a bankruptcy case.[4] The Supreme Court held that Criminal Restitution obligations may nevertheless be dischargeable in Chapter 13 cases, which allow a broader discharge than under other chapters (Pa. Dep't. of Pub. Welfare v. Davenport, 495 U.S. 552, 563 (1990) (discharge of welfare fraud Restitution obligation permitted under Chapter 13 but not Chapter 7 or 11)). This ruling was superseded by statute, at least as to Criminal Restitution and as to Civil Restitution awards resulting from willful or malicious conduct that resulted in personal injury or death. Criminal Victims Protection Act of 1990, Pub. L. No. 101-581, 104 Stat. 2865 (1990); 11 U.S.C. § 1328(a) (3), (4) (2017).

Ultimately, the bankruptcy or other court must determine whether the stay applies to a particular proceeding; and the bankruptcy courts must determine whether to grant relief from the stay and whether to impose sanctions for violations of the stay.

2.4 Primary Players

A bankruptcy case is designed to be a collective proceeding that provides a single forum for the aggregation of all of the Debtor's Property rights, the resolution of interparty disputes and third party litigation, and the allowance of Claims. Thus, generally speaking, any party with a claim to the res (the Bankruptcy Estate) has a right to be heard before the res is carved up for distribution. Fundamentally, a bankruptcy case is an arena for competition among the various constituents of the Debtor both to maximize the value of the estate (through various means such as a sale, a merger, or the Debtor's retention of its Property) and to allocate the resulting proceeds of the estate.

Crime Victims who qualify as Creditors or Interest Holders have the right to participate in the bankruptcy case and to share in distributions in accordance with the priorities set forth in the Bankruptcy Code. Victims, however, may receive distributions from forfeited assets in addition to or in excess of the amounts they would have received as Claimants holding Claims or Interests in the bankruptcy case. These distributions from sources outside of the bankruptcy case may directly conflict with the bedrock policies of ratable distribution and "absolute priority" under the Bankruptcy Code. This is particularly true if equity investors, who would be paid last in the bankruptcy case, are paid first, or exclusively, as Victims of securities or investment fraud.

From the Forfeiture perspective, distributions from a Restitution fund or other Victim recovery fund do not affect the Bankruptcy Estate because the fund is considered to be owned and controlled by the government. If the fund does not belong to the Debtor, then

---

4. See Gruntz, 202 F.3d at 1085; United States v. Robinson (In re Robinson), 764 F.3d 554, 560 (6th Cir. 2014) ("Though the automatic stay prohibits the enforcement of prepetition judgments against property of the estate, § 3613 allows the government to collect criminal restitution despite 'any other Federal law.' This language overrides the application of § 362(a)'s various stays, which distinguish among the debtor in personam, property of the debtor, and property of the estate.").

distributions do not come from Property of the Bankruptcy Estate, regardless of the fact that the funds did at least ostensibly belong to the Debtor before Forfeiture.[5] Creditors and other parties in interest in the Insolvency Proceedings have trouble accepting that Forfeiture can legitimately remove and distribute assets that appeared to belong to the Debtor, that they relied on in dealing with the Debtor, and that would have been included in the Bankruptcy Estate but for the Forfeiture. From the bankruptcy perspective, all parties in interest and all Property are consolidated in a single forum, where their rights are to be addressed under a single, comprehensive, statutory distribution scheme without regard to whether a party qualifies as a Victim under Forfeiture laws. Consequently, in parallel Insolvency Proceedings and Forfeiture Proceedings, the various bankruptcy/insolvency constituents (frequently acting as a unified group) often compete with the government for control and distribution of the underlying res.

2.4a Debtors, Debtors in Possession, and Trustees

The bankruptcy case and Bankruptcy Estate are administered in a fiduciary capacity by a Chapter 7 Trustee or, in a Chapter 11 case, by a Chapter 11 Trustee or the DIP (a Debtor that remains in the possession of its estate). 11 U.S.C. §§ 704, 1107 (2017).

Although appointment of a Trustee is automatic in Chapter 7 cases, Trustees are generally not appointed in Chapter 11 cases, in which the DIP presumptively manages the Bankruptcy Estate. In a Chapter 11 case, appointment of a Trustee removes the Debtor from management of the entity. The Debtor's management (or the Debtor, if an individual) may be ousted on motion by a Creditor or other party in interest or, under compelling circumstances, sua sponte by the court. A Trustee will be appointed if the court finds "cause," usually in the form of evidence of fraud or mismanagement, or if a Trustee is otherwise in the interests of Creditors. 11 U.S.C. § 1104(a) (2017). In addition, the United States Trustee (as distinguished from the case Trustee, as noted in section 2.4c) is *required* to seek the appointment of a Trustee if it has "reasonable grounds to suspect" that any of the Debtor's management or other governing members participated in actual fraud, dishonesty, or criminal conduct in the Debtor's management or the Debtor's public financial reporting. 11 U.S.C. § 1104(e) (2017). Unlike DIPs, Trustees are required to be bonded, which provides the Bankruptcy Estate an added layer of protection for faithful exercise of duties. 11 U.S.C. § 322(a) (2017).

Although Trustees are relatively rare in ordinary Chapter 11 cases, appointment of a Trustee (and thereby, ousting of the Debtor from possession) is routine in parallel proceedings in which the collapse of the enterprise arose from fraud by the Debtor or its management. Trustees are appointed in almost every case involving parallel criminal prosecution or Forfeiture Proceedings because the pendency of such proceedings is usually considered sufficient cause to conclude that the Debtor is not a proper fiduciary of the estate.

If a Trustee is appointed, the Debtor's few remaining duties include: (i) appearing for examination under oath at the meeting of Creditors required under Bankruptcy Code section 341(a); (ii) filing the schedules of assets and liabilities and certain other required

---

5. *See* Ad Hoc Adelphia Trade Claims Comm. v. Adelphia Commc'ns Corp., 337 B.R. 475, 478 (S.D.N.Y. 2006) ("[A]ny payments from the restitution fund would be from 'a fund to be created and owned by the Government,' not a distribution of assets of the debtors' estates as part of a plan of reorganization.").

disclosures; and (iii) surrendering to the Trustee any and all Property of the Bankruptcy Estate (other than exempt Property in an individual Debtor case). In almost all other respects, the duties, rights, and remedies created under the Bankruptcy Code are exercised by the Trustee. The bankruptcy Trustee, as fiduciary of the Bankruptcy Estate, has the right to assert competing Claims to Property that is the subject of a Forfeiture Proceeding.[6]

2.4b Examiners

As a more modest alternative to the appointment of a trustee in a Chapter 11 case, the Bankruptcy Code permits the court to appoint a neutral expert to serve as an *examiner* "to conduct such an investigation of the debtor as is appropriate, including an investigation of any allegations of fraud, dishonesty, incompetence, misconduct, mismanagement, or irregularity in the management of the affairs of the debtor of or by current or former management of the debtor." 11 U.S.C. § 1104(c). The United States Trustee selects the Examiner following consultation with the principal parties in interest.

The appointment of an Examiner is warranted if it is in the best interests of creditors, shareholders, and the estate.[7] The bankruptcy court determines the appropriate scope of the examination, leaving some discretion to tailor the Examiner's role or (according to some cases), refuse to appoint an Examiner altogether.[8] Unlike a Trustee, an Examiner does not supplant the DIP, although the court has the power to order the Examiner to perform those duties of a trustee that the court directs the debtor in possession not to perform. 11 U.S.C. § 1106(b). This type of Examiner, whose duties exceed the more limited investigatory role, is often referred to as an "Examiner with expanded powers." It is unclear, however, whether an Examiner (like a Trustee) is able to waive the Debtor's attorney-client privilege, particularly as to communications within the scope of the Examiner's investigation.[9]

2.4c United States Trustee

The *United States Trustee* (*US Trustee*), as distinguished from the bankruptcy case Trustee, is a regional officer of the DOJ appointed by the Attorney General of the United States. The US

---

6. *See, e.g.*, United States v. Erpenbeck, 682 F.3d 472, 477 (6th Cir. 2012) (Chapter 7 trustee falls "within the class of third parties to whom the government owes direct notice" because he has "an interest in the seized article").

7. Section 1104(c)(2) technically mandates appointment of an Examiner, if requested by a party in interest, in all cases in which the Debtor's fixed debts for borrowed money (*i.e.*, *not* for goods, services, or taxes) exceed $5 million. In practice, however, motions relying on this subsection are rare and, even when made, are not always granted, despite the apparent mandatory nature of this provision. *See, e.g.*, In re Residential Capital, LLC, 474 B.R. 112, 199–120 (Bankr. S.D.N.Y. 2012) (surveying cases addressing whether court has ability to refuse the appointment of an examiner, even if statutorily warranted, where the facts and circumstances render the appointment inappropriate).

8. *See In re* Mirant Corp., 314 B.R. 555, 557 (Bankr. N.D. Tex. 2004) (Bankruptcy Code permits "a designer approach to assignments given examiners").

9. *Cf.* Commodity Futures Trading Comm'n v. Weintraub, 471 U.S. 343, 351–352 (1985) (trustee may waive privilege; "Because the attorney-client privilege is controlled, outside of bankruptcy, by a corporation's management, the actor whose duties most closely resemble those of management should control the privilege in bankruptcy. . . ."); *In re* Boileau, 736 F.2d 503, 506 (9th Cir. 1984) (declining to rule on the general authority of an Examiner to waive the attorney-client privilege, but permitting waiver in the particular circumstances of the case).

Trustee is responsible for, among other duties, selecting, appointing, and supervising private Trustees to serve in all Chapter 7 cases and in those Chapter 11 cases in which the court has ordered appointment of a Trustee. This office of the DOJ is also responsible for maintaining the overall integrity of the administrative side of the bankruptcy system. It was created in 1978 to serve as the nonjudicial watchdog of the bankruptcy system. The principal, but by no means only, functions of the US Trustee program are to: (i) appoint and supervise panel and standing Trustees in Chapter 7, 12, and 13 cases; (ii) form official committees in Chapter 11 cases; and (iii) monitor the employment and compensation of court officers (i.e., Trustees, Examiners, ombudsmen, committees, and the professionals retained by any of them). 28 U.S.C. § 586 (2017). The US Trustee is charged with a general systemic role in the overall integrity and administration of the bankruptcy process. It also has standing to raise and be heard on any substantive issue in any particular case or proceeding under the Bankruptcy Code. 11 U.S.C. § 307 (2017). The US Trustee program is divided into twenty-one regions, each with a US Trustee appointed for a five-year term by the Attorney General. Each region comprises one or more judicial districts, some within several states.[10]

As part of its administrative and oversight responsibilities within the bankruptcy system, the US Trustee is also responsible for referring crimes arising in connection with bankruptcy cases to the US Attorney for investigation. Such crimes include hiding material assets, defalcation during the case, and similar wrongdoing. 18 U.S.C. §§ 151–158 (2017); *see also* 18 U.S.C. §§ 1961, 2516, 3057, 3284 (2017). Thus, the US Trustee may play a key role in parallel Insolvency Proceedings and Forfeiture Proceedings. The US Trustee Program Policy and Practices Manual (*UST Manual*) contains procedures for the US Trustee's conduct in those situations where both criminal and civil investigations/cases are in progress simultaneously. (*See* Appendix F.) The UST Manual expressly addresses case management issues that arise from parallel proceedings involving bankruptcy crimes. It provides only general guidance that might be relevant with respect to the more global intersections presented by parallel bankruptcy and Forfeiture Proceedings.

2.4d Ombudsmen

The Bankruptcy Code also provides for appointment by the US Trustee of an expert *ombudsman* to protect specified interests, typically involving customer and patient privacy considerations during the bankruptcy case.

- A consumer privacy Ombudsman may be appointed to review and protect "personally identifiable information," such as customer lists or stored customer data, that are subject to a prepetition policy of the Debtor prohibiting their transfer or sale. Such appointments usually arise in the context of a proposed sale of such assets. 11 U.S.C. §§ 101(41A), 332, 363(b)(1)(B) (2017).
- If the Debtor in a case under Chapter 7, 9, or 11 is a "health care business," appointment of a patient care Ombudsman is mandatory to monitor the quality of patient care, unless the appointment is not necessary for the protection of patients under the specific facts of the case. 11 U.S.C. §§ 101(27A), 333 (2017).

---

10. The judicial districts for the states of Alabama and North Carolina are excluded from the US Trustee system. Bankruptcy administrators employed by the court in those districts carry out functions analogous to those of the US Trustee.

There are no specific Bankruptcy Code provisions addressing the use of Ombudsmen in parallel Insolvency Proceedings and Forfeiture Proceedings for purposes other than in the context of patient care and personally identifiable information. Nevertheless, to the extent that other privacy or consumer concerns arise in parallel proceedings, these provisions could serve as a model for the appointment of Ombudsmen under Bankruptcy Code section 105.

2.4e Creditors and Interest Holders

Stated simply, Creditors hold Claims, defined in the Bankruptcy Codes as any right to payment (whether unsecured or secured, liquidated or unliquidated) or to an equitable remedy for breach of performance if such breach gives rise to a right to payment. 11 U.S.C. § 101(5) (2017). Interest Holders assert Equity Security interests, which include shares in a corporation or similar security; interests of limited partners in limited partnerships; or warrants or other rights related to purchase, sell, or subscribe to either of the foregoing. 11 U.S.C. § 101(16), (17) (2017).

Both Creditors and Interest Holders are parties in interest with the right to raise, appear, and be heard on any matter in a Chapter 11 case. 11 U.S.C. § 1109(b) (2017). The distribution rights of Creditors and Interest Holders are more fully elaborated in sections 2.6 and 2.7.

2.4f Committees

A *committee* is an official or unofficial group of Creditors or Interest Holders that may advocate on behalf of its constituency in a bankruptcy case. Members of official Committees are fiduciaries to their constituency; members of unofficial Committees typically are not.

2.4f(i) Creation and Role in the Case

The Bankruptcy Code promotes the formulation of consensual Plans of reorganization under Chapter 11 by requiring the formation of a Creditors' Committee (assuming sufficient Creditor interest) and by permitting the formation of an Equity Security holders' Committee if a distribution to Interest Holders appears possible. 11 U.S.C. § 1102(a)(1) (2017). The US Trustee selects the members of the Committee(s).

An unsecured Creditors' Committee usually comprises three to seven unsecured Creditors, usually representative of different types of Claims (e.g., loans, trade Claims, or tort Claims) but weighted toward the largest Claims of each type. The Committee members are fiduciaries to the constituency they are appointed to represent. The Committee may retain attorneys and other professional advisors at the expense of the Bankruptcy Estate. It has standing to make certain types of motions, object to the Debtor's proposed actions, and conduct its own investigations, although its primary role is negotiating a Plan with the Debtor. 11 U.S.C. § 1103(c) (2017).

2.4f(ii) Multiple Official Committees

The Bankruptcy Code permits the formation of more than one official Committee if a single unitary Committee cannot adequately represent the interests of all Creditors. 11

U.S.C. § 1102(a)(2) (2017). Generally, formation of multiple Committees is disfavored due to cost and other considerations. Nevertheless, where Creditors' interests vary dramatically, separate Committees may be necessary. For example, in cases in which possible modification of pension and retiree health benefits are central issues, the US Trustee often appoints a Committee of current or retired employees of the Debtor. See 11 U.S.C. § 1114.

2.4f(iii) Unofficial (Ad Hoc) Committees

In addition to the official Chapter 11 Committees, Creditors and Interest Holders may organize informally as unofficial (ad hoc) Committees, provided that they file the required disclosure notices. Fed. R. Bankr. P. 2019(b). By forming unofficial Committees, groups of Creditors or Interest Holders with a common agenda may join forces and share expenses without the limitations imposed upon members of official Committees, including accountability as fiduciaries and oversight by the US Trustee. Unofficial Committees are commonly organized by groups of bondholders, unions, employees, tort claimants, secured loan syndicates, and other distinct subcategories of investors or financial institutions.

2.4f(iv) Significance for Parallel Proceedings

Usually, official Creditors' Committees will favor application of the bankruptcy priorities to the distribution of assets, because applying Forfeiture priorities will generally mean that a subset of Claimants, namely, Victims, would receive disproportionately more than general trade and other Creditors. In parallel proceedings, either official or unofficial Committees of Victims may be formed to advocate for their interests vis-à-vis Creditors and Interest Holders.

2.4g Other Parties in Interest

The phrase *party in interest* is used throughout the Bankruptcy Code. Although not expressly defined, the term specifically includes a Debtor, Trustee, Creditor's Committee, Creditor, Interest Holder, and indenture trustee. 11 U.S.C. § 1109(b) (2017). More generally, any person or entity that has a pecuniary interest or other financial stake in the outcome of a particular matter pending before the bankruptcy court is granted the right to be heard. *Id.* The SEC similarly has the right to be heard but does not have a right of appeal. 11 U.S.C. § 1109(a) (2017).

The general public and citizens in the community do not qualify as Parties In Interest. The purpose of the pecuniary interest test is to insulate the bankruptcy process from undue interference, litigation, and appeals pursued by persons who would not be directly financially affected by the court order. Thus, Party In Interest does not include individual customers of a utility in bankruptcy, nor persons who are merely "concerned" with the outcome of the bankruptcy court's rulings.[11] Where parallel proceedings are pending, the

---

11. Memorandum of Decision Regarding Motion for Order Vacating Appointment of Committee of Ratepayers at 12–13, *In re* PG&E Corp., 2019 Bankr. LEXIS 1706 (Bankr. N.D. Cal. May 28, 2019) (ratepayers are not creditors and, thus, are not eligible for appointment to an official committee); *In re* Goldman, 82 B.R. 894, 896 (Bankr. S.D. Ohio 1988) (concluding that one who merely has an option to purchase property that was now part of the estate was not a Party In Interest because "'party in interest' . . . does not encompass entities that are merely 'concerned' with the results of a debtor's bankruptcy proceedings.").

bankruptcy court may need to consider what additional entities have a sufficient pecuniary interest to appear and be heard in the bankruptcy case.

2.4h The Role of Counsel

2.4h(i) Fiduciary Responsibilities

A Trustee (or DIP) is a fiduciary on behalf of the Bankruptcy Estate for the benefit of Creditors, Interest Holders, and other Parties In Interest. Counsel for the Trustee or DIP is a fiduciary for the Bankruptcy Estate and does not represent the Debtor's principals or management (who may retain their own counsel, if appropriate).[12] Similarly, counsel for an official Committee represents the Committee in its role on behalf of all unsecured Creditors, not in the Committee members' individual capacities.

2.4h(ii) Retention and Payment

The employment of counsel by a Trustee, DIP, or official Committee is subject to stringent disclosure and disinterestedness requirements under the Bankruptcy Code. 11 U.S.C. §§ 327, 1103 (2017). Only professionals retained under the applicable provisions of the Bankruptcy Code are entitled to compensation from the Bankruptcy Estate. Compensation is permitted only by court order, to the extent reasonable, following the professional's interim and final fee applications. Parties In Interest may object to fee applications. 11 U.S.C. §§ 330, 503 (2017).[13]

2.4i The Role of the Bankruptcy Court

Under the former Bankruptcy Act, bankruptcy judges were responsible for both judicial and administrative functions within the bankruptcy system. The Bankruptcy Code intentionally eliminated bankruptcy judges' administrative role with respect to the direct supervision of Trustees, accounting, and asset management, and assigned that responsibility to the newly created US Trustee. Under the Bankruptcy Code, the bankruptcy court decides whether a Trustee is necessary in a Chapter 11 case. The US Trustee, however, appoints the Trustee, oversees that Trustee's administration of the Bankruptcy Estate, audits Trustee records, oversees the first meetings of Creditors, and monitors the integrity of the system. Previously, under the Bankruptcy Act, the bankruptcy judge (known as a "referee" rather than judge under the Bankruptcy Act) would have served each of those functions.

---

12. *See, e.g.*, Everett v. Perez (*In re* Perez), 30 F.3d 1209, 1219 (9th Cir. 1994) ("While he must always take his directions from his client, where counsel for the estate develops material doubts about whether a proposed course of action in fact serves the estate's interests, he must seek to persuade his client to take a different course or, failing that, resign.").

13. Davis v. Elliot Mgmt. Corp. (*In re* Lehman Bros. Holdings Inc.), 508 B.R. 283, 296 (S.D.N.Y. 2014) ("Although official committee membership alone cannot be a sufficient condition for reimbursement of professional fee expenses . . . to the extent the Individual Members qualify under § 503(b)(3)(D) by virtue of having made a 'substantial contribution' to the bankruptcy case, they may have their professional fee expenses paid under § 503(b)(4)."). The costs of defending a fee application are not payable under the Bankruptcy Code. Baker Botts LLP v. ASARCO LLC, 135 S. Ct. 2158, 2169 (2015).

In general, the Bankruptcy Code contemplates that the bankruptcy judges engage in judicial rather than administrative matters. In other words, their task is to conduct hearings and rule on disputed matters brought before them after notice and an opportunity for Parties In Interest to be heard and to apply the Federal Rules of Evidence and procedural rules in the same manner as district court judges. 11 U.S.C. § 102(1).

Somewhat ironically, the bankruptcy judge's administrative and judicial functions were statutorily bifurcated (in an effort to assure that bankruptcy judges were primarily judges, not administrators) during the same period when federal district courts and state courts began to take more active "managerial" control over their cases, in contrast to their earlier, relatively disinterested, reactive approach to party-initiated case management.[14] Over time, the Federal Rules of Civil Procedure amplified the role of judicially directed initial status conferences and pretrial conferences. Similarly, the Bankruptcy Abuse Prevention and Consumer Protection Act of 2005 specifically amended the Bankruptcy Code to encourage bankruptcy judges to hold early case status conferences and engage in the kind of active case management that had become the accepted role of federal district court judges in other types of civil litigation. 11 U.S.C. § 105(d). Actively setting deadlines, encouraging settlement discussions, and working with counsel to increase the effectiveness and decrease the costs of pretrial processes are still "judge's" work, however, quite distinct from the kind of financial and operational administration of Trustees and Debtors that were carved out of the bankruptcy judges' responsibilities under the Bankruptcy Code.

Because of the nature of bankruptcy cases, bankruptcy courts are called upon to determine whether the Trustee/DIP has exercised reasonable business judgment in approving settlements, accepting offers to sell Property, obtaining financing, and retaining and paying professionals. These types of matters are not typical of civil litigation before district courts and are often referred to as "administrative" matters because they are not necessarily disputed by any party. They do, however, require notice and the opportunity for a hearing before the court, and they may lead to contested matters that require discovery and evidentiary hearings. For this reason, such "administrative" motions require court review and approval. The key distinction from the pre-Code era is that, under the Bankruptcy Code, bankruptcy courts only decide matters brought before them by motion or complaint on notice (but for narrowly defined sua sponte powers).

2.5 Property of the Estate

The commencement of a bankruptcy case creates an "estate." 11 U.S.C. § 541(a) (2017). Section 541 of the Bankruptcy Code specifies what Property of the Debtor becomes Property of the Bankruptcy Estate upon the commencement of the case. The scope of the estate is broadly construed.[15] The estate includes, among other tangible assets and intangible rights owned by the Debtor as of the commencement of the case: (i) any interest

---

14. *See* Judith Resnik, *Managerial Judges*, 96 Harv. L. Rev. 374 (1982). The Bankruptcy Code contemplates similar managerial responsibilities for bankruptcy judges to "ensure that the case is handled expeditiously and economically." 11 U.S.C. § 105(d).

15. United States v. Whiting Pools, Inc., 462 U.S. 198, 209 (1983) (even property held by taxing authorities constitutes property of the estate where debtor retains a beneficial interest).

in Property that is recovered by the estate from a third party using the avoidance, turnover, offset and related recovery powers under the Bankruptcy Code; (ii) all postpetition proceeds of Property of the estate; and (iii) all Property that the estate acquires after the commencement of the case. 11 U.S.C. § 541 (2017).

2.5a State Law Role in Determining Property of the Estate

The Bankruptcy Code broadly defines what Property of the Debtor becomes part of the Bankruptcy Estate. The Code does not, however, define what constitutes "property" in the first place. That issue is a matter of non-bankruptcy law, which establishes the nature, scope, and extent of a Debtor's underlying interest in Property. In other words, the threshold question of whether a Debtor has Property that passes into the estate depends, in the first instance, on whether the Debtor has cognizable title to the Property under state law. Butner v. United States, 440 U.S. 48, 55 (1979).

2.5b Forfeiture Proceedings and Property of the Estate

Whether something constitutes Property of the Bankruptcy Estate as of the petition date depends on the precise nature of the Debtor's interest in that Property on that date. It is thus possible that Property previously forfeited by the Debtor under a civil or criminal Forfeiture Proceeding may be excluded from the Bankruptcy Estate (or, more precisely, may never become part of the Bankruptcy Estate in the first instance). The issue of whether Forfeited Property becomes Property of the Bankruptcy Estate is likely to be vigorously contested among the Creditors, the Victims, and the government. These intersections are more fully elaborated in section 1.1 and chapter 3.

2.5b(i) Constructive or Express Trusts

With respect to Property in which the Debtor holds only bare legal title, such as Property the Debtor holds in trust for the benefit of another party, only the Debtor's bare legal title becomes Property of the Bankruptcy Estate. The Bankruptcy Estate excludes any beneficial or equitable interest in the Property that the Debtor does not hold. 11 U.S.C. § 541(d) (2017). For example, if the Debtor is the trustee under an express trust for the benefit of a third party, the beneficial interest in the trust is not part of the estate. The determination that a trust exists precludes the bankruptcy court from controlling or administering the beneficial interest in the trust's assets.

Consequently, constructive trust theories are often advanced but typically fail in parallel Insolvency Proceedings and Forfeiture Proceedings. Third-party Claimants (such as Victims of crimes or fraud) often advocate state law trust theories in an effort to remove assets from the Bankruptcy Estate on the theory that the Debtor holds only legal title and no beneficial interest in the asset. Establishing that the Debtor holds the asset in trust for those entities as beneficiaries would deprive the Bankruptcy Estate of the ability to administer the underlying asset and instead reserve its value for the benefit of the Victims who claim to be the beneficiaries of the trust.

Constructive trust theories are creatures of state law, with elements that vary from state to state. In general, however, it is extremely difficult for a Creditor, Victim, or other Claimant to establish that the Debtor holds an asset under a constructive trust for their benefit. This follows primarily because most constructive trust theories require an ability to trace the assets, the lack of an adequate remedy at law, a confidential relationship, and fairness to others who are similarly situated. The last element is particularly difficult to establish in a typical bankruptcy case, especially one involving allegations of fraud or other activity that adversely affected large groups of Claimants.

2.5b(ii) Forfeiture and the Relation Back Doctrine

The "bare legal title" issue is one of the most critical sources of friction between Insolvency Proceedings and Forfeiture Proceedings. As discussed in chapter 3, the government usually argues that Forfeiture of Property divests the beneficial interest of the holder (i.e., the Debtor/defendant) as of the commission of the crime and vests ownership of that Property in the government on that date (under the Relation Back Doctrine).[16] Thus, even though the Debtor/defendant may retain both title of record and possession of the Property at issue on the date of the bankruptcy filing, the government's position is that the government's title "relates back" to the date of the offense, such that the Bankruptcy Estate holds bare legal title, at best.

The scope of the Relation Back Doctrine and its application in each case are often highly contested and profoundly affect the scope of the Property subject to the competing proceedings. Disputes about its application are likely, and will require determinations by courts in one or more of the parallel proceedings, or settlement under a Coordination (Cooperation) Agreement or the like. Because a Bankruptcy Estate comprises only Property of the Debtor as of the commencement of the case, the Relation Back Doctrine means at least in theory that Property forfeited or forfeitable as a result of a pre-bankruptcy crime or event never becomes Property of the Bankruptcy Estate. The Relation Back Doctrine may apply even if, as of the bankruptcy petition date, the Debtor/defendant had not yet been charged with a crime and no determination had been made that the Debtor/defendant committed a crime.

The Relation Back Doctrine is limited in several respects, including by uncertainty whether commingled Property or Substitute Property relates back, particularly if not identified prior to the filing of a bankruptcy case. First, to obtain clear title to forfeited Property, the government must provide notice to third parties to permit the assertion of any competing interests in the Property.[17] Moreover, some cases distinguish between the traceable fruits of the criminal activity (Proceeds) and other Property (not direct Proceeds

---

16. *See, e.g.*, United States v. Frykholm, 362 F.3d 413, 415 (7th Cir. 2004) ("Title to all forfeitable assets vests in the United States as soon as criminal proceeds are invested; a judgment of forfeiture just confirms that this has occurred."); Ad Hoc Adelphia Trade Claims Comm. v. Adelphia Commc'ns Corp., 337 B.R. 475, 478 (S.D.N.Y. 2006) ("Moreover, it is worth noting that if Adelphia had rejected the government's proposal and the government succeeded in forfeiting its assets, the government's interest in the assets would have been superior to those of the creditors in any case."); Gowan v. Patriot Group, LLC (*In re* Dreier LLP), 452 B.R. 391, 411 (Bankr. S.D.N.Y. 2011) (title vests in government at the time of the fraud). *See also* Luis v. United States, 136 S. Ct. 183 (2016) ("If we analogize to bankruptcy law, the Government, by application of § 853(c)'s relation-back provision, becomes something like a secured creditor with a lien on the defendant's assets superior to that of most any other party.").

17. United States v. Erpenbeck, 682 F.3d 472, 475 (6th Cir. 2012); United States v. Frykholm, 362 F.3d 413, 416 (7th Cir. 2004) (participant in Ponzi scheme could not establish a third-party interest as a bona fide purchaser for value).

of the crime) that the government may seize to satisfy a Forfeiture judgment. For instance, when Forfeitable Property has been commingled with other Property that cannot readily be segregated, the government may proceed against any other Property of the defendant (i.e., Substitute Property). Substitute Property may constitute the overwhelming portion of the Forfeitable Property, and yet it may not be subject to the Relation Back Doctrine, at least if the bankruptcy case is filed before the Substitute Property has been identified.[18] The interaction between these doctrines may significantly affect the scope of the Bankruptcy Estate and the reach of the Forfeiture.

2.5c Turnover of Property to the Trustee

The Trustee (or DIP in a Chapter 11 case) has the responsibility and power to collect all Property of the Bankruptcy Estate. The "turnover" remedy is available to maximize the estate, including the following powers:

- to compel any third party in possession, custody, or control of any Property of the estate to deliver and account for such Property (or the value of the Property), unless the Property has "inconsequential" value (11 U.S.C. § 542(a) (2017));
- to compel third parties that owe a matured debt to the Debtor to pay the Trustee instead, unless the obligor has setoff rights based on a corresponding Claim against the Debtor (11 U.S.C. § 542(b) (2017));
- to seek an order to compel any attorney or accountant that holds books, records, documents, or papers related to the Debtor's Property or financial affairs to deliver or disclose such recorded information to the Trustee (11 U.S.C. § 542(e) (2017)). This turnover duty is subject to any applicable privilege; however, the Trustee has the power to waive the Debtor's privilege; and
- to compel a custodian appointed under non-bankruptcy law with respect to the Debtor, Property of the Debtor, or Property of the estate, such as a Receiver or an Assignee under a general ABC, to turn over that Property to the Trustee. Such custodians have an affirmative statutory duty to turn over the Property in their possession and control immediately upon being notified of the bankruptcy filing, but the bankruptcy court may allow the custodian to remain in possession under some circumstances, subject to the oversight of the bankruptcy court (11 U.S.C. § 543 (2017)).

2.5d Avoiding Powers (Clawbacks)

The Bankruptcy Estate can also be augmented by the Trustee's power to avoid preferential or fraudulent transfers made by the Debtor before the commencement of the case. The avoidance powers ensure that Creditors are treated fairly by requiring that Property preferentially or fraudulently transferred to selected persons on the eve of bankruptcy be

---

18. *See* United States v. Erpenbeck, 682 F.3d at 477 (Relation Back Doctrine applies only to tainted property, not to Substitute Property); *contra* United States v. McHan, 345 F.3d 262, 272 (4th Cir. 2003); United States v. Rothstein, Rosenfeldt, Adler, P.A. (*In re* Rothstein, Rosenfeldt, Adler, P.A.), 717 F.3d 1205, 1212–1214 (11th Cir. 2013) (considering when property becomes so commingled that it may be forfeited only as Substitute Property, rather than as Proceeds, Facilitating Property, or Relation Back Property).

restored to the estate for the benefit of all Creditors. If the Trustee successfully avoids a transfer, he also enjoys the ability to recover the Property transferred or the value of such Property for the benefit of the estate. 11 U.S.C. § 550(a) (2017). As with the other rights and duties of a Trustee under the Bankruptcy Code, a DIP may also exercise the Trustee's avoiding powers.

A *preference* is a transfer (typically, a payment on account of a pre-existing debt), made by an insolvent Debtor to a Creditor within 90 days before the filing of the petition, that enables the recipient to recover more than it would have otherwise received in a hypothetical liquidation under Chapter 7. 11 U.S.C. § 547(b) (2017). There are many defenses to the avoidance of a Preference, most importantly including transfers made in the ordinary course of business. 11 U.S.C. § 547(c) (2017). If the recipient is an insider, e.g., an officer or director of a corporate Debtor, or close relative of an individual Debtor, or someone else capable of exercising control over the Debtor (11 U.S.C. § 101(31) (2017)), the preference period is extended from 90 days to one full year. Potential liability for Preferences has nothing to do with fault and everything to do with timing of payments.

Trustees may also seek to avoid fraudulent transfers. A *fraudulent transfer* is a transfer made (or an obligation incurred) by a Debtor within two years (or within up to six years depending on which law applies) before the bankruptcy filing that is either: (i) made with an actual intent to hinder, delay, or defraud Creditors; or (ii) made in return for less than reasonably equivalent value when the Debtor was insolvent, regardless of the Debtor's intent. 11 U.S.C. §§ 544, 548 (2017). Unlike Preferences (which impose essentially "no fault" liability), actual fault on the part of the transferor or recipient may be at issue. Recovery may invoke the specific Bankruptcy Code avoidance provision under 11 U.S.C. § 548 (2017), or state law provisions "stand in the shoes of" power under 11 U.S.C. § 544 (2017).

Section 548 provides for a two-year reach-back period, but automatically confers standing on the bankruptcy Trustee. Section 544 enables the Trustee to use the Trustee's so-called "strong arm" powers to reach back up to four to six years, depending upon the state's particular statute of limitations period. Under section 544, however, the Trustee can only pursue causes of action that could have been brought under state law by an unsecured Creditor that was both a Creditor on the date of the transfer *and* remained unpaid as of the date of the bankruptcy filing. 11 U.S.C. § 544 (2017).[19]

Fraudulent Transfer actions are particularly potent tools in Ponzi scheme-related bankruptcy cases, because those Debtors are often insolvent from very early in the venture, which enables the Trustee to recover distributions and transfers going back many years. Avoidance powers often play a prominent role in parallel proceedings because they give the Trustee the power to "clawback" distributions that were made before the bankruptcy filing. This extraordinary power is generally not available to the government implementing a Forfeiture Order. It often provides a powerful incentive and starting point from which the parties to the parallel proceedings may negotiate Coordination (Cooperation) Agreements.

---

19. *See* United States v. Frykholm, 362 F.3d 413, 417 (7th Cir. 2004) ("[B]ankruptcy would have enabled the trustee to recoup the sums distributed to the first generation of investors . . . Those payments could have been reclaimed under the trustee's avoiding powers and made available to all of the bilked investors.").

2.6 Claims and Interests

Creditors hold Claims against the Debtor, while Interest Holders hold Equity Securities in the Debtor. Under the Bankruptcy Code, anyone that has a Claim against the Debtor qualifies as a Creditor. 11 U.S.C. § 101(10) (2017).

A Claim is broadly defined under the Bankruptcy Code to mean virtually every right to payment (regardless of state law definitions of the term "claim") that arose before the commencement of a bankruptcy case. 11 U.S.C. § 101(5) (2017). Equity Security is broadly defined to include all stock or shares in a corporation, an interest in a limited partnership, or a warrant or other right related to either of the foregoing. 11 U.S.C. § 101(16), (17) (2017).

Whether a Claim arose before the date of the order for relief is often a vexing question. Many courts consider that a Claim has arisen under bankruptcy law if the claimant can "fairly contemplate" the existence of the Claim although it may not yet have accrued under non-bankruptcy law.[20] This test is important because it delineates the broad reach of the bankruptcy discharge. (Only "Claims" are eligible to be discharged in bankruptcy cases; postpetition obligations are generally not dischargeable.)

2.6a Creditors and Victims

Whereas the bankruptcy process broadly includes all holders of Claims and Equity Securities, the Victims entitled to participate in the Forfeiture process are defined by the fortuities of the charging decision and the terms of any plea bargain.

The cast of Creditors and Interest Holders competing for a distribution from the Bankruptcy Estate in an Insolvency Proceeding often overlaps with but does not mirror the group of Victims potentially entitled to a distribution in a Forfeiture Proceeding. Although Creditors and Interest Holders in an Insolvency Proceeding include all holders of Claims and Equity Securities, Victims entitled to distribution under Forfeiture and Disgorgement principles will include only parties defined as Victims with respect to the particular crime of conviction or other offense. Some Victims under Forfeiture definitions may also be Creditors or Interest Holders under insolvency definitions, and vice versa.

The government must show a causal connection between the specific conduct underlying the offense of conviction and the Victim's losses. Hence, the government's discretion to prosecute only selected charges, and the defendant's ability to negotiate a plea for a subset of those charges, may exclude from the pool of Victims persons (including some Creditors and Interest Holders) who might otherwise have been entitled to distribution had other choices been made with respect to the charging decision and plea bargain terms.[21]

Nevertheless, Victims who may not otherwise be entitled to Restitution under the specific charges may qualify for compensation through the Forfeiture Remission process.

---

20. *See* ZiLOG, Inc. v. Corning (*In re* ZiLOG, Inc.), 450 F.3d 996, 999–1001 (9th Cir. 2006) (whether employment discrimination claim qualified as administrative priority or post-confirmation obligation depends upon whether it was within the "fair contemplation" of the employee before confirmation).

21. *See* United States v. Freeman, 741 F.3d 426, 434 (4th Cir. 2014) (differentiating Creditors from Victims on the basis that awards of Restitution must compensate "only for the loss caused by the specific conduct that is the basis of the offense of conviction") (quoting Hughey v. United States, 495 U.S. 411, 413 (1990)).

The Remission regulations authorize compensation for any Victim of the offense underlying the Forfeiture or a related offense. 28 C.F.R. § 9.8(b) (2017).

The courts coordinating these cases must find solutions within the framework of the governing statutes. Those statutes generally do not allow the courts to apply broad equitable remedies to reconcile statutory incompatibilities. Coordination (Cooperation) Agreements, together with careful statutory parsing where appropriate, are a desirable means of fostering settlement.

2.6b Allowance and Determination

To share in a distribution from the Bankruptcy Estate, a Creditor or Interest Holder must hold an "allowed" Claim or Equity Security. Moreover, in a Chapter 11 case, only the holder of an allowed Claim or Equity Security is entitled to vote on a Plan. 11 U.S.C. § 1126(a) (2017). Thus, the allowance or disallowance of Claims is a key process in any bankruptcy case.

Ordinarily, the Debtor must disclose all of its known or potential Creditors and Interest Holders (whether acknowledged or disputed) in schedules or lists filed with the court at the outset of the case. Fed. R. Bankr. P. 1007. Unless the schedules filed in a Chapter 11 case accurately list the amount of a Creditor's Claim and do not identify the Claim as unliquidated, disputed, or contingent, the Creditor is required to file a formal proof of Claim supported by prima facie evidence. A filed proof of Claim will supersede any Claim that is scheduled by the Debtor.

Generally speaking, a scheduled Claim or filed proof of Claim is deemed allowed unless a Party In Interest (typically the Debtor or another Creditor) files an objection to the Claim. 11 U.S.C. § 502(a) (2017). Ultimately, the Creditor has the burden of proof to establish the merits of its Claim under applicable state or federal law. *In re* Allegheny Int'l, Inc., 954 F.2d 167, 173–174 (3d Cir. 1992); *In re* Holm, 931 F.2d 620, 623 (9th Cir. 1991).

Objections to Claims initiate contested matters, in which the parties may conduct discovery. The bankruptcy court determines the validity and amount of the Claim after such evidentiary hearing as may be necessary. *See* Fed. R. Bankr. P. 3007, 9014, 7026–7037. In very large bankruptcy cases, the court may establish a Claims resolution facility to manage a high volume of Claims. These facilities adapt alternative dispute resolution methods to the particular needs of the case. These methods typically include the use of structured negotiation and mediation rules designed to reduce the cost of the fact-finding and determination process. Unless the parties stipulate otherwise, however, the bankruptcy court will ultimately hear and determine the allowance of each disputed Claim.

In Forfeiture Proceedings, in contrast, the Restitution and Remission processes are largely handled administratively rather than judicially. The rules regarding the Remission and mitigation process are not statutory, but rather are set forth in 28 C.F.R. §§ 9.1–9.9 (2017). Similarly, the implementing policies are not statutory, but are published in the *Asset Forfeiture Policy Manual*. General, but not particular, information is available online for each significant Remission case.[22] Nevertheless, the methods of identifying Victims and establishing a Claims submission and review process tend to be ad hoc and vary from case to case depending on the circumstances. Some variant of a Claims resolution process,

---

22. *See* Remission, DOJ (last updated April 11, 2017), https://www.justice.gov/criminal-afmls/remission (listing websites for active, large Remission cases).

under the aegis of an administrator, may be used. Unlike Insolvency Proceedings, however, Victims do not typically have an absolute right to a full trial before the court. Instead, the Claims administrator makes a report and recommendation to the Asset Forfeiture and Money Laundering Section (AFMLS) of the DOJ on each petition. The chief of AFMLS makes the final decision on the amount of any distribution on a Victim's claim, and no appeals are available. Information about individual Victims is not publicly available and cannot be released without their permission.[23] This factor prevents a bankruptcy Trustee from determining who is being paid through the Remission process, and thus determining whether additional payment is warranted on account of Claims filed in the bankruptcy case by persons who are also Victims for Forfeiture purposes.

2.7 Distribution

After the liquidation of a Debtor's Property is complete in a Chapter 7 case, or the Plan is confirmed in a Chapter 11 case, the Trustee can make distributions to Creditors from Property of the Bankruptcy Estate. The Bankruptcy Code establishes detailed protocols governing these distributions. The following discussion briefly summarizes essential principles, to the extent that those principles affect interactions between Bankruptcy Proceedings and Forfeiture Proceedings.

2.7a Maximization and Equitable Distribution Principles

The principal objective of every bankruptcy case is to maximize value and make fair and equitable distributions to Creditors and Interest Holders. If that can be done while preserving employment and maintaining the enterprise value, the Debtor will typically choose to keep the continued operation of the business, either by reorganization under a Plan as a standalone company (usually owned by the Creditors of the Bankruptcy Estate) or by a sale of the business as a going concern, either during the case or under a Plan, to a new owner. If, on the other hand, the business cannot continue or the Debtor cannot afford the expense of Chapter 11, then a filing under Chapter 7 is likely. The goal under either chapter, of course, is to generate a return to Creditors and Interest Holders, although usually Interest Holders receive nothing.

Two overarching principles determine what distributions are made, in what order, in what amount, to which Creditors and Interest Holders.

First, the Bankruptcy Code's modified "absolute priority rule," if truly absolute, would mandate that each Claim or Equity Security having a certain priority be paid in full before any Claim or Equity Security having a lower priority receive any distribution. This rule is not truly absolute, however, because it allows deviations based upon compliance with certain minimum requirements and agreement within certain constraints. *See, e.g.,* 11 U.S.C. § 1129(a)(7), (8), (b) (2017).

Second, the Bankruptcy Code's "priority" rules reflect legislative policy determinations that certain categories of Claims are entitled to more favorable treatment than other categories. 11 U.S.C. § 507 (2017).

---

23. These restrictions are due to the protections provided by the Privacy Act, 5 U.S.C. § 552(a) (2017), and the Crime Victims' Rights Act, 18 U.S.C. § 3771 (2017).

2.7b Bankruptcy Priorities

A bedrock principle of the bankruptcy process is ratable distribution among Creditors of equal priority. In general, the rights of secured Creditors (with a lien on specific collateral) are senior to all other Creditors with respect to their collateral. 11 U.S.C. §§ 507, 1129(a) (2017).

Claimants whose entitlements arise during the administration of the bankruptcy case for the benefit of the estate are entitled to payment ahead of prepetition unsecured Creditors. 11 U.S.C. § 503 (2017). The rights of Creditors are, in turn, senior to the rights of Interest Holders.

Even within these general categories of Creditors and Interest Holders, however, specific Claimants or subgroups of Claimants may take priority over others based upon priority and subordination principles. 11 U.S.C. §§ 507 (priorities), 510 (subordination) (2017). For example, certain categories of prepetition "priority" unsecured Claims (including certain taxes, family law obligations, wage and benefit obligations, etc.) are entitled to be paid prior to prepetition "general" unsecured Claims. 11 U.S.C. § 507 (2017).

2.7c Automatic Subordination of Certain Victim Claims

Among unsecured Creditors, the absolute priority rule does not distinguish between tort Creditors and contract Creditors, nor between slip-and-fall tort Creditors and those that may hold fraud Claims. Nevertheless, a unique subordination rule applies in bankruptcy to Claims arising from the purchase or sale of securities.

Under the Bankruptcy Code, Claims arising from securities fraud are automatically treated differently than other Claims. Claims asserting damages arising from the purchase or sale of a security are statutorily subordinated to all Claims or Equity Securities that are senior or equal to the underlying security. 11 U.S.C. § 510(b) (2017). Thus, Claims for damages in connection with a secured bond offering would be subordinated to the bond Claims themselves. Similarly, Claims for fraud in the issuance of common stock would be subordinated to unsecured Claims, but because no class is junior to common stock, the stock fraud Claims would have the same priority as common stock. This provision prevents an Equity Security holder from couching its interest as an unsecured "claim" for damages arising from fraud, rather than accepting treatment of the security according to its terms, in an attempt to leap-frog ahead of its cohorts.

Distributions to Victims in a Forfeiture Proceeding are often at odds with the strict ranking of Claims and Equity Securities in an Insolvency Proceeding. In Forfeiture Proceedings, the Victims entitled to recovery may include defrauded investors whose Equity Security recoveries would statutorily be subordinated to Creditors' Claims in the bankruptcy case.

Although Creditors may object in bankruptcy cases to payments made to (arguably junior) Victims through the Forfeiture process, most cases reconcile the conflict based on the different recovery source (i.e., a government fund versus Property of the Bankruptcy Estate).[24] The funds administered through the Forfeiture fund would, however, have been administered in the bankruptcy case if the Property had not been forfeited. Unlike other governmental reimbursement funds that are funded by fees paid by the regulated

---

24. *See* Ad Hoc Adelphia Trade Claims Comm. v. Adelphia Commc'ns Corp., 337 B.R. 475, 478 (S.D.N.Y. 2006).

industry, Victim asset recovery funds are generated by removing assets that would otherwise be administered in a different forum (i.e., the Bankruptcy Court) in a manner that likely would have resulted in substantively different distributions to Claimants. This reality makes the initial determination of the propriety and scope of the Forfeiture essential to the administration of the parallel proceedings.

2.7d Chapter 7 Distributions

In a Chapter 7 case, distributions follow a strict ranking under which all senior Claims must be paid in full before any distributions may be made to the next tier of Creditors. Generally speaking, Claims are ranked as follows: (i) secured Claims, up to the value of the secured Creditor's interest in the collateral; (ii) administrative expenses, namely, those costs incurred by the Bankruptcy Estate following the commencement of the case, such as goods and services provided by vendors after the petition date and the fees of professionals retained by the officers of the court (i.e., a Trustee, an Examiner, a Committee, or an Ombudsman); (iii) priority Claims, such as employee wages earned within six months before the commencement of the case; (iv) all other unsecured Claims; and (v) Equity Securities. 11 U.S.C. § 726(a) (2017).

Claims for a "fine, penalty or forfeiture" that are not compensation for an actual pecuniary loss are treated specially under the Bankruptcy Code. Such punitive Claims are payable after all unsecured Claims are paid in full (including late-filed Claims), but before interest is paid to unsecured Creditors and before any surplus in the estate is remitted to the Debtor. 11 U.S.C. § 523(a)(7) (2017).

The fundamental rationale for such treatment lies in the fact that such Claims are excluded from the discharge (with the possible exception of some Civil Forfeiture Claims under Chapters 12 and 13)[25] and, hence, will survive the bankruptcy case and remain payable by the Debtor from future earnings or income.

Thus, although the bankruptcy distribution scheme contemplates that forfeiture Claims will be paid *after* general unsecured Claims, the Bankruptcy Code does provide for forfeiture Claims to be ratably paid from the Bankruptcy Estate. 11 U.S.C. § 726(a)(4) (2017). Therefore, when the government obtains a judgment forfeiting Substitute Property that is part of the Bankruptcy Estate, the government may pursue a Claim in the Insolvency Proceeding. Nevertheless, the inclusion of Forfeiture Claims under the Bankruptcy Code's classification scheme is generally not considered an obstacle to (nor inconsistent with) the government's ability to seek the removal, ab initio, of Forfeited Property from the Bankruptcy Estate.[26] Thus, when the government's Forfeiture precedes the bankruptcy case or relies on Relation Back to remove the estate's assets ab initio, the government may effectively reverse the Bankruptcy Code's priority scheme by Forfeiting assets and applying them at the government's discretion, possibly including to pay Victims who in the bankruptcy case would hold Equity Securities, before Creditors deemed senior under the bankruptcy distribution scheme are paid in that proceeding.

---

25. *See* discussion *supra* section 2.3.f.
26. *See* United States v. Rothstein, Rosenfeldt, Adler, P.A. (*In re* Rothstein, Rosenfeldt, Adler, P.A.), 717 F.3d 1205, 1210–1211 (11th Cir. 2013).

2.7e Chapter 11 Distributions

Sometimes liquidation cases are filed under Chapter 11 instead of Chapter 7 to provide more flexibility under a Plan with respect to distributions to Creditors than would otherwise be permitted under the Chapter 7 distribution regime. In Chapter 11 cases, as long as Creditors have been classified properly and accept the Plan by the requisite majorities, the Plan may accord different treatment to similar classes and different treatment to Creditors within a single category but different classes. For instance, a Plan may provide that, "for administrative convenience," smaller Creditors may be separately classified and treated. Other classification schemes among similarly situated Creditors (and varying distributions to those different classes) are also generally permitted under a Plan, unlike under a Chapter 7 case, as long as the classification scheme has a legitimate economic or business justification. 11 U.S.C. §§ 1122–1124 (2017).

Distributions in Chapter 11 generally depend on Creditor acceptance of the Plan. Nevertheless, Bankruptcy Code section 1129 protects dissenting Creditors and Interest Holders by establishing limitations and safeguards that set the outer boundaries of Chapter 11 flexibility. Absent Creditor acceptance, the only path to confirmation is compliance with the "cramdown" provisions of the Bankruptcy Code. These require that the plan is "fair and equitable" to, and does not "discriminate unfairly" against, each rejecting class. 11 U.S.C. § 1129(b) (2017). These standards essentially incorporate the absolute priority rules of Chapter 7 and require either that the senior Creditors be repaid in full or that no junior class receive or retain any Property under the plan.

Forfeiture Proceedings may affect both liquidating businesses and businesses attempting to reorganize under Chapter 11 and survive. Case management strategies will vary significantly in these two highly divergent types of cases.

Coordination in the liquidation of Ponzi schemes and other nonviable business entities. Chapter 11 cases entangled with parallel Forfeiture Proceedings may involve businesses that are wholly illegitimate and part of the Debtor/defendant's fraud, such as Ponzi schemes. Such fraudulent businesses are usually shuttered immediately. The Chapter 11 Trustee then may seek to recover transferred Property and to maximize the value of the potentially scant amount of non-fraudulent Property that remains. (*Madoff* and other Ponzi schemes are examples.) In these liquidating cases, parallel proceeding coordination is important for several reasons, including:

- to determine what causes of action may be pursued solely by the Trustee, rather than the government (such as avoiding powers unique to bankruptcy Trustees);
- to determine whether the government may assert any interest in proceeds the Trustee recovers from the exercise of avoiding powers or other causes of action;
- to determine whether the government has forfeited any Substitute Property to which the Trustee has a colorable claim on behalf of the Bankruptcy Estate;
- to determine whether certain assets can be administered more efficiently in the bankruptcy case; and
- to reduce the waste associated with extensive litigation over conflicting schemes of asset administration and distribution.

Coordination in the reorganization or sale of potentially viable business entities. In addition to these important reasons for coordination of parallel proceedings where the entity is liquidating, coordination is a crucial imperative where the Chapter 11 case involves a legitimate operating business that has become entangled in a Forfeiture Proceeding.

This typically occurs as a result of fraud, securities law violations, or criminal activity by a defendant who holds an ownership interest in the business. (*Dreier*, *Rothstein*, and *Adelphia* are examples.) These cases will typically require the sale of the business as a going concern, whether during the case or as part of a Plan. 11 U.S.C. §§ 363, 1123 (2017). Only the bankruptcy court will be in a position to sell such assets if the Forfeiture Proceedings have not yet resulted in a final judgment. In any such sale process, the government's interests and concerns will need to be accommodated. For example, in the *Adelphia* case, the criminal cases against the principals of Adelphia were in progress during the Chapter 11 case and a final judgment of Forfeiture had not yet been entered. To maximize the value that could be realized from the businesses, the parties resolved the matter by allowing the sale of the NHL hockey team and the cable communications business as part of the bankruptcy process, with the proceeds to be allocated as agreed.[27]

2.7f Other Chapters

In addition to Insolvency Proceedings under Chapter 7 and 11, a Forfeiture Proceeding may occasionally proceed alongside a Chapter 13 case.[28] Chapter 13 is designed for individual Debtors with regular income and debts below certain statutory thresholds. Forfeiture Proceedings will seldom, however, implicate cases under Chapter 12 (family farmers). Although not common, Chapter 15 (ancillary proceedings concerning foreign Debtors) may be implicated when foreign or domestic Forfeiture Proceedings affect entity groups or their assets that cross international borders. Chapter 12 and 13 cases offer somewhat broader discharges than Chapter 7 or 11 cases. 11 U.S.C. §§ 1228, 1328. Some Restitution and other fines may be dischargeable in those chapters, even though they are not dischargeable in cases under Chapter 7 or 11.

2.7g Claims Trading

In a bankruptcy case, Creditors are usually entitled to monetize their distribution rights by selling their Claims to third parties, who may or may not already hold Claims in the case. Such *claims trading* in distressed debt is ubiquitous in bankruptcy cases and is expressly permitted under applicable rules. Fed. R. Bankr. P. 3001(e). Claims Trading allows a holder who cannot wait months or years to receive a distribution in an Insolvency Proceeding to monetize its entitlement and receive payment in an amount and on terms the seller and buyer agree. If a Creditor sells its Claim, the buyer stands in the shoes of the seller for most purposes and is, for example, entitled to assert the Claim (subject to all defenses that would be valid against the seller), vote the Claim in respect of any Plan of reorganization, and receive distributions on account of the Claim.

In contrast, the Forfeiture process typically only recognizes the potential entitlements of Victims, and not their assignees, when determining the recipients of distributions in Forfeiture Proceedings.[29] Given the absence of transparency in Forfeiture

---

27. *See* Appendix C for further background on the *Adelphia* proceedings.
28. *See, e.g.*, United States v. Robinson (*In re* Robinson), 764 F.3d 554, 560 (6th Cir. 2014) (defendant, unable to satisfy criminal Restitution judgments, filed a Chapter 13 case).
29. *See* United States v. Freeman, 741 F.3d 426, 434 (4th Cir. 2014) (restitution may compensate "'only for the loss caused by the specific conduct that is the basis of the offense of conviction'") (quoting Hughey v. United States, 495 U.S. 411, 413 (1990)).

distributions, it is unclear whether the governmental agencies have honored or could honor assignments, and if so on what terms. (For example, because this information is not publicly available, it is not possible either to verify or debunk suggestions that a fund administrator in one case chose to honor assignments to family members or estates of deceased Victims but not to honor assignments to unrelated third-party assignees.) Consequently, Claimants/Victims may have great difficulty monetizing potential entitlements in a Forfeiture Proceeding. The buyer/transferee/assignee may be unable to enforce any assignment because it is not strictly a "Victim" under the Forfeiture distribution statutory framework.

The fact that Forfeiture law does not honor assignments may create other policy concerns as well. Unregulated contracts of assignment may impose burdens on the Victim (as seller/assignor) that are difficult for some Victims to satisfy. These could include, for example, an obligation to file and pursue Claims or petitions for Remission with the forfeiting agencies, or to turn over proceeds mistakenly paid to the assignor. The assignment contracts might also include provisions to reverse the transaction if the Victim/seller is insufficiently diligent in these endeavors, or if the buyer is unable to stand fully in the Victim/seller's shoes in the Forfeiture proceeding.[30] Given the statutory definition of Victim for purposes of Forfeiture distributions, it is unclear whether the parties can resolve these challenges in the context of a court-approved settlement or Coordination (Cooperation) Agreement. The courts overseeing the parallel proceedings should inquire into these issues if possible.

2.8 Discharge and Its Limits

2.8a The Fresh Start

The "fresh start" goal of a bankruptcy case is embodied in the discharge. The discharge, among other effects, operates as a permanent, statutory injunction against the commencement or continuation of any action to collect, recover, or offset any debt that has been discharged. This broad discharge is available to any individual under Chapter 7 or 11 and any entity that confirms a Plan under Chapter 11. Entities that liquidate under either chapter are not entitled to a discharge. A discharge may be denied altogether to an individual Debtor for certain enumerated reasons (such as fraud on the bankruptcy court or concealment of assets). 11 U.S.C. §§ 727, 1141, 1228, 1328 (2017).

2.8b Non-Dischargeable Obligations of Individual Debtors

Forfeiture and fraud Claims are among the favored few types of Claims that can usually survive a bankruptcy filing by, and discharge in favor of, an individual Debtor. The Bankruptcy Code provides that specific types of prepetition debts may be excepted from the discharge granted to an individual Debtor. These include, most notably, debts incurred through fraud. 11 U.S.C. § 523 (2017). Non-dischargeable Claims survive bankruptcy as

---

30. For further information, an American Bar Association publication titled THE BANKRUPTCY CLAIMS HANDBOOK (ABA 2013) provides comprehensive coverage.

enforceable obligations of the Debtor if the Debtor retains any assets or generates future income. These Claims, commonly referred to as non-dischargeable obligations, include certain tax liabilities, domestic support obligations, certain fraud Claims, and student loans. Included among the list of non-dischargeable obligations are Claims that seek a "fine, penalty, or forfeiture payable to and for the benefit of a governmental unit," unless the Claim is "compensation for actual pecuniary loss," in which case it is dischargeable. 11 U.S.C. § 523(a)(7) (2017).

Consequently, an individual convicted of fraud, embezzlement, or defalcation while acting in a fiduciary capacity will generally not receive a discharge of any related Claims filed in a parallel bankruptcy case. Even if a general discharge is granted to the Debtor, the individual will be unable to use the bankruptcy process to discharge any related Claims. Accordingly, if and to the extent the government asserts a fraud or Forfeiture Claim against a Debtor in a bankruptcy case (as distinguished from effecting an actual Forfeiture of Property of the Debtor), such a Claim will not be extinguished.

For example, defendants in a Forfeiture Proceeding commonly agree not only to forfeit specific known and identified Property, but also to the entry of a Forfeiture judgment (the amount of which may be determined in connection with sentencing), with a credit for any forfeited funds. If any assets are subsequently discovered, the Debtor will not be able to use the discharge to shield those assets from the Forfeiture judgment.

2.8c Entity Discharge

Debtors that are entities, rather than individuals, are not subject to the non-dischargeability provisions that apply to individual Debtors. For corporations and other entities, discharge is generally all or nothing. A reorganizing entity may usually obtain a broad discharge of all debts. A liquidating entity is not entitled to a discharge of any debts; however, the corporate shell will retain no assets against which Creditors or Interest Holders could press unsatisfied Claims because all assets have been liquidated and distributed in the bankruptcy case.

Chapter 3

Statutory Framework: Asset Forfeiture Proceedings

3.1 Overview
3.2 Forfeiture Methods and Policies
    3.2a Pre-Seizure Planning Common to Civil and Criminal Forfeiture
    3.2b Criminal Forfeiture
    3.2c Civil Forfeiture
    3.2d Administrative Forfeiture
3.3 Primary Players
    3.3a DOJ Criminal Division
    3.3b US Attorneys
    3.3c US Marshals Service
    3.3d SEC
    3.3e US Trustee
3.4 Property Subject to Forfeiture
    3.4a General Categories of Forfeitable Property
    3.4b Money Judgments
    3.4c Nexus Required for Forfeiture of Facilitating Property
    3.4d Relation Back Doctrine
    3.4e Substitute Property
    3.4f Seizure from Third Parties
3.5 Claims and Defenses
    3.5a Third-Party Claims and Defenses in Criminal and Civil Forfeitures
    3.5b Claims in Administrative Forfeiture
    3.5c Trustees and Creditors as Third-Party Claimants
        3.5c.i Trustees
        3.5c.ii Lienholders
        3.5c.iii General Unsecured Creditors
3.6 Distribution of Forfeited Property
    3.6a Restoration
    3.6b Remission
    3.6c Restitution
    3.6d Victims
3.7 State Law Forfeiture

*****

3.1 Overview

In general, as previously noted, Forfeiture focuses on divesting the defendant and associates of Property used to engage in or facilitate criminal activity and of Property that represents the Proceeds of crime. The federal government may seize assets using criminal Forfeiture, civil Forfeiture, or administrative Forfeiture powers (as defined in sections 3.2b–d), or by ordering Disgorgement of ill-gotten gains in SEC proceedings.

This chapter[1] focuses on federal criminal and civil Forfeiture and Disgorgement, and briefly overviews other Forfeiture powers under federal and state law. The implications in terms of intersections with Insolvency Proceedings are generally the same. The DOJ and the SEC view Forfeiture Proceedings and Disgorgement proceedings as governmental enforcement actions that are excepted from the automatic stay pursuant to 11 U.S.C. § 362(b)(1) (2017). *See* Jahn v. United States (*In re* WinPar Hospitality Chattanooga, LLC), 401 B.R. 289, 293 (Bankr. E.D. Tenn. 2009). The agencies consider these remedies to be essential tools to stop ongoing fraud and to compensate Victims.

Glossary II, *post*, identifies the primary governmental agencies that may be involved, provides their common acronyms, and explains their respective roles in Forfeiture Proceedings and Disgorgement proceedings. Of those agencies, the representatives the courts are likely to encounter in coordinating parallel Insolvency Proceedings and Forfeiture Proceedings are identified in this chapter (at section 3.3). The other agencies typically operate in the background, outside of the court proceedings.

3.2 Forfeiture Methods and Policies

Governmental authority to seize Property through Forfeiture generally arises by statute, as elaborated in this chapter, and is implemented primarily through the Federal Rules of Criminal and Civil Procedure,[2] whereas the SEC considers Disgorgement to be an equitable, rather than a statutory legal, proceeding.[3] In practice, civil Disgorgement and asset Forfeiture are distinct processes that serve different functions. Each, however, intersects with Insolvency Proceedings by contrasting control and distribution of Property for the benefit of Victims or otherwise under governmental distribution policies, to control and distribution of Property according to bankruptcy or other Insolvency Proceeding priorities.

To supplement the governing statutes, the DOJ has developed policies that elaborate the methods, processes, and policies the DOJ employs in implementing both civil and criminal Forfeitures. These policies are set forth at the Asset Forfeiture Policy Manual, DOJ Money Laundering and Asset Recovery Section webpage, and US Attorneys' Manual.[4]

---

1. Chapter 3 is an adaptation of Sarah J. Welling and Jane Lyle Hord, *Friction in Reconciling Criminal Forfeiture and Bankruptcy: The Criminal Forfeiture Part*, 42 Golden Gate L. Rev. 551 (2012). Used with permission.

2. *See also* U.S. Dep't of Justice, Criminal Division, Money Laundering and Asset Recovery Section, Asset Forfeiture & Money Laundering Statutes (2015), https://www.justice.gov/criminal/afmls/pubs/pdf/statutes2015.pdf (consisting of a 356 page brochure of "select" federal Forfeiture statutes).

3. *But see* Kokesh v. SEC, 137 S. Ct. 1635, 1639 (holding that Disgorgement is a "penalty" subject to the five-year statute of limitations under 28 U.S.C. § 2462).

4. Links to these manuals and the DOJ webpage are found in Appendix G. The DOJ has also issued stand-alone publications that address topics that merit extended treatment. *See, e.g.*, Asset Forfeiture Policy Manual (2016); Guide to Interlocutory Sales and Expedited Settlement (2007); and Financial Investigations Guide (1998).

The asset Forfeiture process involves several steps, including planning in advance of the seizure, seizing and taking custody of the Property, notifying interested parties, addressing any Claims and petitions, and determining the disposition of forfeited Property, including remission to Victims, and possible equitable sharing with state and local law enforcement agencies should sufficient funds be available after compensation of Victims.

3.2a Pre-Seizure Planning Common to Civil and Criminal Forfeiture

The US Attorney for the federal judicial district in which the Forfeiture is to occur is responsible for coordinating pre-seizure planning. Pre-seizure planning generally requires coordination among the Assistant US Attorney in charge of the Forfeiture, the Assistant US Attorney in charge of any related criminal matter, investigative agents, and the United States Marshals Service representative. In cases implicating the Financial Institutions Reform, Recovery, and Enforcement Act of 1989, Pub. L. No. 101–73, 103 Stat. 182 (1989) (FIRREA), a federal regulatory agency representative will also be involved. 12 U.S.C. § 1833a(e) (2017). If the proposed Forfeiture spans multiple federal judicial districts, the US Attorney initiating the Forfeiture must coordinate pre-seizure planning in all districts where assets will be seized. *See* United States Attorneys' Manual, §§ 9–111.110.

3.2b Criminal Forfeiture

Criminal forfeiture is an additional penalty sought as part of a criminal prosecution of a defendant. By definition, it is necessarily accomplished by judicial process. It allows the government to take Property from convicted defendants as part of the sentence imposed after conviction. It is another part of the sentence rather than a separate charge in itself. If the government intends to seek Criminal Forfeiture as an additional *in personam* (against the person) remedy, it must provide express notice of its intention to seek Forfeiture of the Property used or derived from the crime. Criminal Forfeiture may be imposed on a defendant after conviction (or in a plea agreement) with respect to an authorizing substantive crime.

Four statutes containing similar Forfeiture provisions serve as the primary authorization for federal Criminal Forfeiture:

- The Controlled Substances Act of 1970, 21 U.S.C. §§ 801–971 (2017) (CSA);
- The Racketeer Influenced and Corrupt Organizations Act of 1970, 18 U.S.C. §§ 1961–1968 (2017) (RICO); and
- Two general Criminal Forfeiture statutes, 18 U.S.C. § 982 (2017), 21 U.S.C. § 853 (2017).

The CSA and RICO Forfeiture provisions, which were adopted contemporaneously, are identical in many ways. Accordingly, courts often find authority under one persuasive under the other. Money laundering has been added more recently; however, its provisions substantially track the other Forfeiture statutes. *See* 18 U.S.C. § 1956 (2017).

Ultimately, Forfeiture is a jury decision. If the defendant is convicted of the underlying crime or crimes, the Forfeiture count is then submitted to the jury. The jury must make predicate factual findings in order to impose Forfeiture. If the jury imposes Forfeiture, the judge has no discretion to override the jury. If the jury finds particular Property forfeitable, the court issues a preliminary Forfeiture Order.

Forfeitures under CSA, RICO, money laundering, and other recently added statutes provide for an ancillary hearing in the event that third parties assert an interest in the Property. After the interests of third parties are addressed, the court issues a final Forfeiture Order.

Any Property forfeited may be distributed, as discussed in section 3.6, at the discretion of the lead governmental agency, among Victims and other governmental agencies. *See* Dep't of Justice, Guide to Equitable Sharing for State and Local Law Enforcement Agencies (2009), *available at* http://www.justice.gov/sites/default/files/usao-ri/legacy/2012/03/26/esguidelines.pdf.

3.2c Civil Forfeiture

Civil forfeiture is either an in rem action against the asset itself or an in personam remedy included as part of a civil enforcement action against a defendant. Like Criminal Forfeiture, Civil Forfeiture is accomplished by judicial process.

In rem Civil Forfeiture: The classic form of Civil Forfeiture is an *in rem* (against the Property) action brought against Property used in the commission of a crime. The Property is the "defendant"; no criminal charge against the owner of record is necessary. These cases, therefore, have names like United States v. $6,976,934.65, Plus Interest Deposited into Royal Bank of Scotland International, Account No. 2029-56141070, Held in the Name of Soulbury Ltd., and Property Traceable Thereto.[5] In these actions, the government is bringing a civil action against the Property directly, seeking to adjudicate all persons' rights in the Property. The government's jurisdiction is based on its seizure of the Property.

In personam Civil Forfeiture: Civil Forfeiture may also be sought as an equitable remedy, in addition to injunctive relief, in an in personam civil enforcement action against an individual or entity, such as in cases involving SEC enforcement. *See, e.g.*, SEC v. Wang, 944 F.2d 80, 85 (2d Cir. 1991) ("The disgorgement remedy ... approved in this case is, by its very nature, an equitable remedy ..."). Historically, this form of Forfeiture was framed as "Restitution," but more recently it has been treated as falling within the Forfeiture ambit. *See, e.g.*, SEC v. Texas Gulf Sulfur Co., 312 F. Supp. 77, 92–94 (S.D.N.Y. 1970); *aff'd in part and rev'd in part*, 446 F.2d 1301, 1307–08 (2d Cir. 1971); *see generally* John D. Ellsworth, *Disgorgement in Securities Fraud Actions Brought by the SEC*, 1977 Duke L. J. 641, 641–642 n.3 (1977).

Criminal and Civil Forfeiture are not mutually exclusive: For many offenses, both Civil and Criminal Forfeiture are available. For example, 21 U.S.C. § 853(a)(1) (2017) authorizes the Criminal Forfeiture of drug proceeds, whereas 21 U.S.C. § 881(a)(6) (2017) authorizes their Civil Forfeiture. The government may elect to proceed under both types of Forfeiture at the same time. Civil Forfeiture offers the distinct advantages of not requiring a criminal conviction and requiring a lower standard of proof, i.e., preponderance of the evidence versus beyond a reasonable doubt. On the other hand, to prevail on a Civil Forfeiture, the government must more tightly tie the Property to the criminal activity.

---

5. United States v. $6,976,934.65 Plus Interest Deposited into Royal Bank of Scot. Int'l, 478 F. Supp. 2d 30 (D.C. 2007).

General rules for Civil Forfeitures: The general rules governing federal Civil Forfeiture of Property are set forth in 18 U.S.C. § 983 (2017), with the exceptions set forth in 18 U.S.C. § 983(i)(2).[6]

2000 CAFRA reforms: The Civil Asset Forfeiture Reform Act of 2000, 18 U.S.C. §§ 981–987 (2017) (CAFRA) introduced procedural and substantive reforms to Civil Forfeitures implemented under Civil Forfeiture statutes. The reforms, among other provisions, increased the government's burden of proof in Civil Forfeiture, eliminated cost bonds, and provided enhanced review mechanisms for Property owners. In 2012, the DOJ rules and regulations regarding seizure and Forfeiture were consolidated and updated to comply with CAFRA. *See* 77 Fed. Reg. 177 (Sept. 12, 2012); 21 C.F.R. §§ 1316.01–1316.68 (2017); 28 C.F.R. §§ 8.1–9.9 (2017).

CAFRA's principal additional protections for third-party Claimants include the following:

- The government must show that the Property is subject to Forfeiture; the government is no longer automatically entitled to Forfeiture upon the filing of the complaint. 18 U.S.C. § 983(c) (2017).
- Claimants no longer have to post a "cost bond" (which typically had been 10 percent of the Property's value) before contesting the seizure. 18 U.S.C. § 983(a)(2)(E) (2017).
- Generally, proceedings to determine the underlying merits must commence within 60 days after the seizure. 11 U.S.C. § 983(a)(1) (2017).
- Indigent Claimants may have a right to be provided with counsel. 18 U.S.C. § 983(b) (2017). Attorneys' rights regarding payment have been strengthened, which facilitates Claimants' access to counsel.

Conversely, CAFRA also increases the scope of Forfeiture. First, it adds many offenses, including mail and wire fraud, that had not previously given rise to Forfeiture. Second, it authorizes Criminal Forfeiture whenever Civil Forfeiture would be available, which obviates prior inconsistencies among the various Forfeiture Statutes.

Use of Civil versus Criminal Forfeiture: Until the year 2000 or so, the government used Criminal Forfeiture less frequently than Civil Forfeiture because Civil Forfeiture actions were easier for the government to win. In Civil Forfeiture actions, among other advantages, the government's burden of proof had been lower (preponderance versus beyond a reasonable doubt), the burden of persuasion shifted from the government to Claimants, and Claimants had no privilege against self-incrimination or right to counsel. This balance shifted when, in 2000 and again in 2006, Criminal Forfeiture powers were expanded and additional protections were applied to Civil Forfeiture. Courts overseeing parallel proceedings today often encounter cases that combine both Criminal and Civil Forfeiture, as well as administrative Forfeiture and Disgorgement, as governmental agencies work in tandem to employ the tools they determine will result in the broadest and most easily enforced Property seizures.

---

6. The actions excluded from 11 U.S.C. § 983 (2017) are specialized Forfeitures under the Tariff Act of 1930, 19 U.S.C. §§ 1001–1683g (2017), and other provisions of 19 U.S.C.; Federal Food, Drug, & Cosmetic Act, 21 U.S.C. §§ 301–399h (2017); 22 U.S.C. § 401 (2017); Internal Revenue Code of 1986, 26 U.S.C. §§ 1–9834 (2017); Trading with the Enemy Act, 50 U.S.C. §§ 4301–4341 (2017); or Int'l Emergency Economic Powers Act, 50 U.S.C. §§ 1701–1708 (2017).

3.2d Administrative Forfeiture

Administrative forfeiture is a statutory power that permits the federal seizing agency to seize and forfeit Property directly without judicial involvement through an in rem administrative proceeding. The authority for a seizing agency to commence an Administrative Forfeiture action is found in the Tariff Act of 1930, 19 U.S.C. §§ 1001–1683g (2017). As provided therein, Property that may be subjected to Administrative Forfeiture includes: (i) merchandise that is prohibited from importation; (ii) a conveyance used to import, transport, or store a controlled substance; (iii) a monetary instrument; or (iv) other Property that does not exceed $500,000 in value. 19 U.S.C. § 1607(a) (2017). In general, properties subject to Administrative Forfeiture must be forfeited administratively, unless one of the statutory exceptions applies. See Asset Forfeiture Policy Manual, Ch. 2, § 2.A.

Expanded administrative powers: Before 1990, virtually all forfeitures of Property valued at more than $100,000 were conducted judicially (through Criminal or Civil Forfeiture). In 1990, however, the law was amended to permit the Administrative Forfeiture of cash and monetary instruments, without regard to value, and of other Property up to a value of $500,000. 19 U.S.C. § 1607 (2017). The legislative history suggests that Congress sought to increase the speed and efficiency of uncontested Forfeiture actions and had confidence that Administrative Forfeiture laws provided adequate notice and other safeguards.

Enhanced protections for Civil Forfeiture lead to increased preference for Administrative Forfeiture: The CAFRA reforms which, as previously noted, enhanced protections for defendants and Claimants, may have encouraged the government to implement Forfeiture administratively when possible, to avoid the demands of judicially monitored Civil Forfeitures.

SEC administrative Disgorgement: Administrative Disgorgement is an analogous non-judicial seizure remedy that the SEC implements to remove ill-gotten gains from the target of a securities law violation action. See, e.g., 15 U.S.C. §§ 77h-l(e), 78u-2e, 78u-3(e) (2017). Unlike Administrative Forfeiture proceedings against the Property itself, however, Disgorgement is typically an additional remedy under an in personam SEC proceeding against an individual or entity. If the SEC anticipates that Claims will be contested, it tends to submit the matter to judicial supervision rather than to employ administrative proceedings to seek Disgorgement.

3.3 Primary Players

Glossary II lists the principal governmental agencies that may be involved in a Forfeiture Proceeding or Disgorgement and their respective roles. The following itemization briefly identifies the primary governmental parties the courts overseeing parallel Insolvency Proceedings and Forfeiture Proceedings may expect to encounter in court.

3.3a DOJ Criminal Division

The Asset Forfeiture and Money Laundering Section of DOJ's Criminal Division coordinates and oversees DOJ forfeiture, including civil and criminal litigation, policy and procedure, multidistrict seizures, equitable sharing, petitions for Remission, international forfeiture, and training.

3.3b US Attorneys

The US Attorneys' Offices prosecute Criminal and Civil Forfeiture actions against defendants and, where appropriate, in rem against Property.

3.3c US Marshals Service

The US Marshals Service generally takes custody of, manages, and disposes of forfeited Property.

3.3d SEC

The SEC applies Disgorgement both administratively and judicially. Between 2010 and 2014, for example, the SEC has obtained $1.8 billion to $2.8 billion annually in Disgorgement orders, which significantly exceeds the amount the agency has been awarded in statutory penalties over the same period. *See* select SEC and Market Data Reports, http://www.sec.gov/about/secreports.shtml.

3.3e US Trustee

The Office of the US Trustee (OUST), an arm of the DOJ, exercises oversight and coordination of activities in the bankruptcy system. The OUST refers criminal matters that come to its attention during the course of a bankruptcy case to the local US Attorney for investigation and prosecution. In the type of Forfeitures this guidebook addresses, OUST involvement typically will be as a resource for the courts and intermediary among the players, rather than an entity implementing Forfeiture. As part of the DOJ, the OUST is an invaluable resource to the courts and parties because its officers appreciate the language and procedures of both the bankruptcy and criminal processes, and the OUST may be encouraged or enlisted to foster communication between the parties to the Insolvency Proceedings and Forfeiture Proceedings.

3.4 Property Subject to Forfeiture

CAFRA lists the types of Property subject to Forfeiture and sets forth certain procedures, such as with respect to stays where parallel criminal and civil proceedings exist. 18 U.S.C. §§ 981–987 (2017). Almost any kind of Property, real or personal, which was used in connection with an offense, is traceable to the gross Proceeds of the criminal activity, or was obtained directly or indirectly from such offense, may be forfeited. In particular, the aggregate effect of the Relation Back Doctrine and Substitute Property doctrines has important implications for Insolvency Proceedings.

3.4a General Categories of Forfeitable Property

Courts encountering Forfeiture Proceedings need to understand: (i) the differences between Facilitating Property, Proceeds, and Disgorgement; and (ii) the manner in which the Relation Back and Substitute Property doctrines may dramatically increase the scope of Forfeitable Property.

Forfeitable Property, that is, Property subject to Forfeiture, falls into two general categories: Proceeds and Facilitating Property.

The category of Proceeds includes:

- *In cases involving illegal goods or services, unlawful activities, and telemarketing and health care fraud schemes*: all gross proceeds, including any Property of any kind obtained directly or indirectly, as the result of the underlying offense, and any Property traceable thereto.
- *In cases involving lawful good or services that are sold in an illegal manner*: the net proceeds acquired through the illegal transactions after deducting the direct costs (but not overhead) incurred in providing the goods or services.
- *In cases involving fraudulently obtained loans or credit*: the net amount of the loan or credit, less any amounts repaid.

Forfeitability of Proceeds is a relatively new concept in criminal law. It first appeared in Criminal Forfeiture statutes in 1970 and has no common law analogue. The statutory language defining Proceeds varies among the statutes. In general, however, Proceeds includes gross receipts rather than net profits. In 2009, Congress adopted this definition in the context of the money laundering crime. *See* 18 U.S.C. § 982 (2017). If there are multiple defendants, they are held jointly and severally liable for all foreseeable Proceeds that result from their crime(s). Some exceptions have been carved out, however.

The second general category of Forfeitable Property, Facilitating Property, includes any Property used or involved in the crime. Again, the statutory language varies. It generally evolved in the context of drug crimes as part of the historical development of Criminal Forfeiture. Facilitating Property typically has a legitimate genesis unconnected to the underlying criminal activity; i.e., because it was not generated by crime, it is not a Proceed of the crime. Nevertheless, when defendants use clean, untainted Property to commit a crime, it becomes Forfeitable under this second category. For example, a defendant who legitimately owns an office building and runs an investment company from the building, but uses the company to operate a Ponzi scheme, may forfeit the building as Property that facilitated the crime.

3.4b Money Judgments

In addition to forfeiting Proceeds and Facilitating Property, the government may seek a monetary Forfeiture judgment in lieu of seizing specific Property. Money judgments are not expressly mentioned in the Forfeiture statutes but are implicitly authorized by the government's power to seize Substitute Property. This power, described in more detail in section 3.4e, affords the government power to seize Substitute Property when the specific Forfeitable Property is unavailable. Because money is just another form of Property, courts have allowed the government to enforce money judgments as Substitute Property.

3.4c Nexus Required for Forfeiture of Facilitating Property

In order for Property to be forfeited as Facilitating Property, there generally must be a "nexus," or substantial connection, between the Property and the crime. The nexus requirement was developed by courts that deemed the requirement to be implied by the statutory language. Generally, the nexus requirement applies to Property forfeited on the theory that it facilitated the crime. If Property is forfeited under the theory that it is

Proceeds, a nexus necessarily exists because the Property was generated by the crime. If the government is seeking a money judgment, as Substitute Property, no nexus between Substitute Property and the crime is necessary.

Civil Forfeiture generally requires a more direct nexus than does Criminal Forfeiture. Property subject to Civil Forfeiture must have a direct connection with the offense. 18 U.S.C. § 981 (2017). Property subject to Criminal Forfeiture is not so circumscribed. Generally, the government is entitled to a rebuttable presumption of forfeitability with respect to any Property of a person convicted of an offense as to which Forfeiture may be imposed, if the Property was acquired during the period of the offense or shortly thereafter, or if the defendant had no other likely source for such Property. *See, e.g.*, 21 U.S.C. § 853(d) (2017) (Criminal Forfeiture for drug crimes). By contrast, Civil Forfeiture for drug offenses requires proof of a direct connection with the offense itself. *See* 21 U.S.C. § 881(a) (2017) (Civil Forfeiture for drug offenses).

3.4d Relation Back Doctrine

The Forfeiture Statutes all provide that "[a]ll right, title, and interest in property [subject to Criminal Forfeiture] vests in the United States upon the commission of the act giving rise to forfeiture." *See, e.g.*, 21 U.S.C. § 853(c) (2017); *see also* Caplin & Drysdale, Chartered v. United States, 491 U.S. 617, 627 (1989) ("[Section] 853(c) reflects the application of the long-recognized and lawful practice of vesting title to any forfeitable assets, in the United States, at the time of the criminal act."). As discussed in chapter 1, the Relation Back Doctrine is the doctrine under which title to Forfeitable Property vests in the federal government at the time the crime is committed or at the time the Property is used to facilitate the crime. Because title vests in the government at the time of the crime, anything that is done to the Property after that, whether by the defendant or a third party, does not change its character—it is still the government's Property.

The effect of the Relation Back Doctrine varies depending on which theory of Forfeiture the government uses. For Proceeds, the Relation Back Doctrine means that Proceeds were never the Property of the criminal defendant because at their creation, i.e., when the defendant generated them through the crime, title vested in the government. The defendant never had any claim of title. For Facilitating Property, on the other hand, Relation Back means that title shifts from the defendant to the government. Facilitating Property legitimately belonged to the defendant up until the time of the crime, but the Relation Back Doctrine legally shifts the title from the defendant to the government when the Property is used in the crime.

The Relation Back Doctrine presents a major source of friction between Insolvency Proceedings and Forfeiture Proceedings. If a bankruptcy petition is filed before the initiation of the Forfeiture Proceedings, all Property in which the Debtor holds legal or beneficial title becomes Property of the Bankruptcy Estate and is thereby subject to the bankruptcy court's in rem jurisdiction, at the instant the case is filed. Invoking the Relation Back Doctrine, however, the governmental agency seeking Forfeiture may seek to dispossess the Debtor/defendant of the Property retroactively, and thus try to extract the Property from the jurisdiction of the bankruptcy court. The government can be expected to posit that: (i) legal title to the Property vested in the government before the bankruptcy was commenced; and (ii) the automatic stay does not preclude the Criminal Forfeiture Proceedings from moving forward.

3.4e Substitute Property

For Criminal Forfeitures, the government may be authorized to seize other Property of the defendant if the specific Property subject to Forfeiture is unavailable. This doctrine of Substitute Property is designed to prevent defendants from evading Forfeiture. Seizure of Substitute Property is meant to deprive the defendant of all Forfeitable Property or its value. Substitute Property includes any Property seized from the defendant in lieu of Facilitating Property or Proceeds (or other Forfeitable Property) if the Facilitating Property or Proceeds "as a result of any act or omission of the defendant—(A) cannot be located upon the exercise of due diligence; (B) has been transferred or sold to, or deposited with, a third party; (C) has been placed beyond the jurisdiction of the court; (D) has been substantially diminished in value; or (E) has been commingled with other property which cannot be divided without difficulty." 21 U.S.C. § 853(p) (2017).

In addition to involuntary seizures of Substitute Property, defendants may agree to provide alternative Property to serve as Substitute Property as part of a plea or consent judgment (possibly in exchange for sentencing accommodations).

The Substitute Property power justifies the entry of monetary judgments. Monetary judgments effectuate the broad remedial purpose of the Forfeiture statutes and "ensur[e] that all eligible criminal defendants receive the mandatory forfeiture sanction Congress intended and disgorge their ill-gotten gains, even those already spent." United States v. Casey, 444 F.3d 1071, 1074 (9th Cir. 2006). With this purpose in mind, all circuits to which the issue of monetary judgments has been presented have approved of their imposition. *See, e.g.*, United States v. Awad, 598 F.3d 75, 78 (2d Cir. 2010); United States v. Vampire Nation, 451 F.3d 189, 201–02 (3d Cir. 2006); United States v. Hall, 434 F.3d 42, 59 (1st Cir. 2006); United States v. Baker, 227 F.3d 955, 970 (7th Cir. 2000). The government's power to seize Substitute Property in effect converts the in rem power to forfeit specific criminal Proceeds and Facilitating Property into an in personam money judgment against the defendant.

At least one court has held that the government cannot apply the Relation Back Doctrine to Substitute Property because the Substitute Property could not be identified until the other Forfeitable Property was identified and determined to be unavailable. Under this analysis, if a bankruptcy case is filed before the Forfeiture Proceeding identifies the Property subject to Forfeiture and then identifies Substitute Property, the government could not use the Substitute Property doctrine to assert that the Property never became Property of the Bankruptcy Estate, as it could do with Facilitating Property and Proceeds. *See* United States v. Erpenbeck, 682 F.3d 472, 477 (6th Cir. 2012); *cf.* United States v. McHan, 345 F.3d 262, 272 (4th Cir. 2003). Nevertheless, case law on this issue remains sparse.

3.4f Seizure from Third Parties

The government can forfeit identified Property the defendant transferred to a third party unless the third party can establish either of the two statutory defenses (noted below). If, however, the third party has since sold or transferred the Property and it is untraceable, the Substitute Property doctrine does not allow the government to seize Substitute Property from third parties. Rather, it must resort to state common law actions of conversion and detinue to recover the money.

Because the government may not seize Substitute Property from third parties, the court must determine exactly what Forfeitable Property remains in the third parties' hands. If the Forfeitable Property is money that has been commingled with other funds, and there has been an outflow of funds from the commingled account, the court must determine if the outflow came from the clean funds or the forfeitable money.

If the forfeitable money is insufficient to satisfy the Forfeiture judgment, the government cannot seize substitute assets or money from third parties to satisfy the judgment.

3.5 Claims and Defenses

The courts overseeing parallel Insolvency Proceedings and Forfeiture Proceedings may be asked to consider not only whether individual entities are entitled to assert Claims against and interests in the forfeited Property, but as a critical threshold matter, whether third parties—including the Trustee, Receiver, lien holders, and general Creditors—were entitled to receive and did receive proper and timely notices of their potential rights to assert such Claims or Interests.

3.5a Third-Party Claims and Defenses in Criminal and Civil Forfeitures

The legal fiction created by the Relation Back Doctrine, i.e., that title to Forfeitable Property vests in the government at the moment it becomes forfeitable, creates significant problems for third parties. Because the defendant did not have clear title to any Forfeitable Property, subsequent transfers to third parties were arguably invalid because the government owned the Property.

The Forfeiture Statutes specify the interaction between the Relation Back Doctrine and the rights of third parties. For example, with respect to drug offenses, under the Relation Back Doctrine, title to any Forfeitable Property vests in the government as of the date of the crime. The defendant has no title and cannot have conveyed any rights in the Property to a third party. Consequently, any Forfeitable Property subsequently received by a third party is subject to Forfeiture to the United States. 21 U.S.C. § 853(c) (2017). This is designed to prevent the defendant from hiding Property by giving or selling it to others.

Third-party Claimants have two defenses to Forfeiture. 21 U.S.C. § 853(n) (2017). A third-party Claimant may defeat Forfeiture if it can satisfy either the "superior interest" defense or the "bona fide purchaser for value" defense. A *superior interest* defense means that, as of the time of the crime, the third party, not the defendant, owned the Property or otherwise had rights superior to those of the defendant. 21 U.S.C. § 853(n)(6)(A) (2017). A *bona fide purchaser for value* defense asserts that the third-party claimant: (i) bought the Property for value (i.e., acquired the Property at arms length for a fair price); and (ii) was reasonably without cause to believe the Property was subject to Forfeiture (i.e., lacked the mens rea necessary to be liable for Forfeiture because the third party did not know about the crime).

The two third-party defenses work differently when applied to the two general categories of Forfeitable Property.

Application of the Superior Interest defense to Facilitating Property: If the government is forfeiting Property based on the theory that it was clean Property but was used to facilitate the crime, the third party may claim that, at the time the defendant used the Property in committing a crime, the third party had an interest in it that was vested or superior to the defendant's interest. This comes up frequently in the cases. An example is where a defendant husband is convicted of a drug crime involving his jointly owned house. In such a circumstance, the co-tenant/wife's half interest is not forfeited.

Application of the Superior Interest defense to Proceeds: By definition, Proceeds do not exist until they are generated as a result of a crime. Under the Relation Back Doctrine, title to the Proceeds vests in the government at the time of the crime. In theory then, the defendant never had any title to the Proceeds; title was in the government from the birth of the Proceeds. If the defendant had no title, any third-party Claimant's title may be superior to the defendant's title. Whether the third party's interest is superior to that of the government is a harder question. The courts that have addressed the issue have held either that a third party cannot acquire a Superior Interest or that any interest acquired is not superior to that of the government. This follows from the nature of the Superior Interest defense as a question of timing.

Application of the Bona Fide Purchaser for Value defense to Facilitating Property: The elements of the defense (purchase for value and mens rea) are the same for both Proceeds and Facilitating Property. Nevertheless, because Proceeds are often in the form of currency, whereas Facilitating Property is usually some form of non-cash personal Property, the structure of the transactions will be different. In part, the analysis depends upon whether: (i) the Facilitating Property itself is of a type that would raise suspicion that the defendant intended to use it in commission of a crime; or (ii) the nature of the transaction is sufficiently suspicious to raise an inference of criminal activity.

- *General use assets*: An inference of potential use for criminal purposes would not ordinarily apply to general use assets such as a house or computer.
- *Specialized use assets*: Some Property by its mere possession or condition should raise some apprehension on the part of a third-party buyer. For example, if the third party knows that the car at issue has hidden compartments, that knowledge might lead a reasonable person to believe that it would be used to hide and transport something illegal.
- *Suspicious circumstances*: Unless the third-party claimant is an institution with a lien against the Property or a pawn shop, the defendant will usually be engaging in a transaction with an individual in a non-traditional, one-on-one context. Because of that greater degree of personal interaction in the sale transaction, courts may be more willing to infer that the third party had reasonable cause to believe that the Property was forfeitable.
- *Suspicious timing or price*: A defendant seeking to convey Property linked to the crime may sell the Property for a price well below its obvious value. If the value given by the third party is clearly inadequate consideration, the transaction may not be considered a bona fide purchase.

Application of the Bona Fide Purchaser for Value defense with respect to Proceeds: With respect to Proceeds, the defendant is likely to be using cash Proceeds to acquire goods and services in a traditional commercial setting. In such a transaction, the ordinary commercial relationship of the parties makes it less likely that a third party will be imputed with reasonable cause to believe that the money would be subject to Forfeiture. If, however, the third party has some personal relationship with the defendant, that might give the third party reason to believe that the defendant was involved in some illegal activity, then the government may be able to establish the requisite mens rea.

3.5b Claims in Administrative Forfeiture

Administrative Forfeiture arises primarily in the context of customs and tax enforcement, as discussed in section 3.2d. A Claimant asserting a right to the return of seized Property may contest an Administrative Forfeiture action by filing a claim containing specified information within the time limits. 18 U.S.C. § 983(a)(2) (2017). If the claim is not filed in accordance with the statute, the seizing agency may enter a declaration of Forfeiture pursuant to 19 U.S.C. § 1609 (2017). The US Attorney's duty to file a Civil Forfeiture action in the district court (rather than proceed by nonjudicial Administrative Forfeiture) does not arise until a proper claim is filed. For example, in Manjarrez v. United States, No. 01C7530, 2002 WL 31870533 (N.D. Ill. Dec. 19, 2002), the district court held that a claim filed by the Claimant's attorney, instead of by the Claimant personally, was not under oath as the statute requires, and therefore was not a valid claim. Manjarrez v. United States, No. 01C7530, 2002 WL 31870533, at *2 (N.D. Ill. Dec. 19, 2002). Accordingly, the 90-day period in which the government was required to commence a judicial Forfeiture action never began to run. *Id.*

If the seizing agency ignores the Claimant's protestations and proceeds with the declaration of Forfeiture without referring the case to the US Attorney for the filing of a complaint, it runs the risk that the Claimant was correct. By that time, it is likely that the 90-day period for commencing a Civil Forfeiture action pursuant to 18 U.S.C. § 983(a)(3) (2017) will have expired. If that is the case, Civil Forfeiture of the Property will be barred by the "death penalty" provision in 18 U.S.C. § 983(a)(3)(B) (2017).

Lengthy and intricate policies govern the interests of third parties. The policies can be found in the Asset Forfeiture Policy Manual, Ch. 4.

3.5c Trustees and Creditors as Third-Party Claimants

3.5c.i Trustees

The timing of the filings and of the Forfeiture Order may significantly impact the bankruptcy Trustee's potential entitlement to assert a Superior Interest in forfeited Property. For example, a bankruptcy Trustee may assert a Superior Interest Claim against the forfeited Property if the government seeks to forfeit the Property under the Relation Back Doctrine as Substitute Property in a situation in which the Insolvency Proceeding obtained in rem jurisdiction over the Property before the government identified the Property as Substitute Property. *See* United States v. Erpenbeck, 682 F.3d 472, 477 (6th Cir. 2012); *cf.* United States v. McHan, 345 F.3d 262, 272 (4th Cir. 2003). If a Trustee or Receiver has a colorable claim that it holds a Superior Interest in the Property on behalf of the Bankruptcy Estate or Receivership estate, and the government is aware of the pendency of the Insolvency Proceeding, the government must give the Trustee or Receiver direct notice of its entitlement to assert that Superior Interest (rather than notice by publication). *Id.*; Fed. R. Crim. P. 32.2(b)(6).

The nature of the Property may affect the Trustee's ability to assert a Bona Fide Purchaser defense. Whether the bankruptcy Trustee might qualify as a Bona Fide Purchaser may turn on 11 U.S.C. § 544 (2017), which accords the Trustee the status of Bona Fide Purchaser with respect to real estate but not with respect to personal Property. *See* 11 U.S.C. § 544(a)(3) (2017).

3.5c.ii   Lienholders

A secured Creditor might qualify as a Bona Fide Purchaser. A secured Creditor who takes a security interest in Property (tangible or intangible) in exchange for value (including an antecedent debt) can be a Bona Fide Purchaser of the Property (e.g., a deposit account). *See* United States v. Huntington Nat'l Bank, 682 F.3d 429, 436 (6th Cir. 2012) (applying 21 U.S.C. § 853(n)(6)(B) (2017)).

3.5c.iii   General Unsecured Creditors

General unsecured Creditors do not qualify as Bona Fide Purchasers (United States v. Campos, 859 F.2d 1233, 1238 (6th Cir. 1988); United States v. Reckmeyer, 836 F.2d 200, 206 n.3 (4th Cir. 1987)), even if they hold a right to setoff (United States v. BCCI Holdings (Lux.), S.A., 961 F. Supp. 287, 295 (D.D.C. 1997)).

It is extremely difficult for a Creditor to assert a Superior Interest under a constructive trust theory with respect to forfeited Property. The establishment of a constructive trust is highly dependent on state law. The elements typically require an ability to trace value to a specific asset, the lack of an adequate remedy at law, a confidential relationship, fairness to others similarly situated, and "clean" hands. Where numerous parties were harmed by the fraud or other activity that led to forfeiture, the "fairness" element generally renders it difficult for one party to leap ahead of others. On constructive trust theories, *see* United States v. BCCI Holdings (Lux.), S.A., 46 F.3d 1185, 1190–1191 (D.D.C. 1995); United States v. Shefton, 548 F.3d 1360, 1366 (11th Cir. 2008); United States v. Ramunno, 599 F.3d 1269, 1275 (11th Cir. 2010); United States v. Wilson, 659 F.3d 947, 955 (9th Cir. 2011).

3.6   Distribution of Forfeited Property

3.6a   Restoration

Restoration refers to the process by which the US Attorney may ask the Attorney General to use forfeited funds to compensate a group of Victims as part of a criminal Restitution order, if no other funds are available. A criminal conviction is the essential predicate for any Restoration request. The Victims to receive compensation must be specifically named in the Restitution order issued with the sentence. *See* Asset Forfeiture Policy Manual, Ch. 13.

The Restoration request. The US Attorney works with the investigative agency to develop a list of Victims to receive compensation, and to specify the funds forfeited in related administrative, criminal, or civil enforcement proceedings. Victims may be required to supply documentation or other information to the US Attorney if they wish to be compensated.

Advantages of Restoration vs. Remission. The Restoration procedure eliminates the need for each Victim to file a separate petition for Remission (see below). Restoration requests are generally processed more quickly than Remission petitions. Nevertheless, the same underlying requirements apply; i.e., the Victim must have been directly harmed in an amount that has been substantiated.

3.6b Remission

Remission refers to the process under which the Attorney General may return or distribute assets to owners, lienholders, or Victims, who qualify under governmental regulations and file appropriate petitions. (*See* Appendix B for a summary of the Remission statutes and regulations.)

Process for making a claim: Upon seizure of the Property, the US Attorney's Office, with the assistance of the investigating agency, is required to identify all potential Victims of the offense and to notify them by mail (or, if unknown, by publication) of the opportunity to make a claim for Remission.

Losses that may be claimed. Only pecuniary losses are compensable. Losses must be substantiated by appropriate documentation.

Distribution. Remission is a discretionary process. The specific details regarding individual distributions are generally not made publicly available. In general, however, if the government remits forfeited Property, the government's administrative expenses are paid first, before any distributions are made to Victims. Innocent owners may also assert the right to return of the Property. If substantiated, they have priority. Next in priority are valid lienholders, to the extent of their liens. Only if available funds remain might the Victims receive compensation. If whatever portion of the forfeited funds has been remitted is not sufficient to repay all losses, then amounts will usually be prorated. Given the discretionary nature of the process, however, a Victim's particularized needs could be taken into account. *See generally* 28 C.F.R. § 9.8 (2017) (Remission procedures for Victims).

3.6c Restitution

Criminal Restitution. Restitution refers to payments the court orders a defendant to make to the clerk of the court, who then makes distribution to the Victims identified in the order, in the amounts ordered. DOJ regulations and policies implement distributions. (*See* Appendix B for a summary of the Restitution statutes and regulations.)

Courts may order Restitution to Victims as part of the sentence, either without the defendant's agreement or by plea agreement. 18 U.S.C. § 3663(a)–(b) (2017). Restitution orders may require:

- return of Property to rightful owners;
- payment of the value of lost Property;
- payment of medical expenses in connection with bodily injury; or
- payment of other compensatory damages.

Pre-sentence reports are supposed to provide a complete accounting of Victim losses and of the defendant's financial situation. Victims are entitled to notice of the conviction, the pre-sentence report, and the deadline to file any separate declaration regarding their own losses. 18 U.S.C. § 3664(d) (2017). Victims may but are not required to participate. 18 U.S.C. § 3664(g)(1) (2017). Restitution payments may differ among Victims based upon their individual needs. 18 U.S.C. § 3664(i) (2017). Disputes regarding Restitution are resolved by a preponderance of the evidence. 18 U.S.C. § 3664(e) (2017). The government has the burden of proof on Victim losses. *Id.* The defendant has the burden with respect to financial ability to pay. *Id.*

Civil Restitution. The same processes and standards for seeking compensation apply to Victims of offenses resulting in Civil Forfeitures. An order for Civil Restitution may be included in civil enforcement judgments.

3.6d Victims

The Forfeiture statutes generally use the same definition of Victims with respect to provisions for Restitution or other compensation:

> [T]he term 'victim' means a person directly and proximately harmed as a result of the commission of an offense for which restitution may be ordered including, in the case of an offense that involves as an element a scheme, conspiracy, or pattern of criminal activity, any person directly harmed by the defendant's criminal conduct in the course of the scheme, conspiracy, or pattern. 18 U.S.C. §§ 3663(a)(2), 3663A(a)(2) (2017).

A person cannot qualify as a Victim, however, if that person:

- knowingly contributed to or benefited from the offense underlying the Forfeiture or was willfully blind to it;
- has recourse to other reasonably available assets or compensation; or
- seeks recovery for torts or physical injuries that are associated with the offense but are not the basis for the Forfeiture.

By statute, Restitution for Victims is generally discretionary with the Attorney General and DOJ, which may choose to retain Forfeited Property for the benefit of law enforcement agencies. *See, e.g.*, 28 C.F.R. § 9.7 (2017). As a matter of policy and practice, the government's costs for Forfeiture Victim recovery programs are paid from Forfeiture funds, then compensation is provided to Victims, and then any remaining funds are subject to equitable sharing with other law enforcement agencies. *See, e.g.*, Asset Forfeiture Policy Manual, Ch. 12, § A.3. Restitution is, however, mandatory for certain Victims, such as those suffering crimes of violence, offenses against Property involving drug-involved premises, tampering with consumer products, or theft of medical products. 18 U.S.C. § 3663A (2017).

General Creditors have no rights whatsoever to distributions from forfeited Property unless they *also* qualify as Victims within the meaning of the applicable Forfeiture statute. This is true even though Victims and general Creditors may have been harmed by the same actions, and even though the crime of conviction (and consequent identification of Victims) may be determined by the government's charging order or the defendant's plea agreement. This is a primary source of substantive and policy tension between Insolvency Proceedings and Forfeiture Proceedings.

3.7 State Law Forfeiture

All fifty states have statutes authorizing Forfeiture, some under limited circumstances, others more broadly. State Forfeiture laws often track federal statutory provisions. *See generally* Dee Edgeworth, Asset Forfeiture: Practice and Procedure in State and Federal Courts (3d ed. 2014); Stefan Cassella, Asset Forfeiture Law in the United States (2d ed. 2007); Forfeiture (2010), *available at* https://ndaa.org/wp-content/uploads/Forfeiture_3_2010.pdf (compendium of forfeiture statutes from all 50 states); *see, e.g.,* Or. Rev. Stat. §§ 131.550–131.604 (Criminal Forfeiture), §§ 131A.005–131A.460 (Civil Forfeiture) (2017).

Chapter 4

Coordination of Multiple Proceedings

4.1 Factors Affecting Coordination

4.2 Rules and Guidelines Applicable to Case Coordination
    4.2a Government Policy Manuals
    4.2b Rules and Procedures Applicable to Coordination of Insolvency and Forfeiture Proceedings
        4.2b.i Civil Rule 16 and Bankruptcy Rule 7016: General Case Management Rules
        4.2b.ii Bankruptcy Code § 105: General Equitable Powers
        4.2b.iii Civil Rule 83 and Bankruptcy Rule 9029: Case-Specific Protocols
        4.2b.iv Bankruptcy Rule 1015: Joint Administration or Consolidation of Bankruptcy Cases
        4.2b.v Bankruptcy Rule 9019: Settlement Approval Authority
        4.2b.vi Federal Rule of Criminal Procedure 57: Local Rules

4.3 Multiple Filings in Federal District and Bankruptcy Courts
    4.3a Cases in the Same Federal District
    4.3b Cases in Different Federal Districts: Venue and Transfer

4.4 Specific Issues in Parallel Civil and Criminal Cases

4.5 Multiple Filings in State and Federal Courts

4.6 Timing of Multiple Filings

*****

4.1 Factors Affecting Coordination

A threshold question in cases involving parallel Insolvency Proceedings and Forfeiture Proceedings is whether they can be coordinated at all. Unlike complex civil cases, such coordination must avoid violating a defendant's constitutional rights in the related criminal case or frustrating a pending criminal investigation. Thus, parallel criminal and civil cases present unique challenges to judges, prosecutors, Trustees, parties, and other stakeholders, who may be unable easily to create joint document depositories, schedule joint depositions, coordinate rulings over discovery disputes, or transfer and consolidate cases across different jurisdictions.

Although coordination in these cases may be a challenge, coordination may serve important goals of bankruptcy and asset Forfeiture—such as maximizing compensation to both the Victims of the Debtor's conduct and other Claimants. From the court's perspective, coordination also furthers the goal of conserving judicial resources. Due to the interplay of the bankruptcy and Forfeiture processes, coordination may significantly enhance the range of possible outcomes beyond what could be achieved by contested court orders dueling across jurisdictions.

Factors favoring coordination efforts: Considerations weighing in favor of coordination of related Insolvency Proceedings and Forfeiture Proceedings include:

- substantial overlap of the Creditors and the Victims seeking distributions;
- substantial overlap of the third parties who may have to return Property subject to Criminal Forfeiture and Clawback proceedings;
- substantial overlap of the Property subject to the Insolvency Proceedings and Forfeiture Proceedings;
- the potential need to operate an ongoing business under supervision of a bankruptcy Trustee or other court-supervised person, and recognition that the government generally restrains but does not seize ongoing businesses before Forfeiture;[1]
- the need to sell or otherwise dispose of the forfeited Property without waiting for completion of contested criminal proceedings and appeals; and
- circumstances allowing for resolution of privilege issues in the production of documents and testimony without violating a party's constitutional rights.

In such cases, coordination may prevent duplicative distributions to Claimants, minimize conflicts between the government and the Bankruptcy Estate, reduce litigation expenses, and maximize net recoveries. Early coordination may also help prosecutors, Trustees, parties, and judges resolve potential scheduling and discovery disputes before they arise.

Factors complicating coordination efforts: In some cases, however, significant factors may potentially weigh against, or at least complicate, coordination, including:

- where the Creditors, Victims, third-party targets, or Property do not substantially overlap, or parties compete for scarce assets;
- when coordination may jeopardize the individual rights of the Debtor or third-party defendants;
- when criminal proceedings require the prosecutor to assume greater control over the collection of information and the negotiation of Coordination (Cooperation) Agreements related to a still-pending criminal investigation;
- ethical guidelines that bar the threat of criminal sanctions in civil settlement negotiations; and
- constitutional considerations that limit the venue of a criminal proceeding to the place where the crime was committed.[2]

Even in the most difficult cases, judges and parties may benefit from taking some initial steps to understand the timing and nature of parallel cases that involve overlapping

---

1. Asset Forfeiture Policy Manual, Ch. 1, § D.4.
2. *See* U.S. Const. amend. VI (affording defendants the right to a jury trial in the state and district where the crime was committed); *see also* United States v. Cabrales, 524 U.S. 1, 9–10 (1998) (limiting prosecution to the state where alleged money laundering took place). Under the Federal Rules of Criminal Procedure, a defendant can move for a change of venue to avoid substantial prejudice, for the convenience of parties and witnesses or in the interest of justice. Fed. R. Crim. P. 21(a)–(b).

evidence, parties, and issues. Courts and parties may rely on a range of tools to accomplish these goals, from formal consolidation to informal coordination through pretrial conferences, as described in the sections that follow.

4.2 Rules and Guidelines Applicable to Case Coordination

4.2a Government Policy Manuals

In the absence of specific statutory or rule provisions governing the intersections between Insolvency Proceedings and Forfeiture Proceedings, official policy manuals are instructive.

On the Forfeiture side, a key reference source is the Asset Forfeiture Policy Manual, published by the DOJ Asset Forfeiture and Money Laundering Section (AFMLS). This manual contains the most current statement of DOJ policies and procedures regarding Forfeiture. The current edition (as of this writing) was published in 2016.[3] It provides detailed policies with respect to all aspects of Forfeiture Proceedings.

On the insolvency side, the US Trustee Manual includes an appendix that presents policy and practice guidance with respect to commonly recurring issues that may arise when the US Trustee or the bankruptcy Trustee has made a criminal referral during a bankruptcy case, and when a Trustee must administer a bankruptcy case while a criminal investigation or case is pending. Among other topics, the appendix addresses information sharing, discovery, protective orders, and special problems arising from the exercise of the Fifth Amendment privilege by individuals associated with the Debtor. This manual provides general guidance that may be relevant in parallel bankruptcy and Forfeiture Proceedings but does not expressly address forfeiture/bankruptcy intersections.

One important common reference source is technically applicable only by analogy to parallel Insolvency Proceedings and Forfeiture Proceedings. The FJC's Manual for Complex Litigation (MCL) is designed to aid in managing interrelated civil cases. It reflects the suggestions and recommendations of its editors, as developed over four editions, for techniques and procedures that have proven to be useful in the management of civil litigation, especially environmental, class action, mass tort litigation, and similar cases. Its primary audience is intended to be federal trial judges, but the MCL notes that the same tools may also aid state courts. The MCL directly addresses only civil litigation because managing parallel civil and bankruptcy or criminal cases presents additional complications arising from differences in rules and case management constraints. Nevertheless, the MCL notes that coordination of related bankruptcy Adversary Proceedings and criminal cases may be desirable. Manual for Complex Litigation, Fourth, § 10.123 (2004). Moreover, the MCL contains many ideas that can be applied to good effect in the coordination of parallel Insolvency Proceedings and Forfeiture Proceedings.

---

3. A link to the online version is included in Appendix I. As the Asset Forfeiture Policy Manual stresses, it does not "create or confer any legal rights, privileges, or benefits that may be enforced in any way by private parties." Asset Forfeiture Policy Manual, Foreword.

4.2b Rules and Procedures Applicable to the Coordination of Insolvency and Forfeiture Proceedings

4.2b.i Civil Rule 16 and Bankruptcy Rule 7016: General Case Management Rules

In the absence of rules designed expressly to govern Insolvency Proceeding and Forfeiture Proceeding intersections, courts have extrapolated tools from the following generally applicable rules.

Civil Forfeiture cases and SEC Receiverships are governed by Federal Rule of Civil Procedure 16. Federal Rule of Bankruptcy Procedure 7016 expressly incorporates Federal Rule of Civil Procedure 16 by reference and makes it applicable to all Adversary Proceedings brought by bankruptcy Trustees to recover assets or avoid transfers. Both rules provide for:

- *Pretrial conferences*: The court may convene one or more pretrial conferences for purposes of expediting the resolution of the matter, establishing judicial control and management, and facilitating settlement.
- *Scheduling orders—mandatory provisions*: The court must issue a scheduling order setting deadlines for joinder of parties, amendment of pleadings, completion of discovery, and the filing of pretrial motions.
- *Scheduling orders—optional provisions*: The scheduling order may address issues of privilege, protective orders, electronic discovery protocols, dates for one or more pretrial conferences and trial, and "other appropriate matters."

Notably, beyond these standard provisions, Federal Rule of Civil Procedure 16(c)(2)(L) also permits the court to "consider and take appropriate action" with respect to "adopting special procedures for managing potentially difficult or protracted actions that may involve complex issues, multiple parties, difficult legal questions, or unusual proof problems."

Although Federal Rule of Civil Procedure 16 does not expressly refer to intercourt communications or coordination, the flexible approach to case management that it embodies has served as the springboard for the kind of intercourt communication and coordination discussed in this guidebook.

4.2b.ii Bankruptcy Code § 105: General Equitable Powers

In 2005, in order to encourage bankruptcy courts to undertake more active case management, Congress added subsection (d) to section 105 of the Bankruptcy Code. Bankruptcy Code section 105(d)(1) expressly authorizes the bankruptcy court to convene status conferences to "further the expeditious and economical resolution of the case."

Chapter 7 cases usually do not require such judicial intervention, because most are "no asset" cases administered entirely by panel Trustees. In Chapter 12 and 13 cases, Plan confirmation hearings are customarily set within just a few months of filing, again obviating the need for status conferences. Chapter 11 cases, on the other hand, usually take much longer to complete and are more complex in all respects. Judges now customarily hold an early case status conference during the first week of Chapter 11 cases to approve notice requirements, hear the initial round of motions on financing and operational issues, and address similar matters. Either during that initial status conference or a subsequent one, the judge may also set deadlines and procedures for filing and confirming Plans. These conferences provide an excellent opportunity for the court to inquire about the pendency of related proceedings, particularly where fraud or Forfeiture may be an issue.

Scope of section 105 powers: In addition to section 105(d)'s specific authority to hold status conferences and set deadlines, section 105(a) also provides that the bankruptcy court "may issue any order . . . necessary or appropriate to carry out the provisions" of the Bankruptcy Code. This section is usually cited as the basis for the court's exercise of general equitable powers, but its authority is not unlimited: the actions must not contravene any specific provision of the Bankruptcy Code.[4] Section 105 has even (more controversially) been used to justify the injunction of state court criminal proceedings that threaten irreparable harm to the Bankruptcy Estate.[5]

Use of section 105 to support inter-court coordination: Section 105 does not expressly address the issue of inter-court communication and coordination. Nevertheless, such efforts appear to fall well within the boundaries of section 105's powers.

4.2b.iii Civil Rule 83 and Bankruptcy Rule 9029: Case-Specific Protocols

Federal Rule of Civil Procedure 83 and Federal Rule of Bankruptcy Procedure 9029, which is adapted from Rule 83, authorize a bankruptcy judge to regulate practice in any manner consistent with controlling law or rules.

Local Rules: Federal Rule of Civil Procedure 83(a) and Federal Rule of Bankruptcy Procedure 9029(a) authorize the adoption of local rules to govern local procedure, provided that those rules are consistent with and not duplicative of federal statutes or the national rules promulgated by the United States Supreme Court and Congress. Because the bankruptcy courts are units of the district courts, local bankruptcy rules must be formally adopted by the district courts. It would be permissible to include intercourt communication and coordination mandates in local bankruptcy rules to address problems that arise in parallel or multiple proceedings, but such provisions have not been incorporated to date.

Procedure in specific cases: Federal Rule of Civil Procedure 83(b) and Federal Rule of Bankruptcy Procedure 9029(b) both expressly authorize judges to "regulate practice" in their own courtrooms in any manner consistent with federal law, the national rules, and the district's local rules. The proliferation of "local local" rules has historically been premised upon this authority, but many local rules have more recently tried to rein in this practice. Nevertheless, in any given case, Federal Rule of Civil Procedure 83 and Federal Rule of Bankruptcy Procedure 9029 unequivocally authorize a judge who is confronted with the challenges of parallel Insolvency Proceedings and Forfeiture Proceedings to develop protocols and procedures that make sense for the specific problems arising in such cases. Intercourt communication and coordination should fall within the scope of these provisions.

---

4. *See, e.g.,* Canter Family Trust v. Canter (*In re* Canter), 299 F.3d 1150, 1155 (9th Cir. 2002) (section 105 permits injunctive relief to stop parties from pursuing actions in other courts that threaten the integrity of the estate); MacArthur Co. v. Johns-Manville Corp (*In re* Johns-Manville Corp.), 837 F.2d 89, 93 (2d Cir. 1988), *cert. denied*, 488 U.S. 868 (1988) (court had authority under section 105 to approve settlement among third-party insurers under the principle that the court could approve disposition of property of the estate free and clear of liens, claims, or interests); Barbieri v. RAJ Acquisition Corp. (*In re* Barbieri), 199 F.3d 616, 620–621 (2d Cir. 1999) (section 105 does not authorize the court to disregard clear language of the Bankruptcy Code or Federal Rules of Bankruptcy Procedure).

5. *In re* Heincy, 858 F.2d 548, 549–550 (9th Cir. 1988).

4.2b.iv Bankruptcy Rule 1015: Joint Administration or Consolidation of Bankruptcy Cases

Joint administration of cases: Federal Rule of Bankruptcy Procedure 1015(b) authorizes the court to order that multiple related bankruptcy cases be "jointly administered." This procedure applies to cases involving general partners and the partnership, corporations and their affiliates, and spouses. "Joint administration" usually includes use of a single caption to cover all cases, maintenance of a single docket for the filing of all papers that affect all of the cases, and the entry of a single order on a motion that affects all cases. Hearings are held jointly; usually, notice is also joint. Nevertheless, the assets and liabilities of the entities involved remain separate and separately liable for their own debts.

Consolidation of bankruptcy cases involving the same Debtor: If multiple cases are filed as to the same Debtor, those cases may be consolidated under Federal Rule of Bankruptcy Procedure 1015(a). "Consolidation" means that the assets and liabilities listed in both cases would be treated as all applying to the consolidated case. This sometimes occurs when separate voluntary and involuntary petitions are simultaneously filed.

Substantive consolidation of cases involving different Debtors: Federal Rule of Bankruptcy Procedure 1015 does not, however, apply to or authorize the "substantive consolidation" of the assets and liabilities of different Debtors. The equitable doctrine of substantive consolidation is the bankruptcy equivalent of alter ego liability and may be invoked upon proof that multiple Debtors have in fact operated as if they are a single enterprise or that they have so intermingled their business affairs that they cannot effectively be distinguished, provided that the interests of particular Creditors or categories of Creditors can be fairly treated in the consolidation process.[6] This doctrine sometimes comes into play in fraud cases.

4.2b.v Bankruptcy Rule 9019: Settlement Approval Authority

Federal Rule of Bankruptcy Procedure 9019 authorizes the bankruptcy court to approve a compromise or settlement in the case. This includes settlement of pending Adversary Proceedings within the case, but can also include settlement of disputes pending in other courts, before administrative agencies, in arbitrations, or pre-litigation disputes. It can also include settlement of disputes among third parties that directly impact the Bankruptcy Estate.[7] Due to the automatic stay, typically the bankruptcy court must initially authorize a Debtor to enter into the settlement after notice to Creditors and an opportunity for a hearing. Thereafter, the agreed orders or judgments can be entered in the parallel

---

6. The Supreme Court has not adopted a uniform standard for substantive consolidation. The courts of appeals have adopted several different tests. One frequently cited test requires proof that Creditors dealt with the entities as a single economic unit and did not rely on their separate identities in extending credit, or the affairs of the Debtors are so entangled that separating them would be prohibitively costly and consolidation would benefit all Creditors. Union Savings Bank v. Augie/Restivo Baking Co. (*In re* Augie/Restivo Baking Co.), 860 F.2d 515, 518 (2d Cir. 1988). *See also* Owens Corning, 419 F.3d 195, 211 (3d Cir. 2005); Alexander v. Compton (*In re* Bonham), 229 F.3d 750, 766 (9th Cir. 2000); *In re* Hemingway Transp., 954 F2d 1, 32 n.15 (1st Cir. 1992).

7. *See, e.g.*, MacArthur Co. v. Johns-Manville Corp. (*In re* Johns-Manville Corp.), 837 F.3d 89, 93 (2d Cir. 1988), *cert. denied*, 488 U.S. 868 (1988) (court had authority under section 105 to approve settlement among third-party insurers under the principle that the court could approve disposition of property of the estate free and clear of liens, claims, or interests).

proceedings to implement the settlement. In short, Federal Rule of Bankruptcy Procedure 9019 encompasses authority for the bankruptcy court to approve substantive Coordination (Cooperation) Agreements proposed by the Trustee and prosecutor to settle conflicting processes with respect to Property and distributions in the parallel bankruptcy and Forfeiture Proceedings.

4.2b.vi Federal Rule of Criminal Procedure 57: Local Rules

Like Federal Rule of Civil Procedure 83 and Federal Rule of Bankruptcy Procedure 9029, Federal Rule of Criminal Procedure 57(a) authorizes the district courts to develop local rules that apply to the entire court. Federal Rule of Criminal Procedure 57(b) authorizes "local local" rules that apply to an individual judge's docket or protocols that may apply to a particular case.

Also like Federal Rule of Civil Procedure 83 and Federal Rule of Bankruptcy Procedure 9029, Federal Rule of Criminal Procedure 57 authorizes a judge who is confronted with the challenges of parallel Insolvency Proceedings and Forfeiture Proceedings to develop protocols and procedures that make sense for the specific problems arising in such cases. Intercourt communication and coordination should fall within the scope of these provisions.

4.3 Multiple Filings in Federal District and Bankruptcy Courts

If all of the parallel proceedings are pending in the same district, in the same courthouse (or at least in the same neighborhood), and at the same time, then case coordination will at least not be impeded by geographic barriers. Such proximity makes it much easier to hold joint hearings, open multiple channels of communication among judges and attorneys who likely already know each other, and provide direct access to hearings by all parties to all of the proceedings. Of course, institutional barriers may still have to be overcome. Unfortunately, venue rules and other considerations may cause the parallel proceedings to be pending in different jurisdictions without a ready means to bring them together under one roof.

4.3a Cases in the Same Federal District

Insolvency Proceedings and both Criminal and Civil Forfeiture Proceedings that are pending in the same district may, in some circumstances, be heard by a single judge based on principles of judicial efficiency and avoidance of inconsistent rulings. Even within a single district, however, it may be more practical, convenient, or appropriate to allow the parallel proceedings to remain assigned to different judges, who may elect to coordinate either informally or formally by joint coordination or Case Management Orders.

Required notices of related cases: Typically, parties are required by local rule to file a notice of a related civil case when the related cases:

- arise from the same or closely related transactions or events;
- involve the same or substantially similar questions of law and fact; or

- would otherwise result in substantial duplication of labor if heard by different judges.[8]

Such notices of related cases are also commonly required if a Civil Forfeiture Proceeding and a criminal case are pending in the same district.[9] The court may elect to assign the new case to the judge who presides over the existing related case. A party may object that the cases do not qualify as "related." If, despite the notice of a related case, the clerk's office does not assign the new case to the same judge for judicial efficiency, a party may move to have it so assigned.

In addition, a notice of a related case is required in many districts if a newly filed or removed civil action "involves all or a material part of the subject matter of an action" simultaneously pending before a United States court of appeals, bankruptcy court, or other state or federal court or agency.[10] Such a notice is informational only, because the new civil matter cannot be consolidated with cases in other courts or jurisdictions.

Assertion of district court control over related bankruptcy cases or issues: In theory, if the related pending matter is a bankruptcy case in the same district, the district judge who is assigned the new case could theoretically withdraw the reference and hear the bankruptcy case as well. Nevertheless, the circumstances will not necessarily warrant having the district court handle the entire bankruptcy case in addition to the related matter. The district court has three options under these circumstances:

- *Refer questions to the bankruptcy court on specific issues arising in the Civil Forfeiture or criminal case*: The bankruptcy court can provide recommendations with respect to the Bankruptcy Estate in response to specific questions about matters such as Restitution, Forfeiture of assets, identification of what Property belongs to the Bankruptcy Estate, and similar issues.[11] The district court would make the ultimate decision.
- *Withdraw the reference over the entire bankruptcy case*: The bankruptcy case can then be assigned to the district judge who is presiding over the criminal case in the same district for decision on all matters. *See* 28 U.S.C. § 157(d) (2017).[12] The district court may later re-refer the case to the bankruptcy court after resolving whatever disputes necessitated the withdrawal of reference. Withdrawal of the entire bankruptcy case may pose difficult and unexpected challenges for a district judge who may be unfamiliar with the substantive bankruptcy law and procedure issues relating to case administration, and may have a calendar ill-suited to accommodating the frequent shortened-notice matters that are often required to keep an operating business afloat in a Chapter 11 case.
- *Withdraw the reference only with respect to specific issues in the bankruptcy case*: A district court may also withdraw reference but only as to certain discrete Adversary Proceedings or contested matters within the bankruptcy case

---

8. *See, e.g.*, C.D. Cal. L.R. 83-1.3.1, *available at* http://www.cacd.uscourts.gov/court-procedures/local-rules.

9. *See, e.g.*, C.D. Cal. L.R. 83-1.3.2.

10. *See, e.g.*, C.D. Cal. L.R. 83-1.4.1.

11. *See, e.g.*, D. Neb. Gen. R. 1.5, *available at* https://www.ned.uscourts.gov/internetDocs/localrules/negenr_060104.pdf. *See also* 28 U.S.C. § 157(a) (2017).

12. *See also* Nw. Airlines, Inc. v. Los Angeles (*In re* Nw. Airlines Corp.), 384 B.R. 51, 59 (S.D.N.Y. 2008) (withdrawal of reference would promote the goals of efficiency and uniformity); Mishkin v. Ageloff, 220 B.R. 784, 800 (S.D.N.Y. 1998) ("In the final analysis, the critical question is efficiency and uniformity.").

that substantially overlap with the Forfeiture Proceeding. A district court may do so for a number of reasons, including to: (i) ensure consistent outcomes; (ii) assign the case to a judge with more familiarity over the underlying criminal fraud and discovery process; (iii) conserve resources; or (iv) avoid jurisdictional questions involving the bankruptcy court's authority to hear Claims against third parties.[13] In such cases, the bankruptcy court may still retain jurisdiction over matters that relate exclusively to the administration of the Bankruptcy Estate or, in some cases, to the ongoing supervision of a legitimate business enterprise. *See also* Manual for Complex Litigation, Fourth, § 22.53 (2004). For example, when the federal government and the bankruptcy Trustee seek to forfeit and clawback overlapping funds from the same third party at an early stage in the litigation, the district court may withdraw the reference over that particular action to resolve the matter.

Courts should exercise caution when partially withdrawing the reference of jurisdiction, however. It can get very messy, very quickly. Withdrawing the reference over a number of different issues in piecemeal fashion—or deciding such questions after they have substantially advanced through bankruptcy—may waste resources, create more uncertainty, or undermine the progress of the bankruptcy case. Also, when a federal district court partially withdraws the jurisdictional reference, bankruptcy and district judges handling different aspects of the bankruptcy case will likely still need to communicate frequently so that matters before both judges can proceed efficiently and in a coordinated fashion. Moreover, district and bankruptcy judges will have to consider how knowledge already accumulated by the bankruptcy judge can be used in the other proceeding. *See also* Manual for Complex Litigation, Fourth, § 22.52 (2004).

Alternative approaches to coordinated action between district and bankruptcy courts: In cases where courts do not withdraw the reference from the bankruptcy court, district court and bankruptcy court judges in the same federal district still may promote consistency, conserve resources, and maximize compensation to those harmed by a Debtor's conduct in a number of ways.

- *Communication*: District courts may communicate and share pretrial management orders with courts overseeing the bankruptcy or other related actions.
- *Temporary stay*: Judges in newly commenced criminal or bankruptcy cases may decide to stay their own cases to await a decision from a parallel proceeding that has already substantially advanced toward a final resolution.
- *Meet and confer requirements*: Courts in bankruptcy and Criminal Forfeiture Proceedings may adopt special procedures in complex cases involving many different parties, such as to require that parties in the parallel cases meet and confer and delineate at least some of the issues with respect to which the court might request reporting.[14]

---

13. *See, e.g.,* Exec. Benefits Ins. Agency v. Arkison, 134 S. Ct. 2165, 2172 (2014) (bankruptcy courts lack constitutional authority to hear and determine certain types of Bankruptcy Estate suits against third parties).

14. *See, e.g.,* Fed. R. Civ. P. 16(c)(2)(L); 11 U.S.C. § 105(d)(2) (2017); 18 U.S.C. § 3771(d)(2) (2017) (providing an exception when the "number of crime victims makes it impracticable" to enforce victims' traditional rights to appear under federal law).

- *Joint hearings*: Some district and bankruptcy courts may decided to preside jointly over a number of pretrial matters—including those involving overlapping scheduling requests and discovery orders, as well as related assets, third parties, and potential beneficiaries to a distribution. *See* Manual for Complex Litigation, Fourth, § 22.32 (2004). Such joint hearings can encourage additional coordination among parties, may create a process for parties or court-appointed liaisons to apprise judges in parallel proceedings about new developments, and may result in joint opinions or Case Management Orders among the government, Trustee, and other persons. Joint hearings may also be employed to resolve substantive issues that cross the proceedings, including court approval of proposed settlement or Coordination (Cooperation) Agreements that resolve disputes with respect to allocation and distribution of Property. The types of terms these agreements might include are more fully discussed in chapter 5 of this guidebook.

4.3b Cases in Different Federal Districts: Venue and Transfer

It may not be possible to file the Insolvency Proceedings, Civil Forfeiture Proceedings, and Criminal Forfeiture Proceedings in the same district due to conflicting venue requirements. The parties or the courts may have some flexibility to transfer one or more of the proceedings to the venue where another is already pending, but that is not always possible. Venue for both Civil and Criminal Forfeiture Proceedings will usually be appropriate in the district where the offense occurred. For business entities, however, bankruptcy cases will often be filed in the state of incorporation, such as Delaware or New York. Cross-district and cross-state coordination may pose greater challenges, but they are not insuperable. Because the venue options for the criminal prosecution are the most restrictive, the courts might seek to identify means of transferring venue of the other proceedings to the venue of the criminal action, if such transfers would be consistent with the standards applicable to each type of case. Nevertheless, even if it is not feasible to transfer all of the proceedings to the same district, the courts should not allow the mere fact that proceedings are pending in different districts or different states to defeat coordination among the courts and cooperation among the parties.

Proper venue in bankruptcy cases: Individuals rarely have a choice of venue in bankruptcy cases. Entities typically do have several choices of venue and frequently choose among allowable venues based upon strategic considerations. A bankruptcy case may be filed in any federal district court containing the Debtor's "domicile, residence, principal place of business . . . or principal assets in the United States." 28 U.S.C. § 1408(1) (2017). As a result, in some cases, more than one venue may satisfy the statutory requirements for bankruptcy. Corporations and partnerships are "domiciled" in the state in which they are incorporated or organized. For a variety of strategic reasons, a disproportionate number of entities choose to file their petitions in Delaware or the Southern District of New York. In addition, corporate affiliates may generally piggyback their filings in any district in which an affiliate has already filed a case, even if they otherwise have no connection there. In contrast, a corporation with no affiliates and having its principal place of business and assets in one state can only file in that one state, but even it would not necessarily have to file in its headquarters' district. Most individual Debtors, however, have their domicile, residence, principal place of business, and assets all in the same district, and they have no choice about where they file.

Change of venue in bankruptcy cases: If an interested party objects to venue, the bankruptcy court is authorized to transfer venue of the case to a more appropriate district "in the interest of justice or for the convenience of the parties," even if the original filing venue was proper in the first instance. 28 U.S.C. § 1412 (2017). In deciding whether to transfer venue, courts typically consider a number of factors, including the proximity to the court of Creditors and witnesses necessary to administer the Bankruptcy Estate, the location of the Debtor's assets, economic administration of the Bankruptcy Estate, and the necessity for ancillary administration if the Debtor ends up liquidating its assets.[15] *See generally* section 2.3a, *supra*. It may also be possible to transfer particular proceedings arising in or related to a bankruptcy case. 28 U.S.C. sections 1408, 1409, 1410, 1412, and 1452 embody the rules governing venue of bankruptcy cases, proceedings, and related claims and causes of action.

Proper venue in criminal cases: Criminal cases must be filed where the "crime was committed," unless the court orders otherwise, upon the request of the defendant. 18 U.S.C. § 3232 (2017); Fed. R. Crim. P. 18; U.S. Const. amend. VI. Government Criminal Forfeiture Proceedings are not necessarily so limited: they may occasionally take place in more than one venue, particularly where a criminal case takes place in multiple stages in multiple jurisdictions, or where Forfeitable assets are located in different jurisdictions.[16]

Change of venue in criminal cases: Only the defendant can seek a change of venue to a district other than the one in which the crime was committed. Fed. R. Crim. P. 20, 21. The grounds for such a motion include: (i) to avoid prejudice in the district that would deprive the defendant of a fair trial; (ii) the convenience of parties and witnesses; and (iii) in the interest of justice.[17] Prosecutors have no standing to seek a change of venue.[18]

Venue in Civil Forfeiture cases: The district courts generally have jurisdiction of any Civil Forfeiture Proceeding. 28 U.S.C. § 1355(a) (2017). The action may be brought in any district in which any of the acts or omissions giving rise to the Forfeiture occurred, which is the same venue for any criminal prosecution. 28 U.S.C. §§ 1355(b), 1395(a) (2017). Civil Forfeiture actions may also be filed in any other district where the Forfeitable Property is located. 28 U.S.C. § 1395(b) (2017). Regardless of where the proceeding is filed, the court with jurisdiction and proper venue may issue any process that may be necessary to bring the Property to be forfeited before the court.

Change of venue in Civil Forfeiture cases: Like other civil actions, Civil Forfeiture Proceedings may be transferred to any district or division in which they could have been commenced. 28 U.S.C. § 1404(a) (2017). Because Civil Forfeiture Proceedings may be commenced in the district in which the offense occurred, this rule should allow Civil Forfeiture Proceedings to be transferred to the district in which a related Criminal Forfeiture Proceeding is pending.

---

15. Gulf States Exploration Co. v. Manville Forest Prod. Corp., 896 F.2d 1384, 1391 (2d Cir. 1990); *In re* Dunmore Homes, Inc., 380 B.R. 663, 671–72 (Bankr. S.D.N.Y. 2008); Enron Corp. v. Arora (*In re* Enron Corp.), 317 B.R. 629, 638–39 (Bankr. S.D.N.Y. 2004).

16. *See* United States v. Haddix, No. 5:07-137-JMH, 2008 WL 151847, at *2 (E.D. Ky. Jan. 14, 2008) (denying defendant's motion to dismiss the Forfeiture allegation on the ground that the property subject to Forfeiture was the proceeds of a part of the offense that occurred in Indiana, not Kentucky, where the indictment was filed, and that the property was seized in Indiana).

17. *See* Platt v. Minn. Mining & Mfg. Co., 376 U.S. 240, 245–246 (1964).

18. *See, e.g.*, United States v. Cabrales, 524 U.S. 1, 3–4 (1998) (limiting prosecution to the district where alleged money laundering took place).

4.4 Special Issues in Parallel Civil and Criminal Cases

In some circumstances, a bankruptcy case may be transferred to the same district court as a pending criminal case under the factors identified in section 4.3. It may be far more difficult, however, to transfer or commence a criminal case against a corporation or other entity in the same district as a pending bankruptcy case. Several complications may arise.

- *Ineligible venue*: Bankruptcy cases may be filed in the state of incorporation or a variety of other venues; however, the criminal offense may not have occurred in that same venue.
- *Joint defendants' venue rights*: Criminal cases against corporations and entities often involve individual criminal defendants as well. The Sixth Amendment rights of those individuals limit the prosecutors' ability to charge in a jurisdiction other than the one in which the offense occurred.
- *Prosecutorial demands*: US Attorneys' Offices in different jurisdictions have different demands and different caseloads. Many federal prosecutors may allocate resources from office to office in light of their disparate needs.

Different transfer rules in bankruptcy and criminal law may limit options to consolidate cases, as in other complex civil cases. *See* Manual for Complex Litigation, Fourth, §§ 20.12–13 (2004). Despite the challenges inherent in transferring venue, the courts nevertheless still enjoy, and frequently use, their power to coordinate parallel bankruptcy/forfeiture actions informally.

Information sharing. Judicial efforts to coordinate Insolvency Proceedings and Forfeiture Proceedings on an informal basis are consistent with the type of informal judicial coordination the courts employ in complex actions between state and federal courts,[19] and in oversight of parallel agency and criminal Restitution actions.[20] As in other complex cases, the courts may require federal prosecutors and Trustees to produce information to the judges overseeing each case. Although detailed information about the bankruptcy case, including Creditors and Interest Holders is readily available in the bankruptcy filings, information about the status and distributions in a Forfeiture Proceeding is not. The courts could require information to be shared among the judges handling the different proceedings (in camera if necessary), including information about the names of Victims scheduled to receive Restitution, the basis for the awards, and any other related fines or money awarded to or retained by government entities in the public proceeding.[21] Particular challenges arise, however, when the government makes distributions through the Remission process, which is generally not subject to ongoing judicial oversight.

---

19. *See* William W. Schwarzer et al., *Judicial Federalism in Action: Coordination of Litigation in State and Federal Courts*, 78 Va. L. Rev. 1689, 1690 (1992) (noting informal state-federal cooperation, including "calendar coordination, coordinated discovery, joint settlement efforts, and joint motions hearings and rulings"); Byron G. Stier, *Resolving the Class Action Crisis: Mass Tort Litigation as Network*, 2005 Utah L. Rev. 863, 893 (2005) ("[M]any state and federal judges meet and form networked responses to the challenges of mass tort litigation.").

20. United States v. Peterson, 859 F. Supp. 2d 477, 479 (E.D.N.Y. 2012).

21. Such procedures are common when different plaintiffs' attorneys commence separate actions in different jurisdictions. *See* Manual for Complex Litigation, Fourth, § 22.2 (2004) ("Courts routinely order counsel to disclose, on an ongoing basis, past and pending related cases in state and federal courts and to report on their status and results.").

Substantive Resolution. Chapter 5 of this guidebook elaborates the types of procedural and substantive settlement and resolution that intercourt coordination and interparty cooperation may foster. For purposes of this chapter's discussion of procedural coordination, it is useful simply to note briefly that procedural coordination can foster substantive coordination and cooperation as well.

Notwithstanding the limitations of parallel proceeding coordination, any efforts the courts undertake to communicate with each other, coordinate the proceedings, and compel cooperation among the parties may create opportunities for government attorneys, Trustees, and private lawyers to reach substantive solutions, including to consolidate distributions under a single distribution scheme where possible. For example, actions the government and the Trustee both pursue against a third party might produce a joint settlement, which might include an agreement with respect to the mechanics of a single distribution scheme.[22] The parties might also agree that certain Property "belongs" exclusively to the Bankruptcy Estate. In light of the distinct obligations that prosecutors and Trustees owe, however, there may be cases where dual distribution schemes are necessary at least to some extent. The bankruptcy Trustee cannot agree to a distribution under the Forfeiture scheme that violates bankruptcy priorities. The government may be unable to permit a bankruptcy Trustee to administer some of the forfeited Property. In such cases, separate Trustees or special masters may be required to distribute the proceeds under the Forfeiture and bankruptcy systems to Victims and to bankruptcy Creditors and Interest Holders.[23]

4.5 Multiple Filings in State and Federal Courts

Having parallel cases in both federal and state courts presents additional obstacles to coordination. Even as state prosecutors and agencies increasingly pursue Criminal Restitution from corporations and entities facing parallel federal bankruptcy cases or other Insolvency Proceedings, no mechanism exists to remove state criminal actions to federal court for the purposes of transfer and consolidation.[24] (Whether state court Forfeiture and state court Receivership can be transferred within a state depends upon state procedural law.) Informal coordination is most feasible when a single state prosecutor or agency commences an action in the same state as a pending bankruptcy.

When many different state prosecutors or insurance boards commence actions for Restitution or Forfeiture in different states, the need for coordination is especially great.

---

22. *See, e.g.*, Coordination Agreements in United States v. Petters, 2010 WL 4736795 (D. Minn. Nov. 16, 2010); Kelley v. Hofer (*In re* Petters Co.), 440 B.R. 805, 809–810 (Bankr. D. Minn. 2010).

23. For example, in December 2012, Richard C. Breeden was retained to serve as Special Master on behalf of the DOJ to administer the process of compensating the Victims of the *Madoff* fraud from forfeited funds. A separate SIPA Trustee, Irving Picard, was responsible for overseeing the liquidation of the SIPA estate. *See* Summary, US Attorneys Office for the Southern District of New York, Victim and Witness Services, United States v. Bernard Madoff and Related Cases (Aug. 21, 2015), *available at* https://www.justice.gov/usao-sdny/programs/victim-witness-services/united-states-v-bernard-l-madoff-and-related-cases.

24. A state attorney general Restitution action does not qualify as "mass action" for the purposes of removal to federal court under the Class Action Fairness Act, 28 U.S.C. § 1332, because the state attorney general was the only named party and sole real party in interest. Miss. ex rel. Hood v. AU Optronics Corp., 134 S. Ct. 736, 739 (2014).

The difficulties in achieving cooperation, however, are particularly daunting. In such cases, courts may be able to rely on the Debtor's counsel, or a liaison, to keep the courts updated about ongoing proceedings in multiple jurisdictions.

Early communication among bankruptcy and state court judges may also be essential in such cases. As with the concerns once associated with "competitive class actions" in different state courts[25] (*see* Manual for Complex Litigation, Fourth, § 20.311 (2004)), unilateral action by any judge to dispose of assets too soon may fatally undermine future coordination efforts between the government, Trustee, and other parties.[26]

Early appointment of a mediator may be another tool to achieve coordination. A mediator can freely cross jurisdictional boundaries if the parties are willing to, or can be persuaded to, engage in procedural (and substantive) discussions within that framework. Mediators are regularly retained and paid by the Bankruptcy Estate to resolve complex disputes. The mediator model would be appropriate in the case of parallel proceedings because all parties may benefit from the cost efficiencies that come with effective coordination. The bankruptcy court may be an ideal forum for the appointment because all parties' Claims and Interests are brought to bear in the bankruptcy case.

4.6 Timing of Multiple Filings

The timing of multiple filings can substantially impact how parallel case coordination can or should proceed. When the bankruptcy has substantially proceeded before the government commences a criminal action, the government may in some cases be able to permit the distribution of assets through a bankruptcy to conserve resources, without violating Forfeiture laws.[27] Similarly, when the asset Forfeiture Proceeding has progressed substantially, no assets may remain to be distributed through the bankruptcy case, absent significant clawback actions.

When criminal and bankruptcy proceedings commence at about the same time, however, neither proceeding will enjoy an inherent advantage in pursuing common actions against third parties, identifying documents or assets, or employing forensic accountants or other experts. Nevertheless, some advantages inhere in each type of proceeding.

---

25. Rhonda Wasserman, *Dueling Class Actions*, 80 B.U. L. Rev. 461, 462–63 (2000) (detailing problems of waste in dueling class actions); Geoffrey P. Miller, *Class Actions and Jurisdictional Boundaries: Overlapping Class Actions*, 71 N.Y.U. L. Rev. 514, 516 (1996). Although competitive class actions still exist, the Class Action Fairness Act (CAFA) has reduced their number by permitting defendants to remove state class actions to federal court with minimal diversity. 28 U.S.C. § 1332(d) (2017) (granting federal jurisdiction over interstate class actions where the amount in controversy exceeds $5 million and at least one plaintiff and one defendant are citizens of different states).

26. *Cf.* Jordan D. Maglich, *While Rothstein Victims Wait, Appellate Court Hears Argument over Entitlement to Forfeited Assets*, LexisNexis Legal Newsroom, Jan. 10, 2013, https://www.lexisnexis.com/legalnewsroom/securities/b/securities/posts/while-rothstein-victims-wait-appellate-court-hears-argument-over-entitlement-to-forfeited-assets. *See also* Caitlin F. Saladrigas, *Corporate Criminal Liability: Lessons from the Rothstein Debacle*, 66 U. Miami. L. Rev. 435 (2012). The Eleventh Circuit reversed the district court decision to permit the government seizure and distribution, after concluding that the government should not have forfeited Rothstein's assets. United States v. Rothstein, Rosenfeldt, Adler, P.A. (*In re* Rothstein, Rosenfeldt, Adler, P.A.), 717 F.3d 1205, 1214–16 (11th Cir. 2013).

27. *See, e.g.*, 18 U.S.C. § 3663A(c), (B)(3) (2006) (exemptions when there are a large number of victims or when "complex issues of fact" complicate the sentencing process).

In a government Forfeiture Proceeding, the government may be in a superior position to identify and secure remote assets, more expeditiously and inexpensively than a bankruptcy Trustee. Prosecutors may have standing to seek funds against third parties that private plaintiffs cannot.[28] Public authorities also may attach and collect funds from parties using Criminal Forfeiture laws that private plaintiffs cannot.[29]

On the other hand, if the defendant contests the criminal case instead of agreeing to any early plea, the government's ability to dispose of Property—particularly operating companies—may be hamstrung by delays and uncertainties. This kind of situation arose in the *Rigas/Adelphia* cases. In such cases, the bankruptcy court may be more readily able to sell Property for the highest value. In addition, bankruptcy offers other tools for collection and distribution of Property. The bankruptcy court and Trustees, for example, are well versed in the operation and going-concern disposition of ongoing business operations. Moreover, the proceeds of clawback avoidance actions, such as preference actions under 11 U.S.C. § 547(b) (2017) and fraudulent transfer actions under 11 U.S.C. § 544 (2017), are available for distribution to Creditors and Interest Holders in the bankruptcy case, but no such actions are available in the Criminal Forfeiture process.[30]

In some situations, the tools available in the bankruptcy case may obtain Property unavailable to the government and maximize value in ways the government cannot easily do. Both the government and the Trustee may enjoy advantages at different stages of the proceedings, against different parties, involving different Property. Early and ongoing communication between the Trustee and the federal government may reduce conflicts, avoid duplication of tasks, and maximize recoveries for all Claimants, including Victims and Creditors.

---

28. *See, e.g.*, Equal Emp't Opportunity Comm'n v. Wafflehouse, Inc., 534 U.S. 279, 294 (2002) (holding that the Equal Employment Opportunity Commission (EEOC) can recover damages and other relief on behalf of an employee who could not under a mandatory arbitration agreement); Donald C. Langevoort, *Reading Stoneridge Carefully: A Duty-Based Approach to Reliance and Third-Party Liability Under Rule 10-5*, 158 U. Pa. L. Rev. 2125, 2127–2128 (2010); Adam S. Zimmerman & David M. Jaros, *The Criminal Class Action*, 159 U. Pa. L. Rev. 1385 (2011) (describing powers enjoyed by prosecutors to pursue Restitution from third parties).

29. Anthony Martucci, Note, *Advocating for Asset Forfeiture in the Post-Madoff Era: Why the Government, Not a Bankruptcy Trustee, Should Be Responsible for Recovering and Redistributing Assets from Feeder Funds and Net Winners*, 63 Case W. Res. L. Rev. 599 (2012) (describing the superior powers of federal prosecutors in collection under federal asset Forfeiture laws).

30. *See, e.g.*, United States v. Frykholm, 362 F.3d 413, 417 (7th Cir. 2004) ("bankruptcy would have enabled the trustee to recoup the sums distributed to the first generation of investors, who received $5 million or so against $2.5 million paid in. Those payments could have been reclaimed under the trustee's avoiding powers and made available to all of the bilked investors."); SEC v. Madoff, No. 08 Civ. 10791(LLS), 2009 WL 980288, at *1–2 (S.D.N.Y. Apr. 10, 2009); *see also* United States v. Petters, No. 08-364 (RHK/AJB), 2010 WL 2291486, at *4 (D. Minn. June 3, 2010).

Chapter 5

Case Management Orders, Coordination Agreements, and Cooperation Agreements

5.1 Case Management Orders, Coordination Agreements, and Cooperation Agreements: Overview

5.2 Provisions for Initial and Subsequent Status Conferences

5.3 Provisions Regarding Intercourt Communication

5.4 Interparty Communication
    5.4a Facilitating Communication
    5.4b Provisions Regarding Cooperation Among Counsel and Parties
    5.4c Notice and Communication: Victims, Creditors, Interest Holders, and Other Interested Persons
    5.4d Discussions Between the Bankruptcy Trustee and DOJ
    5.4e Participation by Other Stakeholders

5.5 Provisions Regarding Assets and Property
    5.5a Cooperation Regarding Property Recovery
    5.5b Cooperation Regarding Property Management and Preservation
    5.5c Cooperation Regarding Distributions

5.6 Perspectives of Claimants, Victims, and Interest Holders

5.7 Provisions Regarding Distributions

5.8 Provisions Regarding Evidence, Discovery, and Confidentiality
    5.8a Disclosures
    5.8b Confidential Information

5.9 Provisions Regarding Subsequent Case Management: Deferred Docketing

5.10 Provisions Regarding Recognition of Certain Orders in Other Parallel Cases

*****

5.1 Case Management Orders, Coordination Agreements, and Cooperation Agreements: Overview

This chapter elaborates the particular procedural and substantive matters that the courts overseeing the proceedings may be asked to consider or might require the parties to consider in parallel Insolvency Proceedings and Forfeiture Proceedings. As previously discussed, different procedural and substantive rules govern these parallel proceedings, including with respect to the identification of Property subject to the proceeding, the gathering and liquidation of that Property, the identification of entities entitled to distribution, the allowance or determination of the validity of Claims against the Debtor, and ultimate distributions. These tensions present several areas ripe for coordination, including through Case Management Orders, and Coordination (Cooperation) Agreements designed to:

- ensure each court's awareness of the other parallel proceedings;
- reduce the potential for conflicting rulings in the parallel cases; and
- settle substantive issues, including with respect to control, administration, and distribution of Property.

First, the courts overseeing the various proceedings may seek means of ensuring that they are fully aware of the status of the other parallel proceedings and of the extent to which actions taken in each case may affect the other cases.

Second, the courts may seek means of coordinating certain hearings and rulings in an effort to avoid conflicting rulings on issues that arise in two or more of the proceedings. This might be facilitated through a Case Management Order that addresses procedural, evidentiary, and other matters relating to the coordination of the parallel proceedings, including the mechanics of intercourt communication, joint status hearings, and other matters the courts deem necessary and appropriate to facilitate case management.

Third, the prosecutor or forfeiting agency (often the DOJ) and bankruptcy Trustee (or Receiver, Assignee, or SIPA Trustee, depending on the nature of the Insolvency Proceeding) may negotiate and ask the courts to approve a Coordination (Cooperation) Agreement. These terms are used interchangeably to refer to substantive agreements between the governmental agency implementing Forfeiture, on the one hand, and the Trustee overseeing the Insolvency Proceeding, on the other hand, regarding which proceeding will receive what allocation of the designated Property, including any causes of action the defendant/Debtor may hold against third parties under general law or insolvency law's clawback and avoidance powers.

Coordination (Cooperation) Agreements recognize that resolving substantive conflicts between Forfeiture law and bankruptcy (or other insolvency) law through litigation may be expensive and time consuming, such that coordination or settlement may enhance and expedite recoveries for Victims, Creditors, and Interest Holders. Coordination (Cooperation) Agreements may include provisions ranging from simple procedural coordination to substantive settlement of conflicting claims, including the division of responsibility for recovering and distributing Property, and ultimate determinations of which Claimants will receive distribution from which proceedings and Property.

Cooperation in Dreier. For example, in the case of Mark Dreier, District Court Judge Rakoff, who oversaw the criminal proceedings against Marc Dreier in the Southern District of New York, and Chief Bankruptcy Judge Stuart Bernstein, who oversaw the bankruptcy case, conducted a joint hearing to encourage and approve a Coordination (Cooperation) Agreement between the US Attorney and the bankruptcy Trustee. Among other things, the final agreement: (i) confirmed that the Trustee had authority to pursue avoidance actions without the risk of government Forfeiture; (ii) centralized in the bankruptcy proceeding the distribution of artwork and other Property that had been seized by the federal prosecutor in the Forfeiture Proceeding; and (iii) permitted the government to collect over $30 million in assets from GSO Capital Partners, which had invested in Dreier's fictitious promissory notes and had been paid interest and fees. District Court Judge Cedarbaum, who oversaw the Dreier LLP Receivership, also participated in joint hearings in these cases.

Lack of Cooperation in Rothstein. In contrast, the *Rothstein* parallel proceedings in Florida involved extensive litigation and virtually no cooperation between the Insolvency Proceeding and Forfeiture Proceeding. *See, e.g.,* Jordan D. Maglich, *While Rothstein Victims Wait, Appellate Court Hears Argument over Entitlement to Forfeited Assets,* LexisNexis Legal Newsroom, Jan. 10, 2013, https://www.lexisnexis.com/legalnewsroom/securities/b/securities/posts/while-rothstein-victims-wait-appellate-court-hears-argument-over-entitlement-to-forfeited-assets; Caitlin F. Saladrigas, *Corporate Criminal Liability: Lessons from the Rothstein Debacle,* 66 U. Miami. L. Rev. 435 (2012); United States v. Rothstein, Rosenfeldt, Adler, P.A. (*In re* Rothstein, Rosenfeldt, Adler, P.A.), 717 F.3d 1205, 1214 (11th Cir. 2013) (holding that the government should not have forfeited Rothstein's assets); United States v. Tartagliore, 2018 WL 1740532 (E.D. Pa. 2018) (examining *Rothstein*). (The *Dreier* and *Rothstein* cases are summarized in Appendix C.)

Given the inherent complexity of these cases, the focus here is on provisions that are unique to the intersection between Insolvency Proceedings and Forfeiture Proceedings, rather than the types of provisions that are common to litigating other types of complex cases (which are detailed in the MCL). Particular focus is on provisions that have been adopted by and proven helpful to the courts and parties in prior cases. For simplicity, this chapter attempts to discuss various types of provisions separately, although these provisions often are combined into a single order.

5.2 Provision for Initial and Subsequent Status Conferences

In a number of parallel Insolvency Proceedings and Forfeiture Proceedings, courts have mandated specific coordinated reporting deadlines, entered coordinated scheduling orders, and ultimately approved Case Management Orders. Before the courts can enter Case Management Orders addressing interactions among the proceedings, the courts must be aware that cases pending in other fora may affect the matter before each court. This raises several questions, including what factual scenarios might trigger the court's inquiry into the potential existence of parallel proceedings, and how the court might obtain information necessary not only to become aware of the existence of parallel proceedings, but also to determine whether the proceedings are so intertwined as to merit coordination.

Judges overseeing parallel Insolvency Proceedings and Forfeiture Proceedings should consider whether the underlying facts suggest the likelihood of parallel litigation. For example, the court should inquire about parallel proceedings where the facts suggest a Ponzi scheme, securities law violations, fraudulent financial or investment enterprise, or other circumstances likely to give rise to parallel Criminal or Civil Forfeiture or Disgorgement, and bankruptcy or other Insolvency Proceedings. An early status conference may include inquiries and orders designed to facilitate early and ongoing disclosure of potential parallel proceedings of which the parties are aware.

As discussed in chapter 4 (section 4.2b), current procedural rules were not expressly designed to address the complicated intersections between parallel Insolvency Proceedings and Forfeiture Proceedings. Until those rules are amended (if they are), courts will of necessity continue to draw upon existing rules, statutes, and judicial case management practices to provide bases for coordination. In bankruptcy cases, Bankruptcy Code section 105 expressly authorizes bankruptcy courts to exercise their equitable powers to convene such status conferences as may be appropriate in the circumstances of each case. With respect to initial status conference and scheduling orders, one useful approach is for the bankruptcy judge (applying Bankruptcy Code section 105) to order the parties to the bankruptcy case to appear at a status conference and present information regarding the existence and status of parallel proceedings. Analogous reporting may be sought in Receivership proceedings.

Requiring the parties to bring related cases to the court's attention and report whether the parties view coordination as helpful allows the courts to become aware of the other related proceeding but does not require formal coordination where the parties do not anticipate any conflicts. Sometimes concurrent Insolvency Proceedings and Forfeiture Proceedings will not involve disputes with respect to Property title or issues overlap.

A court overseeing a federal Receivership or other civil case may employ Federal Rule of Civil Procedure 16 as a mechanism for structuring meet and confer or disclosures related to the parallel proceedings. Bankruptcy courts may also invoke Federal Rule of Civil Procedure 16 in Adversary Proceedings pursuant to Federal Rule of Bankruptcy Procedure 7016. Federal Rule of Bankruptcy Procedure 7016 does not apply to the main bankruptcy case itself. Caution is warranted when using Federal Rule of Civil Procedure 16 for parallel case coordination, however, because it is designed primarily as a procedural trigger for other procedural matters and obligations. Parties may intentionally seek to delay triggering these obligations for legitimate strategic reasons such that the Federal Rule of Civil Procedure 16 conference may come too late in the process. Absent specific reasons for haste, the court should avoid pressuring the parties to move forward with the case before they are prepared to do so. These constraints may require the court to consider other, perhaps less formal, means of encouraging or mandating disclosures, while nevertheless allowing the court and the parties more flexibility in disclosing relevant information earlier or later in the proceedings.

Courts may consider whether local rules supplement and support the obligation to disclose related Forfeiture or Insolvency Proceedings, if only to make the judges aware of the parallel litigation. When considering the issuance of initial status conference, disclosure, and coordination orders, the court should give parties an opportunity to explain both any hurdles they have already faced and any ongoing limitations that may restrict their ability to share or cooperate as fully as the parties and the court may prefer.

Despite efforts to encourage sharing of resources and coordination of asset collection and distribution, some legitimate obstacles may inhibit effective communication and coordination between the government and bankruptcy Trustees. For example, the government may lack a comprehensive listing of Victims at the time it commences Forfeiture Proceedings, let alone a comprehensive identification of third parties that may claim an interest in the Property. The Trustee overseeing an Insolvency Proceeding may have a more complete list of all Claimants, including Victims, which the government could use for notice purposes in the Forfeiture Proceeding and which ultimately may support efforts to avoid duplication of payments in both proceedings. The Trustee's information may also be useful to the government in identifying third parties with potential interests in the Property.

In many cases, more complete noticing and access to the forfeited Property could be achieved if the parties shared their lists of potential Claimants and Victims early in the case. Nevertheless, in some instances, sharing information too early may jeopardize a government investigation or compromise the rights of defendants or witnesses in a criminal case. The government, for privacy reasons and to protect ongoing investigations, rarely shares information with the Trustee concerning potential Claimants. Bankruptcy Trustees, however, often need information about Victims and amounts they have been paid through the Forfeiture processes to assure that any Victims who are also entitled to be paid as Creditors or Interest Holders do not recover more than their net losses. Courts seeking to encourage cooperation among the parties to reduce expense and enhance ultimate recoveries to Claimants may need to probe to determine whether any apparent hurdles arise from legitimate case-related concerns rather than from a failure to discern the legitimate parameters of permissible sharing, or a lack of experience and guidance concerning the feasible parameters of coordination.

5.3 Provisions Regarding Intercourt Communication

Once a court is aware of parallel proceedings, it might next consider whether it should engage in direct intercourt communication rather than rely solely on status reporting by the parties. A preliminary question is whether *intercourt communication* should be driven by the courts or by the parties' own request. Intercourt Communication includes all means by which the courts overseeing the Insolvency Proceedings and Forfeiture Proceedings may communicate with each other, including informal communication among the judges, formal filed status reports, and joint hearings at the behest of the courts or the parties.

Intercourt Communication is, by nature, discretionary. It is often initiated at the request of one of the parties because not all parallel proceedings have the degree of intersection necessary to justify the burdens of coordination. In other cases, however, communication may be raised by the courts sua sponte where, for example, one of the judges becomes aware of an issue and the need for coordination. It is often helpful, in any event, for the courts to engage in some level of communication to determine the extent to which coordination may be useful. Because no procedural rules clearly define the parameters of direct Intercourt Communications, the courts may prefer that a Case Management Order delineate the degree, manner, and process for its initiation.

Some judges are comfortable communicating with their judicial colleagues overseeing parallel cases on an informal basis, particularly within the same district; others are not inclined to engage in any type of communication except formally in open court.

Communication Initiated by the Bankruptcy Court. The bankruptcy court may be the first court to become aware of the pendency of parallel criminal and possibly additional civil proceedings regarding the Debtor. In most Chapter 11 cases, the topic would likely arise in any early case status conference held pursuant to Bankruptcy Code section 105. After all, the Debtor should be aware of any other proceedings. Alternatively, some other Party In Interest might learn about parallel proceedings in the course of an examination of the Debtor pursuant to Federal Rule of Bankruptcy Procedure 2004, which permits broad-ranging questions as to the Debtor's Property and liabilities, or any matter pertinent to the bankruptcy case. In that event, the bankruptcy court can serve as the fulcrum to initiate intercourt communication.

Communication Initiated by the District Court. Similarly, the judge overseeing the criminal case involving Forfeiture will often become aware of the pendency of a Receivership (for example, initiated by the SEC) or a bankruptcy case. That judge may desire to initiate communication with the court overseeing the Insolvency Proceeding. As previously noted, in the absence of specific procedural rules that mandate, or even expressly authorize, Intercourt Communication in these types of parallel proceedings, the courts have looked to Bankruptcy Code section 105 and Federal Rule of Civil Procedure 16, as well as general principles of parallel proceeding case management.

Communication Initiated by the Bankruptcy Trustee. Bankruptcy Trustees are another likely player to discover the full range of parallel proceedings. The existence of pending lawsuits is typically a topic of inquiry in the mandatory initial meeting of Creditors, overseen by the Trustee. 11 U.S.C. § 341(a) (2017). Trustees frequently initiate contact with the prosecutors or enforcement agencies. If the prosecutor is amenable to communication, the Trustee's outreach may lead to the resolution of many issues through protocols or Coordination (Cooperation) Agreements between the key stakeholders, with the approval of the courts.

Concerns regarding proper procedure and adequate notice may arise when the courts undertake consideration of proposed Coordination (Cooperation) Agreements. When proposed protocols or Coordination (Cooperation) Agreements are presented to the courts, the courts should ensure that careful and complete notice, opportunity for briefing, and a hearing are held in order to permit the raising of objections by nonsignatories.

If the courts involved in the parallel proceedings decide to hold joint hearings, each of the judges technically presides over his or her own case. For example, some courts have conducted joint hearing on requests for approval of Coordination (Cooperation) Agreements, which permits the judges to hear parallel motions simultaneously, avoid duplication of resources, and facilitate joint questioning. Although the parallel cases are being heard together for the administrative convenience of courts, witnesses, and parties alike, the cases are not in any way thereby substantively consolidated under a single judge or court. In other words, each of the cases is listed separately on each court's calendar but is scheduled for the same courtroom. The proceedings are part of the official record of each case, and separate orders are entered on the docket of each case to document any decisions made at the hearing. Of course, the orders are often identical, other than their case captions. Thus, each judge is, at all times, operating within the scope of that court's jurisdiction.

5.4 Interparty Communication

5.4a Facilitating Communication

When the parties first discover the existence of multiple proceedings, they should begin a dialogue without awaiting court direction in that regard. If they do not do so, then the courts should encourage them to talk among themselves.

From the court's perspective, understanding the nature of the intersections among the proceedings may inform the court's role in encouraging these communications and understanding whether communications have been effective. The court may facilitate communication by understanding the types of issues the parties ought to be discussing and determining at a status conference whether those issues have been on the parties' agenda.

Most importantly, early communication between criminal prosecutors and Trustees or Receivers in trying to identify Property and prevent its dissipation provides substantial benefits. In the vast majority of circumstances, these communications begin between the bankruptcy (or SIPA) Trustee and DOJ. Given the typical secrecy surrounding a criminal case, the Trustee may experience difficulty obtaining information from the Office of the US Attorney (OUSA) or even convincing the local US Attorney to discuss the parallel cases. The Office of the US Trustee (OUST) may be an invaluable resource to facilitate communication, translate bankruptcy concepts to the DOJ and Forfeiture concepts to the Trustees, their counsel, and other parties, and facilitate the court's understanding of the intersections between the Insolvency Proceedings and Forfeiture Proceedings. The court and parties should consider reaching out to the OUST early in the process. The OUST may serve as a vital communication link among the parties and Claimants, and may be a vital resource for the courts because of its expertise in bankruptcy matters combined with its status as an arm of the DOJ.

Within the OUST, the Assistant Director for Criminal Enforcement serves as a central point for communications among bankruptcy Trustees, US Trustees, and other arms of the DOJ, including the Office of Asset Forfeiture Policy and Training, and the Executive Office for US Attorneys.

The nature and duration of communication (once initiated), the stakeholders involved, and the outcomes vary substantially, and should be customized to address the particular nature of the dispute and needs of the particular parties. Nevertheless, some issues recur, both in terms of areas where agreement can often be forged and in terms of practical complications that may limit communication. Courts seeking to foster communication and coordination should be aware of these possible constraints and probe the parties regarding whether they impede communication.

Need for prosecutorial secrecy during investigations: Criminal prosecutors typically operate in secrecy, precharging, to protect the criminal process and to prevent a rush to hide or liquidate assets.

Conflicting strategic agendas: Strategic differences may impact the positions of the main parties as well as the rights of third parties. For example, a narrow charging decision or plea agreement may be preferable for the criminal prosecutor seeking a clear and expeditious conviction. Particularly where the alleged wrongdoer will clearly be incarcerated for the rest of his life or an extended period, the prosecutor may feel no need to, and may prefer not to, include every possible charge in the indictment or plea. This charging decision or plea decision will define the limits of the Victims who may receive distributions under Forfeiture law, although the Remission process may also provide compensation to Victims of related offenses. 28 C.F.R. § 9.8(b)(1) (2017). As a result, only a portion of those who were defrauded or otherwise injured may be classified as Victims and compensated in part through the Forfeiture Proceeding, while the remaining Claimants (who may have been similarly and equally harmed, but may not technically be Victims of the specific crimes charged or plea deals reached) may be relegated at best to unsecured Creditor status in the bankruptcy. These latter Claimants may receive no distribution if significant assets have been excluded from the Bankruptcy Estate through Forfeiture, particularly if secured and priority Creditors receive most or all of the distributions from any Property that remains in the Bankruptcy Estate.

Timing issues: The Insolvency Proceeding or Forfeiture Proceeding may precede the other by months or years, or they may be roughly simultaneous. As a practical matter, the later-in-time filer may reach out to begin communications because the parties to the later filed case may know of the existence of the first case and easily identify the key players. Equally important, because the attorneys in the later case can benefit from the work that has already been ongoing in the first-filed matter, they have a strong incentive to seek to collaborate rather than to duplicate the earlier investigation. If, however, the government already has all of the information the prosecutors believe they will need, they may have no incentive to share information, evidence, or lists of potential Claimants with the later appointed bankruptcy Trustee or other agencies. Even where the Insolvency Proceeding is pending prior to the forfeiture, the government may nevertheless decline to communicate and opt instead to remove all or substantially all Property from the Bankruptcy Estate through Forfeiture, Relation Back Doctrine, and Substitute Property concepts.

In short, given the frequent lack of incentive for the government to communicate and share information with the Trustee, the court may find it useful to bring the parties together to determine the extent to which sharing is feasible and desirable.

5.4b Provisions Regarding Cooperation Among Counsel and Parties

Coordination (Cooperation) Agreements in parallel proceedings are highly case-specific, driven not only by the type of proceedings but also by the sequencing and litigation stage of the proceedings. In addition, as with all complex litigation, the personalities of the particular counsel and firms/agencies involved will impact the course of the litigation. Nevertheless, certain types of agreements are particularly common. Typically, Coordination (Cooperation) Agreements will include provisions regarding identification, realization, and preservation of Property.

Identification of Property: Coordination (Cooperation) Agreements often include provisions requiring that the parties will coordinate and cooperate regarding the identification, preservation, and realization of Property that the other may have an interest in. *See, e.g.*, United States v. Petters, No. 08-5348 ADM/JSM, 2017 WL 4325684, at *2 (D. Minn. Sept. 27, 2017). Interparty communication and negotiation toward Coordination (Cooperation) Agreements can facilitate the narrowing of issues with respect to Property and distributions and may bring into sharper focus areas of discord, such as whether the government's theory of Relation Back and Substitute Property legitimately excludes certain Property from the Bankruptcy Estate.

Property generally falls into one of three categories: (i) Bankruptcy Estate Property clearly not subject to Forfeiture; (ii) Property clearly subject to Forfeiture; and (iii) "hybrid" Property. The parties should be encouraged to determine what tools in each entity's arsenal can best enhance recoveries.

Bankruptcy Estate Property would typically include Property that the government has no tools to pursue, such as perhaps clawback avoidance recovery powers. These assets should clearly vest in the Bankruptcy Estate. Nevertheless, the Trustee will want the assurance of an agreement and court order that any funds the Trustee recovers using these powers will not be subject to Forfeiture.

Conversely, the government's reach may be greater than the Trustee's with respect to recovery of Property held by third parties but not within the reach of clawback avoidance powers.

Hybrid assets may include bank accounts, investments, and other funds that could arguably fall in either category depending on how the line is drawn between the crime Proceeds and Facilitating Property on the one hand, and the legitimate aspects of the business enterprise being administered in the bankruptcy case on the other.

Information sharing and confidentiality provisions: Coordination (Cooperation) Agreements usually include provisions for information sharing, such as imposing a duty to keep other representatives and the courts apprised of all relevant and material developments in the proceedings. Given the nature of the parallel proceedings, information-sharing agreements will typically provide for confidentiality of non-public information and trade secrets, as well as a process for hearing objections. Experience in existing cases suggests that the governmental agencies involved may be willing to talk but not to share information. The nature and extent of the government's ability and desire to cooperate and comply with sharing agreements or orders may therefore be a useful topic for the courts to explore with the parties.

Administration and disposition of Property: Coordination (Cooperation) Agreements may provide mechanisms to address conflicts regarding Property allocation and efficiencies in Property recovery, preservation, or liquidation. Such agreements may serve as a starting point for considering which representative/proceeding is best positioned to respond to issues arising with particular sets of Property. The treatment of any Property proceeds in several phases: the Property must be identified, located, brought within the proceedings, and allocated. Moreover, depending upon the type of Property, there may be a desire to sell the Property or (if it is a business entity) to restructure and operate the Property for some time either to obtain a better sale price or to preserve the entity as a revenue stream for Claimants, who might otherwise receive far less in an immediate liquidation.

Early in the litigation, communication may focus on how the parties will assist each other in the recovery of identified Property as the case develops. Coordination (Cooperation) Agreements may address the mechanics of how the parties will cooperate toward the preservation of Property, including whether legitimate business operations may be continued and if so, under whose oversight.

Over time, there may be a transformation in which the stakeholders begin to focus upon questions of superior liquidation or restructuring capacity as between the proceedings. Given this complexity and these shifts, the respective abilities of the Trustee and the government to identify and pursue certain Property, and to maximize the return on that Property, may change over time. The initial allocation of responsibilities should be without prejudice to future rights if circumstances change, both to enhance efficiency and to maximize recovery. Coordination (Cooperation) Agreements may require cooperation while reserving rights for subsequent resolution, and may provide mechanisms to address potentially conflicting Claims against and Interests in the Property. The parties may seek the court's approval of these agreements to avoid subsequent challenge. *See, e.g.,* United States v. Petters, No. 08-5348 ADM/JSM, 2017 WL 4325684, at *2 (D. Minn. Sept. 27, 2017).

Procedures for resolving disputes about particular Property: Because some Property may be forfeitable (as Proceeds, Facilitating Property, Substitute Property, or using the Relation Back Doctrine) but also be part of a legitimate business enterprise, the court may create procedural mechanisms that encourage discussion between the Trustee and DOJ to negotiate agreements regarding which Property should be placed within either the

Forfeiture or Bankruptcy Estate accounts. Where such determinations impact the recoveries for Creditors and Victims, courts should also devise mechanisms to consider notice to and objections from Claimants, including Creditors and Victims.

Allocation and sharing of costs: Coordination (Cooperation) Agreements may include cost-sharing provisions. Costs and fees for Trustees in bankruptcy are often determined according to a fixed schedule. The costs of Criminal Forfeiture, Restitution, Remission, and Victim recovery fund programs are paid in different ways, such as shifting governmental resources away from other activities and to a process devoted to Victim compensation. Protocols that include some provisions for the allocation of costs should reflect the desire to compensate parties for work actually performed in that joint process, while maximizing the potential recovery to Claimants in the process.

5.4c Notice and Communication: Victims, Creditors, Interest Holders, and Other Interested Persons

The criminal, bankruptcy, and civil litigation systems each have well-established notice requirements, based upon both statutory and constitutional obligations. Where these proceedings not only overlap but also involve the assertion of Claims and Interests by differing parties, notice becomes far more complex. Parties in interest may have different rights to receive notices and to be heard depending on whether an item of Property is administered in the Forfeiture Proceeding or the Insolvency Proceeding. Providing a full explanation of each of these notice requirement regimes is beyond the scope of this project. For an excellent overview of the requirements, deadlines, exceptions to, and sanctions for violation of notice requirements, see Wayne R. La Fave et al., Criminal Procedure § 19.2 (6th ed. 2016); Moore's Federal Practice §§ 4.1–4.121 (2017); Collier on Bankruptcy §§ 342.01–342.09 (2017).

Particular bankruptcy notice considerations: Three bankruptcy notice requirements are particularly relevant in cases related to white-collar crime. First, notice is required to the Debtor of the filing of an involuntary bankruptcy against a Debtor whose Creditors fear may be the subject of a criminal investigation. Second, notice is required to Creditors at the outset of the case to inform Creditors of the filing, existence of the bankruptcy automatic stay, and potentially the need to file a Claim against the Bankruptcy Estate. Third, many actions in bankruptcy require notice to nonmoving parties, a hearing, and court approval before the bankruptcy Trustee can take certain actions such as the sale of substantially all of the assets of the estate. *See* Fed. R. Bankr. P. 2002.

Notice and distribution complexities are exacerbated by differences between the Insolvency Proceeding and Forfeiture Proceeding regimes in their recognition and identification of parties and transferees. Perhaps most notably, many parties entitled to notice in a bankruptcy case are not entitled to notice in a Forfeiture Proceeding. Employees, trade Creditors, and shareholders, for example, will not be entitled to notice of Forfeiture unless they qualify as Victims.

Perhaps as significantly, the status of transferees (including entities that purchase Claims or Interests from Creditors or Interest Holders) complicates distributional considerations. Transferees who acquire Claims may be entitled to notice and distribution in the Insolvency Proceeding but may not be entitled to notice or recovery in a Forfeiture Proceeding. In bankruptcy cases, Creditors are allowed to transfer their Claims to third parties, who may then file notice of the transfer and be recognized in the proceedings as standing in the original Creditors' shoes for notice and distributional purposes. In contrast, the statutes and policy statements governing recovery from Forfeiture funds generally restrict recovery to the original Victim. Consequently, if a Victim monetizes or sells its right to payment from a Forfeiture Victim recovery fund, the transferee may have no right to notice and no right to recovery. This result may upset the expectations of buyers of Victims' bankruptcy Claims unless the terms of their assignment agreement require the Victim to pay over Forfeiture distributions.

Additional complexity in terms of communicating with parties in interest arises from the fact that differences in the treatment of Victims/Creditors/Claimants may lead to the appointment of different representatives in different proceedings who lack legal standing in the other proceedings. Representatives of interest groups may have standing to be heard in one proceeding but not others.

Also, in both Insolvency Proceedings and Forfeiture Proceedings, notice and distribution complexities are exacerbated by the existence of unknown or presently unidentifiable Claimants. The complexities of notice and the practical reality that thousands of potentially interested parties may be seeking ongoing information about the status of the various proceedings often warrant the establishment of means of communication that go well beyond mandatory notice requirements.

The sheer complexity and uncertainty of these cases often confuse potential Claimants, many of whom may not be represented by counsel. The result may be literally thousands of inquiries by telephone, letter, and email, many asking the same basic questions. To create better, more comprehensive, and consistent avenues of communication with potentially interested parties, the Trustee and government in larger cases have often established—and widely advertised—case-specific websites where parties may obtain case information, including information regarding how to assert Claims and Interests, and expectations with respect to the timing, amount, processes, and methods of distributions. *See, e.g.,* Madoff Victim Fund, Department of Justice Asset Forfeiture Distribution Program, http://www.madoffvictimfund.com/ (last visited October 5, 2017) (DOJ website); The Madoff Recovery Initiative, Substantively Consolidated SIPA Liquidation of Bernard L. Madoff Investment Securities LLC & Bernard L. Madoff, http://www.madoffTrustee.com/ (last visited October 5, 2017) (SIPA Trustee website).

The parties may seek the courts' assistance in approving forms of mass notice and means of mass communication. Particularly in large cases, the DOJ and Trustee may ask the court to approve unconventional means of communicating with and distributing monies to these large groups of Claimants and Victims. For example, in *Rigas/Adelphia*, the Criminal Forfeiture fund committed significant public resources to alert Victims of their rights through mass mailings, toll-free phone services, and "Victim–witness coordinators."[1] The approach is consistent with federal laws that increasingly require the government to identify and notify potential Victims about important events that take place throughout the government's case (18 U.S.C. §§ 3771(a)(2)–(a)(4), 3771(c)(1) (2017)),[2]

---

1. *See, e.g., The Need for Increased Fraud Enforcement in the Wake of the Economic Downturn: Hearing Before the S. Comm. on the Judiciary*, 111th Cong. 4 (2009) (statement of Rita Glavin, Acting Assistant Att'y Gen., Criminal Div., United States Dep't of Justice), *available at* https://www.judiciary.senate.gov/download/testimony-of-witnesspdf-2009-02-11.

2. *See, e.g.,* Douglas Evan Beloof, *The Third Model of Criminal Process: The Victim Participation Model,* 1999 UTAH L. REV. 289, 289 (1999).

give them a "reasonable right to confer" (18 U.S.C. § 3771(a)(5); *see also* 11 U.S.C. § 364(d)(1) (2017); *In re* Dean, 527 F.3d 391, 395–96 (5th Cir. 2008)), and, in some cases, guarantee the right to "full" compensation (18 U.S.C. § 3771(a)(6) (2017); Dolan v. United States, 560 U.S. 605, 612 (2010)).

5.4d Discussions Between the Bankruptcy Trustee and DOJ

Three main topics may characterize early communication between the government and Trustee. The courts may find the list in this section useful as a guide to probe whether the parties have been communicating effectively and to determine whether encouragement toward interparty communication or perhaps direct Intercourt Communication may be useful.

Status and Nature of Pending Proceedings

- How long has each process been proceeding? Are there any additional filings or substantial developments in process?
- Will the Insolvency Proceeding focus simply upon liquidation (under Bankruptcy Code Chapter 7 or 11, or other insolvency law), or is there a possibility of a restructuring? Is there a legitimate and potentially viable business affected by the proceedings? What efforts can be undertaken to preserve the business operations if appropriate?
- Given this constellation of processes, to what extent can the parties engage in information sharing and to what extent are they limited? Are hurdles to communication caused by necessary case constraints or by intransigence?

Identification of Property

- What Property has been identified in each proceeding? Who currently controls each item of Property?
- Is the bankruptcy voluntary or involuntary? In either event, is there a concern with nonidentified or hidden Property? Are the tools of the bankruptcy process or of governmental enforcement better suited to ferreting out and recovering Property?
- Has the Forfeiture process identified any other Property not yet under the control of any proceeding? Has any Property already been seized in the Forfeiture or Disgorgement process? Is there other Property the government intends to forfeit or disgorge?
- Are there any types of Property or causes of action that the Trustee has or will seek to have restored to the Bankruptcy Estate—for example, clawback actions seeking to recover fraudulent conveyances and voidable preferences?

Identification of Parties, Stakeholders

- What types of criminal actions will be pursued? What consequence does this have for the scope of Victims for purposes of Forfeiture? Is there a conviction or plea agreement? Has the Debtor/defendant or related party agreed to a Forfeiture of Property? Do others claim an interest in that Property?
- Who are the bankruptcy Creditors and Interest Holders?
- To what extent do the Victims overlap with the bankruptcy Creditors, and Interest Holders?

The first few meetings, particularly among attorneys who have not worked together previously, will often focus simply on relationship building. After this, counsel will typically move the discussion toward sequencing and other key matters important to the attorneys, given the particular dynamics of their cases. Sequencing discussion will typically involve identifying the key issues for discussion, setting a timeline or schedule for that discussion, and identifying the relevant parties for participation in such a discussion. All of these discussions may have to wait until the government has entered into a plea/conviction with the defendant, due to pre-plea restrictions on what information can be shared.

Criminal Forfeiture occurs in several steps: (i) the preliminary Forfeiture remains contingent until conviction; (ii) the post-conviction pre-sentencing process; and (iii) sentencing and the entry of a final Forfeiture Order. The post-conviction sentencing report makes recommendations regarding the proposed compensation for Victims. The final Forfeiture Order is entered as part of the sentence. The gaps between these steps allow time for discussions about how the parallel proceedings should interact. If the preliminary order suggests that the defendant's interest is subject to Forfeiture and that the bankruptcy is derivative of the defendant's interest, whether the forfeited Property comes into the Bankruptcy Estate depends upon the timing of the proceedings and other factors. During these two periods, the parties and courts should explore whether the government's theory of the interaction of Relation Back and Substitute Property prevents Property from becoming Property of the Bankruptcy Estate or leaves substantial Property for the Bankruptcy Estate, as noted in chapter 2.

5.4e Participation by Other Stakeholders

The Trustee in the Insolvency Proceeding and the DOJ in the Forfeiture Proceeding will typically be the key stakeholders and voices in any Coordination (Cooperation) Agreement or other collaboration. The Trustee and US Attorney should in turn consider whether other parties should be included in the discussions about the terms of any proposed Coordination (Cooperation) Agreement. For example, are there bankruptcy attorneys, litigators, case agents, auditors, investigators, Victims' groups (whether Victims, advocates, or attorneys), or others that have been involved in the case, whose voices might either: (i) resolve issues or contribute to building an understanding or resolving questions faced by the key participants; or (ii) help eliminate later opposition to the Coordination (Cooperation) Agreement?

Below is a listing of questions that the Trustee and US Attorney will typically consider with respect to Victims, Creditors, and other interested persons. The court may use the following list as a guideline to ensure that the parties have fully considered how the proposed agreement might affect other stakeholders before the court approves a Coordination (Cooperation) Agreement.

- Are there other actors with institutionalized roles who will be essential to broader agreement, such as a Receiver, or SEC or SIPA Trustee?
- Are there advisors whose insights may help educate the bankruptcy Trustee and OUSA, or who can appraise the information being provided by the other parties to these discussions?
    o For example, are specialized accountants or actuarial expertise needed? In some cases, the FBI, IRS, or other agencies may be useful in providing these types of experts.

- Are there parties with a legal right to object and be heard, whose buy-in to the Coordination (Cooperation) Agreement and cooperation process would be helpful prior to filing a motion with the court?
  o If the agreement proposes to address choice of law issues, will the selection of law create or preclude particular substantive law Claims or entitlements?
  o If the agreement proposes to address the allocation of costs for investigation; restructuring of a corporation/preservation of Property; or distribution; does the proposed allocation unduly or adversely impact any Creditor, Claimant, Victim, or party?

Who should be at the table depends upon the stage of the case. The concerns, and therefore the participants, may be different at the outset of the case, during the preservation stage, and later in the case, as allocation/categorization of Property and distribution is considered. They may also vary based upon the extent to which the cooperation extends from mere sharing of information about the identification of Property to bargaining over the treatment of particular Property (forfeitable or not) or Claimants (Victim or not).

When a Coordination (Cooperation) Agreement's terms substantively affect ultimate distributions (including by determining whether Property is subject to the Bankruptcy Estate or to Forfeiture), the court should inquire regarding how the agreement may affect other Claimants. For example, how will the agreement impact secured Creditors, unsecured Creditors, and Interest Holders, particularly as regards determinations with respect to the validity of Forfeitures? Does the categorization of Property as either Forfeitable Property or Bankruptcy Estate Property impact the ultimate distributions to Creditors and Victims? Does the agreement fix the treatment of Victims/Creditors, such that it is a de facto priority determination? Does the decision to restructure a corporation or to determine that it has no viability impact distributions?

5.5 Provisions Regarding Assets and Property

Because Insolvency Proceedings and Forfeiture Proceedings offer distinct and unique advantages in the collection, preservation, and distribution of Property, cooperation may foster efficiency and enhance recoveries.

5.5a Cooperation Regarding Property Recovery

The parties may design Property recovery Coordination (Cooperation) Agreements around which entity has the greatest expertise and may foster the greatest efficiencies with respect to particular means of identifying and recovering Property.

In a Forfeiture Proceeding, the government may be in a superior position to identify and secure remote Property more expeditiously and inexpensively than the bankruptcy Trustee or Receiver. Prosecutors may have standing to collect funds against third parties that private plaintiffs cannot. *See, e.g.*, EEOC v. Wafflehouse, 534 U.S. 279, 294 (2002) (allowing the EEOC to recover damages on behalf of an employee who could not); Myriam Gilles & Gary Friedman, *After Class: Aggregate Litigation in the Wake of AT&T Mobility v. Concepcion*, 79 U. Chi. L. Rev. 623, 642–643 (2012) (describing advantages enjoyed by states attorney general in *parens patriae* litigation); Donald C. Langevoort, *Reading Stoneridge Carefully: A Duty-Based Approach to Reliance and Third-Party Liability Under*

Rule 10b-5, 158 U. Pa. L. Rev. 2125, 2127–2128 (2010) (noting different liability outcomes depending on whether action is by a governmental entity or private litigation); Adam S. Zimmerman & David M. Jaros, *The Criminal Class Action,* 159 U. Pa. L. Rev. 1385, 1401–1403 (2011) (describing prosecutors' powers to pursue Restitution from third parties).

Public authorities also may attach and collect funds from parties using Criminal Forfeiture laws that private plaintiffs cannot. Yet, because each regime offers different tools, cooperation can often expand the available pool of Property and improve distributions.

Forfeiture also grants other powers that are not available in bankruptcy. In particular, the government has greater power to seize and restrain Property as part of over 200 Mutual Legal Assistance Treaties (MLATs) around the world. In contrast, Trustees need to hire private counsel to initiate litigation to recover the Property on the grounds that it is Property of the Bankruptcy Estate in a United States bankruptcy case. The DOJ can rely upon the MLAT and the foreign government's obligations thereunder, which may offer a vastly simpler process.

In contrast, clawback avoidance actions (such as preference actions under 11 U.S.C. § 547(b) and fraudulent transfer actions under 11 U.S.C. § 544) can be brought under the Bankruptcy Code to recover certain Property that may not be readily recoverable through the Forfeiture process, as discussed in chapter 2. Where the lead attorneys in both regimes are able to cooperate, they frequently are successful in identifying additional Property, as well as Claimants, that would likely not have been identified or recovered if the processes had proceeded entirely independently. In very complex cases, with thousands of transfers, cooperation can also prove beneficial in reducing investigation and process costs, through coordinated efforts.

Consideration should also be given to whether one regime or the other facilitates the resolution of challenges posed by commingled Property and the complexity of tracing. Where tracing is an issue, the DOJ may have greater expertise in using the investigative powers of the government together with the Relation Back Doctrine to identify and pursue hidden Property in sham corporations.

5.5b Cooperation Regarding Property Management and Preservation

In addition to identifying and recovering Property, cooperation may also yield significant benefits with respect to Property management and preservation. The traditional experience of the government in efficiently liquidating individual items of Property, such as vehicles, boats, and bank accounts, has been significantly tested as Forfeiture has expanded into far broader realms of Property. The parties may design Property management Coordination (Cooperation) Agreements around which entity has the greatest expertise and may foster the greatest efficiencies with respect to particular types of Property.

If Property is part of an ongoing business that hopes to reorganize, the bankruptcy court and bankruptcy Trustees have longstanding expertise (under Chapter 11 of the Bankruptcy Code) in operating businesses in bankruptcy. Likewise, bankruptcy Trustees may have greater expertise in winding down and liquidating corporations and business Property.

Tracing and liquidation of certain concrete Property may be equally within the expertise of either proceeding. The courts and parties should explore whether one process or the other might more efficiently manage and administer such Property.

5.5c Cooperation Regarding Distributions

Avoiding Duplication in Distributions. Coordination (Cooperation) Agreements may, and the courts should urge that they do, contain assurances that the parties will adopt and implement means of ensuring the prevention of duplicative payments. Once again, the timing of payments is important to ensure that the distribution processes account for potential distributions already made or to be made under the other distribution scheme.

Consolidation of distribution processes could, in theory, foster efficiency and dramatically reduce the potential for duplicative payments. Several challenges to consolidated distribution must be considered. Although Victims are only entitled to recover their net loss amount under Forfeiture law, privacy laws prevent bankruptcy Trustees from readily determining who has qualified as a Victim or what amounts have been paid in Restitution or Remission.[3] Coordination (Cooperation) Agreements are usually essential to provide the necessary information to compare proposed distributions. Such agreements can also take into account the relative costs involved in the two different distributional processes.

Can a common Trustee be appointed? A common Trustee could consolidate efforts and reduce the risk of double recovery or gaps in assets. Using the same Trustee for both the bankruptcy and Forfeiture might allow the Property to be kept segregated but reduce the need for coordination, risk of duplicative recovery, etc. Regrettably, fiduciary obligations may stand in the way of this type of efficiency because the different regimes ask the fiduciary to serve the interests of different beneficiaries.

Should distribution occur in phases? Some cases have deferred potential disputes over distribution by bifurcating the cooperation process into two or three separate phases: (i) identification and seizure; (ii) liquidation or operation of the Property; and (iii) Claims and entitlements determination and distribution. This structure allows early cooperation that may be beneficial but reserves distribution decisions until a later point in the proceedings when greater information may be available. Such an approach may allow the deployment of the various tools unique to each process, focusing upon the comparative strengths of each process with respect to Property identification, transfer of title, and sale of Property (or, in the case of ongoing concerns, management and restructuring of the business), without determining ultimate entitlements. Nevertheless, because early determinations of control over Property may entrench positions, particularly when one party has devoted resources to Property recovery and management, bifurcation agreements must be delineated in ways that clearly preserve rights, provide for adjustments and cost shifting if necessary, and avoid challenges from objectors disfavored by any reallocation during the Claims and entitlements determination and distribution phase.

5.6 Perspectives of Claimants, Victims, and Interest Holders

Ideally, the key parties should be encouraged to engage in a multiparty process in which they begin a dialogue but ultimately incorporate the reasonable positions of objectors, even if these entities are not official signatories to the agreement. If the objectors' views remain in conflict with the major parties' agreement, then the court will ultimately need

---

3. *See, e.g.,* Privacy Act, 5 U.S.C. § 552a (2017); Crime Victims' Rights Act, 18 U.S.C. § 3771 (2017).

to determine whether to approve the agreement. If it does so, it becomes a court order like any other, subject to the applicable standards of review. In most cases, recognition that a court order will follow may bring the parties into the negotiation process and result in an agreement that the courts can approve. These agreements have substantial force once approved, given the level of discretion accorded the US Attorney and bankruptcy Trustee to shape their respective processes, especially when combined with the court order. Thus, while there is a theoretical avenue for appellate review, in practice the viability of appeal has been viewed as substantially limited.

5.7 Provisions Regarding Distributions

As discussed in chapter 2, Insolvency Proceedings follow well-established processes and priority schemes under which all stakeholders' interests are considered, ranked, and compensated under a time-tested statutory scheme. This scheme is often inconsistent, however, with the Forfeiture Proceeding's focus solely on the defendant and Victims.

A number of federal statutes make compensation for Victims an important criminal justice priority. Chief among these are:

- The Victim and Witness Protection Act of 1982, Pub. L. No. 97-291, 96 Stat. 1248 (codified in scattered sections of 18 U.S.C.);
- The Victims' Rights and Restitution Act of 1990, 34 U.S.C. § 20141 (2017);
- The Mandatory Victims Restitution Act of 1996, 18 U.S.C. § 3663A (2017); and
- The Crime Victims' Rights Act of 2004, 18 U.S.C. § 3771 (2017).

With each Act, Congress encouraged, and at times compelled, prosecutors to take a more aggressive role in Victim compensation. The Mandatory Victims Restitution Act of 1996, for example, has been hailed as part of a move "toward a more victim-centered justice system," which would help transform a criminal justice system that Congress believed was ignoring the plight of Victims. Matthew Dickman, *Should Crime Pay?: A Critical Assessment of the Mandatory Victims Restitution Act of 1996*, 97 Cal. L. Rev. 1687, 1688–1689 (2009).

As previously noted, forfeited assets may (but need not) be used to compensate the Victims through Remission and Restoration processes. *See* 21 U.S.C. § 853(i)(1) (2017) (disposition of Criminal Forfeiture proceeds); 18 U.S.C. § 981(e)(6) (2017) (disposition of Civil Forfeiture proceeds). Remission is the means by which forfeited Property is distributed, possibly including to crime Victims. Restoration is the means by which such Property satisfies a Criminal Restitution order in favor of the Victims.

In addition, over the past decade, federal prosecutors have sought compensation in a number of high-profile cases through "non-prosecution" and "deferred prosecution" plea agreements and convictions. Non-prosecution agreements are made between the prosecutor and the accused before charges are filed and are generally not subject to court review or approval. Deferred prosecution agreements are made in the prosecutor's discretion after a formal charging document has been filed and are generally not reviewed by the court. As these devices have seen increased usage, the DOJ Asset Forfeiture Program has increased correspondingly. While recoveries remained fairly constant from 2000 to 2005, Forfeitures doubled in 2006 and have continued at an increasing pace to a record $1.684 billion in 2011. *See Reports*, DOJ, *available at* https://www.justice.gov/afp/reports-0 (last visited October 5, 2017).

A fundamental recurring theme in the tension between Insolvency Proceedings and Forfeiture Proceedings is the potential inequity arising from the treatment of Victims, as compared with the other Claimants and Parties in Interest. On the most literal and narrow reading, "Victim" is limited to the Victims of the particular crimes charged, which may not embody the complete set of parties harmed by the wrongdoing. This narrowness therefore can create inequities between injured persons, to the extent that a decision is made to charge only certain crimes. It also can create tensions between Victims of the scheme and other Creditors if virtually all Property has been forfeited, leaving nothing for Creditors who are not also Victims. A number of Ponzi scheme prosecutions assume this type of distribution. While at first blush, one might argue that Victims should be paid before Creditors, this may run counter to Bankruptcy Code distributive principles, which establish a complex and comprehensive scheme for priority of distribution based upon state law and federal equitable principles. 11 U.S.C. § 507 (2017). It may also be counter to the reality that Creditors may have relied in good faith on the legitimacy of the business in determining to extend credit and may have been harmed by the collapse of the business to the same extent or more than defrauded investors who qualify as Victims under the particular crime of conviction or plea agreement.

The definition of Victim may have worked adequately for crimes where individual Victims are easily identified, such as bribery or robbery, in which equity may favor crime Victims over Creditors. The *Rothstein* case and others, however, suggest that the equities may not be so straightforward in typical fraud cases. (See discussion of the *Rothstein* case in Appendix C.) Both Forfeiture and bankruptcy have mechanisms to subordinate or disallow Claims by persons who were complicit in the wrongdoing in connection with the fraud that caused the business failure. Some Victims, for example, may be sophisticated investors who arguably may have been in a better position to protect themselves and realize that something was amiss, in contrast to innocent trade Creditors who may have had far less ability to discover the fraud. *See, e.g.*, Nancy B. Rapoport, *Black Swans, Ostriches, and Ponzi Schemes*, 42 Golden Gate L. Rev. 627, 638 (2012). Moreover, different charging decisions might have resulted in different pools of Victims, perhaps including the law firm's employees, including secretaries and janitors with no reason to suspect a fraud and no method for risk-spreading, and other Creditors.

For massive entity frauds, the statutory definition of Victim may bring the objectives of the two systems into conflict. Because bankruptcy and Forfeiture developed separately, and the interactions between Insolvency Proceedings and Forfeiture Proceedings are only recently being tested, it is unclear how Congress intended the broad Forfeiture powers and definitions of Victim to mesh with the bankruptcy priority scheme, where both systems lay claim to the same Property. The primary goals of Forfeiture are to disrupt and dismantle criminal enterprises, deter crime, and restore Property to Victims. By contrast, the Bankruptcy Code is designed to establish an orderly system of repayment for Creditors and Interest Holders of an insolvent concern. Because the two systems have different, valid, and important objectives, they may naturally have different results in parallel cases. The challenge is to resolve these competing objectives where the pool of Property from which distributions can be made falls far short of what would be required to compensate all innocent parties, including Creditors, Victims, and others. These competing objectives can give rise to a contest for control over any particular asset.

The best way to address these issues has generally proven to be in a settlement or Coordination (Cooperation) Agreement. Such an agreement may embody a more considered determination of which Property to hold in Forfeiture and what to leave in the Bankruptcy Estate in order to permit a more equitable result in Distribution to the various Claimants. The DOJ may allow the case to continue in bankruptcy where the Victims will receive a greater payout in the bankruptcy system and potentially far faster than through Forfeiture. This might be accomplished by negotiating to permit this process, subject to a cap on fees, or even dropping the Forfeiture entirely where the bankruptcy process will allow a better recovery for the Victims than the narrow Forfeiture definition would. Yet, where there are different distribution schemes and groups of Claimants, deferral of one process to the other becomes more complex. The DOJ and Trustees have expressed a sense of frustration that they wanted to do the right thing but could not violate the statutory regimes they each serve to do so.

The entry of the preliminary Forfeiture Order terminates the defendant's rights to the Property. Consequently, although third parties may assert a Superior Interest in the Property prior to the final hearing, the Trustee (and Bankruptcy Estate), whose rights are derivative of the Debtor/defendant's, cannot. *See* 11 U.S.C. § 323(a) (2017). This suggests that for there to be a meaningful discussion, not merely a discretionary/one-sided decision by the government to relinquish certain Property, the intervention needs to occur earlier in the process. Traditionally, however, the entry of a plea and preliminary Forfeiture have been paired, and direct intervention by third parties in the process is prohibited.

5.8 Provisions Regarding Evidence, Discovery, and Confidentiality

As noted in chapter 4, criminal cases against corporations and entities may involve individual criminal defendants with venue rights that limit the prosecutors' ability to charge in the same jurisdiction that gives rise to a private lawsuit. U.S. Const. amend. VI (affording defendants right to trial in the state or district where the "crime shall have been committed"); United States v. Cabrales, 524 U.S. 1, 8 (1998) (limiting prosecution to the district where alleged money laundering took place); Platt v. Minn. Mining & Mfg. Co., 376 U.S. 240, 245 (1964). As a result, these proceedings may involve not only criminal, civil, and bankruptcy proceedings, but different district courts around the country, or even the world. This can result in differences between jurisdictions with respect to what evidence may be sought and what disclosures must be made, and may result in potentially conflicting rulings by different courts on parallel discovery motions. The courts may want to encourage the parties to overcome these barriers by entering into Coordination (Cooperation) Agreements to streamline the process.

As discussed in chapter 4, these complexities warrant judicial exercise of the courts' power to coordinate parallel Insolvency Proceedings and Forfeiture Proceedings informally, as they do in complex actions between state and federal court, as well as between courts that oversee parallel agency and criminal Restitution actions. *See* United States v. Peterson, 859 F. Supp. 2d 477, 479 (E.D.N.Y. 2012) (considering victim impact in approving a settlement agreement in an SEC civil action parallel to a criminal action); William W. Schwarzer et al., *Judicial Federalism in Action: Coordination of Litigation in State and Federal Courts*, 78 Va. L. Rev. 1689, 1690 (1992) (noting informal state-federal cooperation, including "calendar coordination, coordinated discovery, joint settlement efforts, and joint motions hearings and rulings"); Byron G. Stier, *Resolving the Class Action Crisis:*

Mass Tort Litigation as Network, 2005 UTAH L. REV. 863, 893 ("[M]any state and federal judges meet and form networked responses to the challenges of mass tort litigation.").

5.8a Disclosures

As noted in chapter 4, government attorneys and Trustees can be obliged to disclose information to the courts overseeing each case, including the names of Victims scheduled to receive Restitution, the basis for the awards, and any other related fines or money awarded to government entities in the public proceeding. *Cf.* Manual for Complex Litigation, Fourth § 22.2 (2004). The court may consider whether any disclosures should be in camera. Disclosures may provide a basis for government attorneys and Trustees to determine whether or not to consolidate settlement funds through a single scheme.

In practice, conflicts may arise regarding the extent of discovery that is desirable. Typically, the DOJ must be concerned with ensuring that disclosures made will not jeopardize its criminal investigation. In contrast, typically the bankruptcy Trustee is concerned with expediting its discovery in order to gather and distribute Property as expeditiously as possible.

5.8b Confidential Information

If it becomes necessary to share confidential information, the Coordination (Cooperation) Agreement should include a confidentiality provision. Common interest agreements are a useful framework for developing confidentiality standards for parallel proceedings. Such provisions can include promises not to share non-public information with third parties, standards for treatment of confidential documents, protection of attorney work product, and a process for objections to the sharing of specified information, where it would cause harm to either of the sets of proceedings.

5.9 Provisions Regarding Subsequent Case Management: Deferred Docketing

When a bankruptcy case is pending, the schedules of assets and liabilities filed in the case are designed to identify all potential Creditors and Interest Holders. If the courts are concerned that injured parties may not yet be aware of their injuries, the courts can establish deferred dockets to toll the statutes of limitation until after such injuries are known. This system is most often used in latent toxic tort cases but could be applied in the context of an elaborate Ponzi scheme, financial fraud, or other complex criminal or securities matter in which awareness of the injury and identification of the injured parties may not be readily apparent. *Cf., e.g., In re* Asbestos Prods. Liab. Litig. (No. VI), No. MDL 875, 2002 WL 32151574, at *1 (E.D. Pa. Jan. 16, 2002), *vacated by* In re Asbestos Prods. Liab. Litig. (No. VI), No. MDL 875, 2009 WL 2222977 (E.D. Pa. July 17, 2009); *In re* Asbestos II Consolidated Pretrial, 142 F.R.D. 152, 153–154 (N.D. Ill. 1991); Peter H. Schuck, *The Worst Should Go First: Deferral Registries in Asbestos Litigation*, 75 Judicature 318 (1992); Manual for Complex Litigation, Fourth § 40.52, ¶ 9 (2004).

Bankruptcy courts have devised mechanisms for addressing the concerns that unknown injuries may present. *See* Manual for Complex Litigation, Fourth Ch. 22

(mass tort case management); Laura B. Bartell, A Guide to the Judicial Management of Bankruptcy Mega-Cases (Federal Judicial Center, 2nd ed. 2009). These issues tend to be less problematic in cases involving financial fraud injury than in cases involving latent tort injuries.

5.10 Provisions Regarding Recognition of Certain Orders in Other Parallel Cases

Coordination (Cooperation) Agreements typically include a promise that each signatory will honor specifically identified resolutions and/or settlements approved by other courts involved in the case. These provisions are fairly straightforward if the subject orders and resolutions have already been approved or are being approved simultaneously. Nevertheless, such agreements must consider how the agreed terms might affect unresolved issues in each proceeding, including how Property should be allocated and how they would be transferred pending the resolution of any unresolved legal issues to be considered by each of the courts involved. Moreover, it may be difficult to include promises to honor future orders or resolutions, unless the parameters thereof are carefully delineated.

Glossary I

Terms, Definitions, and Acronyms

Where this Glossary refers to a term defined by statute or rule, the guidebook uses the terms as defined therein. This Glossary includes definitions of other key terms as they are used in this guidebook.

ABC: an assignment for the benefit of creditors.

Adversary Proceeding: an individual lawsuit that arises under the Bankruptcy Code or arises in or relates to the main bankruptcy case.

Assignee: an individual or entity to whom all of the debtor's assets are assigned in an assignment for the benefit of creditors, who liquidates the assets, gives notice to all creditors to file claims, and then distributes the proceeds.

Assignment for the Benefit of Creditors: an insolvency proceeding governed by state law, rather than federal bankruptcy law, in which the business debtor assigns all of its assets to an assignee, who liquidates the assets, gives notice to all creditors to file claims, and then distributes the proceeds. *See, e.g.,* Cal. Code Civ. Proc. §§ 1800–1802 (2017).

Bankruptcy: any domestic or cross-border bankruptcy or insolvency proceeding, including liquidation or reorganization under the federal Bankruptcy Code, 11 U.S.C. §§ 101 et seq. (2017).

Bankruptcy Estate: all of the debtor's interests in property, wherever located and by whomever held, as of the commencement of the bankruptcy case and during the case. *See* 11 U.S.C. § 541(a) (2017).

Bona Fide Purchaser for Value: a third-party claimant who: (i) bought property for value (i.e., acquired the property at arms' length for a fair price); and (ii) was reasonably without cause to believe the property was subject to forfeiture (i.e., lacked the mens rea necessary to be liable for forfeiture because the third party did not know about the crime).

CAFRA: the Civil Asset Forfeiture Reform Act of 2000, 18 U.S.C. §§ 981–987 (2017).

Case Management Order: an order addressing procedural, evidentiary, and other matters relating to the coordination of parallel proceedings, including the mechanics of intercourt communication, joint status and other hearings, and other matters the courts deem necessary and appropriate to facilitate case management.

Claim: in an insolvency proceeding, includes any right to payment owed by the debtor. *See* 11 U.S.C. § 101(5) (2017).

Claimant: an individual or entity seeking compensation or reimbursement from property that is subject either to a forfeiture proceeding or an insolvency proceeding, or both, whether as a creditor, interest holder, or victim.

Claims Trading: occurs in a bankruptcy case when creditors and interest holders monetize their distribution rights by selling their claims or interests to third parties, who may or may not already hold claims or interest in the case.

Clawbacks: proceedings, generally initiated as part of a bankruptcy case, in which the trustee or other representative seeks to recover on behalf of the bankruptcy estate, payments made or property transferred by the debtor to a third party prior to the bankruptcy filing.

Committee: an official or unofficial group of creditors or interest holders that may advocate on behalf of its constituency in a bankruptcy case.

Coordination Agreement or Cooperation Agreement: a substantive agreement between the governmental agency implementing forfeiture, on the one hand, and the trustee or receiver overseeing the insolvency proceeding, on the other hand, regarding which proceeding will receive what allocation of the designated property, including any causes of action the defendant/debtor may hold against third parties under general law or insolvency law's clawback and avoidance powers.

Creditor: an individual or entity asserting a claim against the debtor in an insolvency proceeding. *See* 11 U.S.C. § 101(10) (2017). Creditors include secured and unsecured lenders, trade creditors, contract counterparties, tax authorities, and holders of tort claims, among others.

CSA: the Controlled Substances Act of 1970, 21 U.S.C. §§ 801–971 (2017).

Debt: any liability on a claim.

Debtor: an individual or entity that is the subject of an insolvency proceeding. *See* 11 U.S.C. § 101(13) (2017).

Debtor in Possession: a debtor that remains in possession of its estate. *See* 11 U.S.C. § 1107 (2017).

DIP: a debtor in possession.

Disgorgement: a judicial or administrative process by which the SEC may seek to aid defrauded investors by divesting a wrongdoer of ill-gotten gains obtained in violation of federal securities laws.

DOJ: the United States Department of Justice.

Equity Security Interest: any shares in a corporation or similar security; interests of limited partners in limited partnerships; or warrants or other rights related to purchasing, selling, or subscribing to either of the foregoing. *See* 11 U.S.C. § 101(16), (17) (2017).

Examiner: a neutral expert appointed by a bankruptcy court "to conduct such an investigation of the debtor as is appropriate, including an investigation of any allegations of fraud, dishonesty, incompetence, misconduct, mismanagement, or irregularity in the management of the affairs of the debtor of or by current or former management of the debtor." *See* 11 U.S.C. § 1104(c) (2017).

Facilitating Property: property used or involved in the commission of the crime.

FIRREA: the Financial Institutions Reform, Recovery, and Enforcement Act of 1989, Pub. L. No. 101-73, 103 Stat. 182 (1989).

Forfeitable Property: all property obtained as part of the criminal enterprise, including all substitute property, facilitating property, proceeds, and relation back property.

Forfeiture: a criminal, civil, or administrative process (including disgorgement) by which a governmental entity obtains control over specified property of a targeted entity.

  Criminal Forfeiture: an additional penalty sought as part of a criminal prosecution of a defendant.

  Civil Forfeiture: either an in rem action against the asset itself or an in personam remedy included as part of a civil enforcement action against a defendant.

Administrative Forfeiture: a statutory power that permits the federal seizing agency to seize and forfeit property directly without judicial involvement through an in rem administrative proceeding.

Forfeiture Order: an order issued in a forfeiture proceeding that authorizes or directs the government to seize identified property.

Forfeiture Proceeding: any criminal, civil, or administrative asset forfeiture or disgorgement proceeding by any governmental entity, including the US Department of Justice, Securities and Exchange Commission, or other federal, state, territorial, or foreign governmental entity.

Fraudulent Transfer: a transfer made (or an obligation incurred) by a debtor within two years (or within up to six years, depending on which law applies) before the bankruptcy filing that is either: (i) made with an actual intent to hinder, delay, or defraud creditors; or (ii) made in return for less than reasonably equivalent value when the debtor was insolvent, regardless of the debtor's intent. *See* 11 U.S.C. §§ 544, 548 (2017).

Insolvency Proceeding: any domestic or cross-border bankruptcy or insolvency proceeding, including liquidation or reorganization under the federal Bankruptcy Code, 11 U.S.C. §§ 101 et seq. (2017), federal or state receivership law, assignment for the benefit of creditors under state law, and liquidation under the Securities Investor Protection Act, 15 U.S.C. §§ 78aaa–78111 (2017).

Intercourt Communications: all means by which the courts overseeing insolvency proceedings and forfeiture proceedings may communicate with each other, including informal communication among the judges, formal filed status reports, and joint hearings at the behest of the courts or the parties.

Interest Holder: any holder of an equity security of the debtor, or anyone who asserts an ownership interest in the debtor or the debtor's property.

Ombudsman: an expert appointed by the US Trustee to protect specified interests, typically involving customer and patient privacy considerations during a bankruptcy case.

Party in Interest: in a Chapter 11 bankruptcy case includes a debtor, trustee, creditors' committee, creditor, interest holder, and indenture trustee. *See* 11 U.S.C. § 1109(b) (2017).

Plan or Plan of Reorganization: in a Chapter 11 bankruptcy case sets forth, among other things, classes of claims or interests in the debtor's estate, proposed treatment of claims or interests, and means for the plan's implementation.

Preference: a transfer (typically, a payment on account of an preexisting debt) made by an insolvent debtor to a creditor within 90 days before the filing of the petition that enables the recipient to recover more than it would have otherwise received in a hypothetical liquidation under Chapter 7. *See* 11 U.S.C. § 547(b) (2017).

Proceeds: any property of any kind obtained directly or indirectly as the result of the underlying offense and any property traceable thereto.

Property: (i) in forfeiture proceedings, assets that have been forfeited or disgorged and are under the court's in rem jurisdiction or the control of the enforcement agency; and (ii) in insolvency proceedings, assets in which the debtor had an interest on the date the case was commenced, together with other assets recovered under insolvency law that come within the insolvency court's in rem jurisdiction.

Receiver: a neutral third party appointed pursuant to court order to take possession or control of assets or a business in a receivership, and report directly to the court.

Receivership: an equitable state or federal insolvency proceeding in which the court appoints a neutral third party as receiver to take possession and control of assets or a business, and report directly to the court.

Receivership Order: the scope and nature of a receiver's powers in a receivership.

Relation Back Doctrine: a legal fiction under which the title to forfeitable property vests in the federal government at the time the crime is committed or at the time the property is used to facilitate the crime. *See, e.g.*, 21 U.S.C. § 853(c) (2017).

Relation Back Property: property subject to forfeiture under the relation back doctrine.

Remission: the process through which the Attorney General may return assets to owners, lienholders, or victims who qualify under governmental regulations and file appropriate petitions.

Restitution: payments the court orders a defendant to make to the clerk of the court, who then makes distribution to the victims identified in the order, in the amounts ordered.

Restoration: the process by which the United States Attorney may ask the Attorney General to use forfeited funds to satisfy a restitution order, if no other funds are available.

RICO: the Racketeer Influenced and Corrupt Organizations Act of 1970, 18 U.S.C. §§ 1961–1968 (2017).

SEC: the United States Securities and Exchange Commission.

SIPA: the Securities Investor Protection Act, 15 U.S.C. §§ 78aaa–78lll (2017).

SIPC: the Securities Investor Protection Corporation.

Substitute Property: a sum of money provided by a defendant and accepted by the relevant agency in lieu of other forfeitable property or a forfeitable partial interest in otherwise non-forfeitable property.

Superior Interest: in criminal forfeiture proceedings, the interest held by a third party, not the defendant, who owned property at the time of the crime or otherwise had rights superior to those of the defendant. *See* 21 U.S.C. § 853(n)(6)(A) (2017).

Trustee: unless otherwise apparent from the context, a private individual appointed to administer a Chapter 7 or 11 bankruptcy case to manage and maximize the bankruptcy estate.

United States Trustee or US Trustee: the regional officer of the DOJ appointed by the Attorney General of the United States, who is responsible for, among other duties, (i) selecting, appointing, and supervising a panel of private trustees to serve in all Chapter 7 cases and in those Chapter 11 cases in which the court has ordered appointment of a trustee; and (ii) maintaining the overall integrity of the administrative side of the bankruptcy system. 28 U.S.C. § 586 (2017).

Victim: an individual or entity that is directly and proximately harmed as the result of the commission of an offense providing for forfeiture, and that either has a statutory right to compensation as such, or may be allowed compensation in the discretion of the governmental agency at issue.

Glossary II

Federal Governmental Agencies Involved in Forfeiture and Parallel Proceedings

The agencies listed here include those principally involved in parallel Forfeiture Proceedings and Insolvency Proceedings. Not all of these agencies are likely to have representatives that appear in district or bankruptcy court judicial proceedings, but they are all involved in law enforcement forfeiture actions. Chapter 3 identifies the principal agency representatives the judge typically will encounter in court.

A. Agencies Inside the Department of Justice

The following agencies and sections participate in both nonjudicial and judicial forfeiture proceedings in aid of their law enforcement objectives. The descriptions provided herein were retrieved from the US DOJ website. *See Asset Forfeiture Program, Participants and Roles*, U.S. Dep't of Justice, https://www.justice.gov/afp/participants-and-roles (last updated April 9, 2018).

Money Laundering and Asset Recovery Section (MLARS), formerly known as Asset Forfeiture and Money Laundering Section (AFMLS), of DOJ's Criminal Division holds the responsibility of coordination, direction, and general oversight of the Justice Asset Forfeiture Program. MLARS handles civil and criminal litigation, provides legal support to the US Attorneys' Offices, establishes policy and procedure, coordinates multidistrict asset seizures, administers equitable sharing of assets, acts on petitions for remission, coordinates international forfeiture and sharing, and develops training seminars for all levels of government.

Asset Forfeiture Management Staff (AFMS) has responsibility for management of the Assets Forfeiture Fund, the Consolidated Asset Tracking System (CATS), program-wide contracts, oversight of program internal controls and property management, interpretation of the Assets Forfeiture Fund statute, approval of unusual Assets Forfeiture Fund uses, and legislative liaison on matters affecting the financial integrity of the Justice Asset Forfeiture Program.

Bureau of Alcohol, Tobacco, Firearms and Explosives (ATF) enforces the federal laws and regulations relating to alcohol, tobacco, firearms, explosives, and arson by working directly and in cooperation with other federal, state, and local law enforcement agencies. ATF has the authority to seize and forfeit firearms, ammunition, explosives, alcohol, tobacco, currency, conveyances, and certain real property involved in violation of law.

Drug Enforcement Administration (DEA) implements major investigative strategies against drug networks and cartels. Enforcement operations have resulted in significant seizure and forfeiture activity. A significant portion of DEA cases are adopted from state and local law enforcement agencies.

Federal Bureau of Investigation (FBI) investigates a broad range of criminal violations, integrating the use of asset forfeiture into its overall strategy to eliminate targeted criminal enterprises. The FBI has successfully used asset forfeiture in white collar crime, organized crime, drug, violent crime, and terrorism investigations.

United States Marshals Service (USMS) serves as the primary custodian of seized property for the Justice Asset Forfeiture Program. USMS manages and disposes of the majority of the property seized for forfeiture.

United States Attorneys' Offices (USAOs) are responsible for the prosecution of both criminal and civil actions against property used or acquired during illegal activity.

B. Federal Agencies Outside the Department of Justice

The following agencies participate in judicial forfeitures only. Unless otherwise indicated, the descriptions provided herein were retrieved from the US DOJ website. *See Asset Forfeiture Program, Participants and Roles*, U.S. Dep't of Justice, https://www.justice.gov/afp/participants-and-roles (last updated April 9, 2018).

Department of State, Bureau of Diplomatic Security (BDS) investigates passport and visa fraud and integrates asset forfeiture into its strategy to target the profits made by vendors who provide fraudulent documentation or others who utilize fraudulent visas and/or passports to further their criminal enterprises.

Defense Criminal Investigative Service (DCIS) is the criminal investigative arm of the Inspector General of the Department of Defense. The DCIS's mission is to protect America's war fighters by conducting investigations and forfeitures in support of crucial national defense priorities that include homeland security/terrorism, product substitution, contract fraud, public corruption, computer crimes, and illegal technology transfers.

Food and Drug Administration (FDA)'s Office of Criminal Investigations has made seizures involving health care fraud schemes, counterfeit pharmaceuticals, illegal distribution of adulterated foods, and product tampering.

United States Department of Agriculture (USDA)'s Office of the Inspector General (OIG)'s mission is to promote effectiveness and integrity in the delivery of USDA agricultural programs. Forfeiture is an important tool in combating criminal activity affecting USDA programs.

United States Postal Inspection Service (USPIS) makes seizures under their authority to discourage profit-motivated crimes such as mail fraud, money laundering, and drug trafficking using the mail.

Securities and Exchange Commission (SEC) may seek judicial seizure of businesses and assets by means of federal receivership actions to halt ongoing civil or criminal fraud schemes involving securities and other financial instruments and investments within its sphere of regulation. *See, e.g., Receiverships*, SEC, https://www.sec.gov/divisions/enforce/receiverships.htm (last modified March 20, 2019) (providing links to websites for particular receiverships in SEC enforcement cases created by the SEC staff).

C. Agencies Involved in Bankruptcy Cases

Office of the United States Trustee (OUST) is a unit of the US Department of Justice which is responsible for investigation, oversight, and reporting of bankruptcy crimes or other malfeasance arising in bankruptcy cases. It also appoints and has administrative oversight of the private trustees who are appointed in Chapter 7, 11, and other bankruptcy cases. The Executive Office of the US Trustee is based in Washington, DC, and establishes policy for the regional offices. The twenty-one regional offices are each headed by a United States Trustee who is appointed by the Attorney General of the United States and oversees the functions of the OUST in that region. The OUST does not have direct criminal authority, but rather refers criminal cases to the US Attorney for prosecution. *See* 28 U.S.C. § 586 (2017); *U.S. Trustee Program, About the Program*, U.S. Dep't of Justice, https://www.justice.gov/ust/about-program (last updated March 6, 2019).

D. State Agencies Involved in Forfeiture

The state agencies involved in forfeiture will vary based on state law, but they typically will involve the Office of the Attorney General.

Appendix A

American Bar Association House of Delegates Resolution 102A (February 2014) and Report and Recommendation

American Bar Association Section of Business Law
Resolution 102A, Adopted February 2014

RESOLVED, That the American Bar Association urges executive, judicial and legislative governmental bodies at the federal, state, and territorial levels to engage in actions designed to reduce unnecessary tension, expense and litigation and to foster inter-court, inter and intra-agency, and inter-party cooperation and coordination in cases where parallel actions or proceedings arise under both (i) bankruptcy or insolvency law and (ii) asset forfeiture or analogous regulatory enforcement law.

FURTHER RESOLVED, That these actions by governmental bodies should include, as appropriate to those bodies' respective charges and missions:

(1) education and training;
(2) development and implementation of policies, procedures, guidelines and protocols for:
    (a) internal processes within those governmental bodies;
    (b) interaction with other governmental bodies; and
    (c) interaction with other external parties and entities, including creditors, victims, class representatives, holders of interests and others with an interest in parallel proceedings arising under both bankruptcy or insolvency law and asset forfeiture or analogous regulatory enforcement law;
(3) enactment of appropriate statutory amendments;
(4) adoption of appropriate evidentiary and procedural rules; and
(5) negotiation of appropriate international, cross-border and multi-lateral agreements, including Mutual Legal Assistance Treaties.

REPORT

This Resolution is designed to reduce uncertainty and to minimize expense, litigation and wasted resources resulting from conflicts between asset forfeiture proceedings and bankruptcy proceedings involving the same parties or assets. It does so by encouraging the development of protocols and processes to foster cooperation among the courts, parties, agencies and entities involved in parallel proceedings that involve both bankruptcy (or analogous insolvency proceedings) and asset forfeiture (or analogous regulatory enforcement proceedings).

A. Context

The tensions arising from the interaction of bankruptcy proceedings and asset forfeiture proceedings form the basis for this Resolution. For simplicity, this Report discusses those tensions in the context of financial fraud, which is the primary arena in which these tensions have become apparent in recent years. These tensions may, however, arise in any situation in which an entity or its assets are subject to both (i) a domestic or cross-border bankruptcy or insolvency proceeding, including receiverships, assignments for the benefit of creditors, and liquidation proceedings under the Securities Investor Protection Act, and (ii) a regulatory enforcement action that includes criminal or civil asset forfeiture by any governmental entity including the Department of Justice, Securities and Exchange Commission, or other federal, state, territorial, foreign, or international governmental entity (for example, under 18 U.S.C. §§ 981, 982, 1963 and 21 U.S.C § 853; 28 U.S.C. § 2461).

Fraud, Crime and Bankruptcy

In the wake of the great recession, a substantial number of high profile parallel criminal prosecutions and individual and business bankruptcies have arisen from allegedly fraudulent financial or securities schemes. Examples include the nationally infamous cases involving Madoff (New York), Adelphia/Rigas (Pennsylvania), Petters/Lancelot (Minnesota), Dreier (New York) and Rothstein (Florida), and the more locally shocking cases of Monroe Beachy (Ohio), Lydia Cladek (Florida), Samantha Delay-Wison (Anchorage), and Nick Cosmo/Agape (Long Island). Until fairly recently (within the past decade, most notably), the intersection between criminal law and bankruptcy law in cases of fraud was relatively routine and non-controversial. Criminal law approaches fraud, in its many forms, as a crime—an act that harms society and calls for public vindication. Criminal law prosecutes the fraudster, and perhaps sentences him/her to prison and likely to restitution. Despite the possibility of a restitution order, criminal law has had no direct impact on the fraudster's assets and little impact on the fallout caused by the collapse of the fraudster's enterprise until recently. These matters were left to other law, including contract, tort, collection and bankruptcy law. To bankruptcy law, fraud is simply one item on a lengthy list of ways to create debt. If a fraudster, or his business, files bankruptcy, bankruptcy law treats the fraudster and the entities harmed by fraud in accordance with bankruptcy's fundamental objectives. Commonly synthesized as the "twin pillars" of modern bankruptcy law, these are: (i) the right to a "fresh start" for the "honest but unfortunate" individual debtor or financial rehabilitation for the business debtor, and (ii) creditors' rights to restorative and distributive justice, expressed in terms of collective enforcement, maximization of value, and equitable distribution. If a fraudster files bankruptcy, bankruptcy law denies discharge to the dishonest debtor and/or the fraudulently incurred debt, and generally permits criminal prosecution or regulatory enforcement action to proceed umestricted by the "automatic stay," which halts most actions against a debtor in bankruptcy. (11 U.S.C. §§ 362 (b)(I), 523(a)(2), (a)(4), (c), 727, 1141(d).) Bankruptcy law's comprehensive processes for asset collection (11 U.S.C. §§ 540–549), claims resolution (11 U.S.C. §§ 521–523), and distribution (11 U.S.C. §§ 503, 727, 1129), provide detailed systems for addressing the complex interactions among diverse interests affected by the collapse of the enterprise. These systems include provisions addressing the rights and obligations arising out of criminal or other regulatory enforcement proceedings, such as restitution and injunctive relief. Analogous, comprehensive processes define insolvency proceedings under other federal, state, foreign, and international law.

Critical Developments in Criminal Law and Regulatory Enforcement

Two significant developments have brought criminal law (and other regulatory enforcement law) into the realm of asset collection and distribution in new ways that put it on a collision course with bankruptcy law. Analogous changes occurred roughly simultaneously under other regulatory enforcement law.

First, during the past several decades, criminal law has embraced the notion of victims' rights. In this regard, restitution orders have become standard in many federal sentences, including in fraud cases. Restitution does not, however, give the government power to seize a defendant's assets and "restore" or "remit" them to "victims." This is where the second development, regarding forfeiture, comes into play. Forfeiture allows the government to seize property that was involved in, facilitated, or is the proceeds of a wide array of crimes. In 2000, and again in 2006, Congress expanded criminal forfeiture to include a lengthy list of federal crimes, including an extensive array of frauds. Today, the government routinely seizes property as a mandatory component of many federal sentences. (18 U.S.C. §§ 981, 982, 1963; 21 U.S.C § 853; 28 U.S.C. § 2461.) When coupled with restitution, remission and restoration, forfeiture allows the government to take a defendant's assets and use them to compensate victims. Criminal forfeiture, together with analogous civil enforcement provisions, today require the government to fashion reasoned means of distributing literally billions of dollars of ill-gotten gains. These changes have altered the landscape because forfeiture no longer operates solely in discrete situations in which a fairly straightforward process is used to gather illicitly obtained property and returns it to its rightful owner, or uses its value to compensate the victims of a crime. When fraud infiltrates a business' operations, it is not uncommon for the business itself and one or more of its principals to be subject to forfeiture and voluntary or involuntary bankruptcy proceedings. In a typical bankruptcy case, the Bankruptcy Code, first, attempts to gather all of the debtor's property in one forum for equitable distribution. In this regard, bankruptcy law differs from forfeiture law, at least in theory, because forfeiture is limited to property tied to the particular crime(s) of conviction. Nevertheless, the enlarged definition of crimes for which forfeiture is authorized, combined with broad concepts such as substitute property, facilitating property, proceeds, and relation back, may result in broad forfeitures of virtually all of the assets that otherwise might be administered in a bankruptcy case. In the case of fraud, depending on the crimes charged (securities fraud, mail fraud, wire fraud, etc.), the forfeitable property that was involved in, facilitated, or constituted proceeds of the crime may include virtually all of the assets of the (possibly legitimate) business. This is especially true in a Ponzi scheme where there arguably are few if any "clean" assets.

Second, the Bankruptcy Code seeks to gather all of the debtor's stakeholders in one forum. Claimants generally cannot opt out of the bankruptcy process, and typically will be bound by the discharge even if they decline to participate. (11 U.S.C. §§ 524, 1141 (2012).) In this regard, bankruptcy law again differs from forfeiture law because bankruptcy law is not limited to distributing property to "victims" whose injuries relate directly to the specific crime(s) of conviction. Rather, it proceeds under a broad structure that includes all of the fraudster's stakeholders without regard to whether their claims or interests arise directly from the fraud. In contrast, under forfeiture law, the definition of "victims" (again, in reference to the crimes of conviction) may include vast numbers of shareholders, investors and others who claim to have been duped. The definition of victims might not, however, include many others who suffered harm from the business collapse, such as suppliers, utilities, trade creditors, employees, and lenders whose dealings with what they perceived to be a legitimate business unwittingly enabled the fraud to continue.

Third, after all of the assets and stakeholders have been brought together in the bankruptcy forum, the Bankruptcy Code mandates distribution according to a carefully constructed and detailed distribution scheme. (11 U.S.C. §§ 726, 1129(a)-(b) (2012).) In so doing, it creates an "absolute priority" system under which debt must be paid in full before equity takes a share, analogous to the familiar notion that an insolvent entity may not distribute dividends to shareholders when it is unable to pay creditors. These distributive precepts may come into tension with forfeiture law, however, particularly if forfeited assets are distributed to "victims" under priorities (or exclusivities) that differ markedly from the distributions that would have been made under bankruptcy law. As a consequence of these different approaches, important substantive conflicts may arise with respect to fundamental determinations of entitlement and distribution under bankruptcy and forfeiture law. Moreover, because the parallel proceedings in forfeiture and bankruptcy cases may be subject to divergent evidentiary and procedural rules and standards, uncertainties arise with respect to fundamental aspects of evidence gathering, sharing, and preservation. The absence of clearly applicable procedural rules leaves the courts with, at best, limited guidance with respect to the resolution of these conflicts or even the scope of their ability to communicate across courts.

B. Essential Premise of This Resolution

This Resolution is designed to reduce the tensions between forfeiture law and bankruptcy law, and thereby reduce unnecessary litigation and waste of resources. It does so by encouraging the development of protocols and processes to facilitate communication, cooperation and coordination among the parties to forfeiture and bankruptcy proceedings. Coordination is possible because, although bankruptcy law and criminal law wield different tools, they hold firmly to the same fundamental principles regarding financial fraud: the dishonest cheat should pay; those harmed by fraud should be compensated. It is not enough to agree upon these principles, however. The restorative and distributive rules of bankruptcy law and forfeiture law vest in highly developed statutes. Those statutes evolved from different sources, for different reasons, and are in many ways irreconcilable today. Consequently, it is incumbent upon those who practice and make policy in these areas to collaborate across disciplines to reconcile competing processes where possible, identify points of tension where necessary, and advocate for change where appropriate. In the absence of clear rules, protocols, processes or guidelines, the level of communication, cooperation and coordination in these cases has necessarily been ad hoc. Consequently, resources that otherwise might be used to compensate those harmed by the underlying conduct may instead be wasted on litigation or other efforts to resolve uncertainties regarding how these divergent legal schemes interact.

C. Recommended Actions

This Resolution does not propose substantive reconciliation of the tensions between forfeiture law and bankruptcy law. Rather, it encourages the entities with a stake in these proceedings to move away from the type of costly litigation and ad hoc coordination that currently defines these proceedings toward the development of coherent policies, protocols, and governing principles.

D. Essential Entities

The essential entities to whom this Resolution is directed include the direct stakeholders as well as rulemaking and lawmaking bodies. Specifically, this Resolution urges that the Recommended Actions be undertaken by:

- the Department of Justice (including without limitation its Criminal Division Asset Forfeiture and Money Laundering Section, Office of International Affairs, Civil Division Commercial Litigation Branch, National Advocacy Center, and Victims' Rights Ombudsman), United States Attorneys, Executive Office of the United States Trustee, Executive Office of the United States Attorney,
- Securities and Exchange Commission, Securities Investor Protection Corporation,
- Federal Judicial Center,
- Federal Bankruptcy Courts, Federal District Courts, State Courts,
- trustees, receivers,
- appropriate committees of the Federal Judicial Conference of the United States,
- Congress,
- and federal, state and territorial governmental, judicial and legislative bodies and agencies.

E. Related ABA Resolutions

This Resolution is consistent with and furthers the objectives of previous American Bar Association Resolutions that encourage the development of (i) processes to facilitate inter-court coordination, and (ii) guidelines governing asset forfeiture and victim protections. A critical gap remains, however, because none of those prior resolutions address forfeiture or parallel proceedings in the context of the interaction of forfeiture proceedings and bankruptcy proceedings. Relevant or analogous prior Resolutions are set forth here alphabetically.

Civil and Criminal Forfeiture. Urge the United States Department of Justice and state and local prosecutor agencies to promulgate guidelines to govern the use of civil or criminal forfeiture. 91M104A

Conduct of Litigation Filed in Federal, State and Territorial Courts. Supports the establishment of methods of cooperation and coordination between federal (including bankruptcy), state and territorial courts for the conduct of litigation filed in federal (including bankruptcy), state and territorial courts arising out of common facts. Supports the exploration of methods for consolidation of such litigation for some or all purposes within the context of constitutional limitations. 92MI20A

Crime Victims. Urge trial judges to encourage processes which inform and educate victims of crimes about programs, procedures and restitution, while observing the legal rights of criminal defendants and assuring impartiality to all who appear before them, including the use of videos, brochures and educational materials, presented to victims by law enforcement officials, at an early stage of the criminal proceeding. 98M104B

Cross-Border Class Actions in U.S. and Canada. Adopts as best practices the *Protocol on Court-to-Court Communications in Canada-US. Cross-Border Class Actions* and *Notice Protocol: Coordinating Notice(s) to the Class(es) in Multijurisdictional Class Proceedings*, dated August 2011 and urges courts and counsel in cross-border class-action cases involving the United States and Canada to adopt the *Protocols*. IIAlOIC

Federal Asset Forfeiture Laws. Urge that federal asset forfeiture laws be amended to comply with the Statement of Principles on the Revision ofthe Federal Asset Forfeiture Laws, dated November II, 1995. 96MI13A

Parallel and Concurrent Proceedings. Urge appropriate committees of the Judicial Conference of the United States to address problems that may arise as a result of parallel and concurrent civil and criminal proceedings, including amendment to relevant federal procedural rules. 93M108B

F. Related ABA Activities

This Resolution is consistent with and furthers the initiative of the Business Law Section, which has been exploring these complex questions and working to facilitate these objectives through its Working Group on White Collar Crime, Asset Forfeiture and Business Bankruptcy. The Working Group, which was formed in October of 2010, exists under the aegis of the Committee on Bankruptcy Court Structure and Insolvency Processes, works in close conjunction with the Business Bankruptcy Committee, and coordinates with other committees of the Business Law Section and Criminal Justice Section. It brings together in dialogue individuals representing the principal entities and interest groups addressing these concerns, including the Essential Entities, in working toward the objectives of this Resolution.

Respectfully submitted,
Dixie L. Johnson, Chair
Business Law Section
February 2014

Appendix B
Brief Summaries of Key Forfeiture Statutes

I. Civil Forfeiture Statutes and Rules

18 U.S.C. § 981 (2017). Civil forfeiture.

(a) Property subject to civil forfeiture includes all proceeds and property used in commission of the offense giving rise to forfeiture.
(b) Property subject to forfeiture under (a) generally may be seized by Attorney General, Secretary of the Treasury, or US Postal Service as applicable.
(c) Seized property is deemed to be in the custody of the seizing official, who may store it in an appropriate location, subject to further order of the court.
(d) Any applicable customs laws apply to seized property.
(e) Seizing officer may retain or transfer the property to any other state or federal law enforcement agency involved in the seizure, subject to various terms and conditions, to ensure the equitable allocation of proceeds; allocation is not subject to court review.
(f) The United States' title in forfeited property relates back to date of act giving rise to forfeiture.
(g) Civil forfeiture proceedings may need to yield to criminal proceedings.
(h) Venue is appropriate where defendant/property owner is found or where the criminal prosecution is pending.
(i) Certain circumstances permit property transfer to cooperating foreign agencies.
(j) Terms "Attorney General" and "Secretary of the Treasury" include their delegates.
(k) Forfeiture of funds is available via interbank accounts.

18 U.S.C. § 983 (2017). General rules for civil forfeiture proceedings.

(a) Procedures for seizure (notice, claim, and complaint).
(b) Representation and rights to appointed counsel for parties with standing to contest civil forfeiture.
(c) Burden of proof.
(d) Innocent owner defense.
(e) Motion to set aside forfeiture.
(f) Release of seized property.
(g) Proportionality: right to contest whether forfeiture was constitutionally excessive.
(h) Civil fine may be imposed on claimants asserting frivolous claims.
(i) Civil forfeiture statute defined: includes all civil forfeiture statutes, except under Titles 19, 21, 22, 26, and 50.

Fed. R. Civ. P., Supp. Rule G. Forfeiture Actions in Rem.

(1) Rule governs forfeiture actions in rem arising from federal statutes.
(2) Verified complaint must be filed with required information, including grounds for jurisdiction and description of the property with reasonable particularity.
(3) Judicial authorization and execution of process; arrest warrants for personal property.
(4) Notice by publication and to known potential claimants.
(5) Responsive pleadings include filing a claim and an answer.
(6) Special interrogatories may be served.
(7) Preserving property; sales: allows issuance of orders to preserve assets not yet in the government's possession.
(8) Motions: specifies procedures for motions to suppress use of the property; to dismiss the action; to strike a claim; to release the property; and to mitigate excessive fines.
(9) Trial: trial by court, absent jury demand under Fed. R. Civ. P. 38.

II. Criminal Forfeiture Statutes and Rules

21 U.S.C. § 853 (2017). Criminal forfeiture.

(a) Property subject to criminal forfeiture: includes proceeds, facilitating property and ownership interest in criminal enterprise.
(b) Meaning of term "property" includes all types of real and personal property.
(c) Third party transfers: United States' title in forfeited property relates back to date of act giving rise to forfeiture. Subsequently transferred property may be recovered from third party transferees unless they are bona fide purchasers for value.
(d) Rebuttable presumption: property either contemporaneously or after-acquired by defendant convicted of a felony is subject to forfeiture, upon proof that no other likely source exists.
(e) Protective orders: United States may obtain protective orders or injunctions to preserve property pending indictment, up to 90 days.
(f) Warrant of seizure: United States may request seizure upon showing of probable cause that property would be forfeitable upon conviction.
(g) Execution: order of forfeiture authorizes Attorney General to seize and hold such property, and use any income therefrom to offset expenses.
(h) Disposition of property: Attorney General has general authority.
(i) Authority of Attorney General to settle, award compensation to victims, preserve, and dispose of forfeited property.
(j) Applicability of civil forfeiture provisions: 21 U.S.C. § 881(d) also applies to criminal forfeiture except to the extent inconsistent with this section.
(k) Bar on intervention: claimants as to the forfeited property are generally barred from intervening in the criminal proceedings or commence a separate action regarding the property.
(l) Jurisdiction to enter orders: districts courts have authority without regard to location of the property.
(m) Depositions: court may order depositions under Fed. R. Crim. P. 15.

(n) Third party interests: describes procedures and rights of third parties to assert claims with respect to forfeited property in which they claim a legal interest.
(o) Construction: liberally construed to effect remedial purposes.
(p) Forfeiture of substitute property: defines and describes procedures and rights with respect to seizure of substitute property.
(q) Restitution for cleanup of clandestine laboratory sites: allows imposition of reimbursement charges for cleaning up methamphetamine labs.

18 U.S.C. § 982 (2017). Criminal forfeiture.

(a) Forfeiture shall be included in sentences for a long list of offenses under Title 18.
(b) Forfeiture of property under this section shall be governed by the Comprehensive Drug Abuse Prevention and Control Act of 1970, 21 U.S.C. § 853 (2017).
(c) Mere intermediaries are not subject to forfeiture of substitute property unless they were involved in three or more separate transactions exceeding $100,000 within any twelve-month period.

18 U.S.C. § 1963 (2017). Criminal penalties.

With the exception of subsection (a), most of the provisions of this section closely track the parallel provisions of 18 U.S.C. § 853 (2017).

(a) Conviction under 18 U.S.C. § 1962 (racketeering) carries maximum term of twenty years to life, plus forfeiture of any interest in property or interest in the criminal enterprise.
(b) Property subject to criminal forfeiture under this section includes any real and personal property.
(c) United States' title in forfeited property relates back to date of act giving rise to forfeiture. Subsequently transferred property may be recovered from third party transferees unless they are bona fide purchasers for value.
(d) Court may issue restraining orders or injunctions to preserve availability of property subject to forfeiture.
(e) Upon conviction under this section, court shall enter judgment for forfeiture; Attorney General authorized to seize and hold such property, and use any income therefrom to offset expenses.
(f) Attorney General has general authority to dispose of and manage forfeited property.
(g) Attorney General is authorized to grant petitions for mitigation or remission; restore forfeited property to victims; protect the rights of innocent parties; settle, award compensation to victims; and preserve and dispose of forfeited property.
(h) Attorney General may promulgate regulations regarding forfeiture.
(i) Claimants are generally barred from intervening in the criminal proceedings or instituting separate suits against the United States regarding the forfeited property.
(j) District courts have jurisdiction to enter forfeiture orders without regard to the location of the property.
(k) Court has authority to order depositions.

(l) Notice, procedures, and rights of third parties to assert claims with respect to forfeited property in which they claim a legal interest.
(m) Forfeiture of substitute property is authorized.

28 U.S.C. § 2461(c) (2017). Mode of recovery.

Government may include notice of forfeiture in any indictment or information in a criminal case involving an offense that is subject to civil or criminal forfeiture.

Fed. R. Crim. P. 32.2. Criminal forfeiture.

(a) Notice to defendant: forfeiture cannot be awarded unless it was included as part of requested sentence in the operative indictment or information.
(b) Entering a preliminary order of forfeiture: specifying procedures for forfeiture determinations.
(c) Ancillary proceeding; specifying procedures for final judgment of forfeiture.
(d) Stay pending appeal: discretionary stay pending appeal.
(e) Subsequently located property; substitute property: specifying procedures for amending forfeiture orders to add or substitute property.

III. Restitution Statutes

18 U.S.C. § 3663 (2017). Order of restitution.

(a) (1) Court may order restitution to any victim of specified offenses as part of the sentence for such offense.
  (2) "Victim" means a person directly and proximately harmed as a result of the commission of an offense for which restitution may be ordered.
  (3) Restitution may be ordered in any criminal case pursuant to a plea agreement.
(b) Restitution orders may require return of property to rightful owner; payment of value of the lost property; payment of medical expenses in connection with bodily injury; or payment of other compensatory damages.
(c) For offenses with no identifiable victim, restitution may be ordered to the United States for the amount of public harm.
(d) Restitution orders to be issued and enforced in accord with 18 U.S.C. § 3664 (2017).

18 U.S.C. § 3663A. Mandatory restitution to victims of certain crimes.

(a) (1) Restitution may be ordered in addition to or in lieu of any other penalty for offenses described in subsection (c).
  (2) Same definition of "victim" as 18 U.S.C. § 3663(a)(2) (2017).
  (3) Restitution may be made to persons other than a "victim" of the parties so agree in a plea bargain.
(b) Same measure of restitution as 18 U.S.C. § 3663(b) (2017).
(c) This section applies to crimes of violence, offenses against property under 21 U.S.C. § 856 (2017); tampering with consumer products; or theft of medical products.
(d) Restitution orders to be issued and enforced in accord with 18 U.S.C. § 3664 (2017).

18 U.S.C. § 3664 (2017). Procedure for issuance and enforcement of order of restitution.

(a) Presentence report to provide a complete accounting of victim losses; any provisions for restitution in plea agreements; and financial resources of defendant.

(b) Court is required to disclose to both parties any portions of presentence report relating to restitution.

(c) This chapter, Chapter 227, and Fed. R. Crim. P. 32(c) shall exclusively govern proceedings regarding restitution.

(d) Notice to be provided to victims regarding conviction, presentence report, and deadline to file separate declaration regarding losses.

(e) Any disputes regarding restitution to be determined by preponderance of the evidence. Government has burden of proof regarding victim losses. Defendant has burden regarding ability to pay.

(f) Full amount of victim's losses to be compensated; availability of insurance coverage not to be considered in determining restitution due to a victim. Manner and schedule of payments to be determined by reference to defendant's ability to pay.

(g) Victims are not required to participate.

(h) Restitution may be joint or apportioned among co-defendants.

(i) Restitution payments may differ among victims depending upon type and amount of loss and their individual circumstances. United States as victim is last in line for payment.

(j) Restitution to victims who have already been compensated by insurance or other source will follow payments to all other victims; shall be net of any compensatory damages recovered in civil suits for the same loss.

(k) Defendant required to notify court and Attorney General of any material change in economic circumstances; notice to be provided to victims by the Attorney General; payment schedule may be modified.

(l) Conviction estops defendant from denying the essential allegations of the offense in any later civil litigation brought by the victim.

(m) Restitution orders enforceable by all reasonable methods, including recording abstracts of judgment.

(n) If person obligated to pay restitution or a fine receives substantial resources from any source, including inheritance, during a period of incarceration, the value of such resources shall be applied to the remaining restitution.

(o) Sentence imposing restitution is a final judgment.

(p) Nothing in this section gives rise to private right of action versus the United States or its employees.

IV. Regulations Governing Remission or Mitigation of Civil and Criminal Forfeitures

28 C.F.R. §§ 9.1–9.9 (2017).

9.1 (a) **Purpose, authority, scope:** sets for procedures for remission or mitigation of forfeitures under DOJ's jurisdiction with respect to individuals who were not involved with and did not know about the conduct involved in the offense.

(b) *Authority to grant*: rests with agency seizing the property.
(c) *Scope*: supersedes prior regulations.
(d) *Effective date*: applies to all forfeiture actions on or after October 12, 2012.

9.2 **Definitions**: mostly drawn from 18 U.S.C. § 983.
Petition: request for remission or mitigation.

9.3 **Petitions in administrative forfeiture cases**
(a) *Notice of seizure*: Notice of seizure and intent to forfeit the property to be given to parties with ownership interest; petitions generally must be filed within thirty days.
(b) *Persons who may file*: anyone with an ownership interest in the property, including lienholders, but not if they have fled the jurisdiction to avoid prosecution.
(c) *Contents of petition*: sets forth basic requirements.
(d) *Releases*: petition must be accompanied by releases by titled or registered owner and any other known claimants of their interests in the property.
(e) *Filing with agency*: sets for requirements for "filing" and proper notice to the agency at issue.
(f) *Agency investigation*: upon receipt of a petition, seizing agency is obligated to investigate merits and submit a report to the ruling official.
(g) *Ruling*: no hearing; ruling on paper submissions and the investigative report.
(h) *Petition granted*: remission or mitigation ruling to be sent to petitioner and US Marshal or other custodian prescribing terms, conditions for release of property.
(i) *Petition denied*: shall explain reasons for denial and procedure for reconsideration.
(j) *Request for reconsideration*: must be submitted within ten days of receipt of notice of denial, and must include new evidence or information not previously considered.
(k) *Restoration of proceeds from sale*: petitioner may seek proceeds if it did not have notice in time to petition before the sale of the property; must file within ninety days of sale.

9.4 **Petitions in judicial forfeiture cases**
(a) *Notice of seizure*: Notice of seizure and intent to forfeit the property to be given to parties with ownership interest; petitions generally must be filed within thirty days.
(b) *Persons who may file*: owner, lienholder, or victim (if the victim has legally cognizable title).
(c) *Contents of petition*: sets for elements that must be included.
(d) *Releases*: petition must be accompanied by releases by titled or registered owner and any other known claimants of their interests in the property.
(e) *Filing petition with Department of Justice*: petitions must sworn by petitioner or counsel; must be submitted to US Attorney in district in which the forfeiture proceedings are pending.
(f) *Agency investigation and recommendation*: seizing agency required to submit report to US Attorney as to whether the petition should be granted or denied; US Attorney then makes recommendation to Chief of Asset Forfeiture and Money Laundering Section for review and action.

(g) *Ruling*: Chief shall rule; no hearing held.
(h) *Petitions under Internal Revenue Service liquor laws*: Chief shall consider petitions as to such seizures only before a decree of forfeiture is entered; thereafter, district court has exclusive jurisdiction.
(i) *Petitions granted*: If Chief grants, decision shall be mailed to petitioner, US Attorney, US Marshal, and the seizing agency, which shall coordinate the release of the property.
(j) *Petitions denied*: Copy of decision to be mailed to petitioner, US Attorney, US Marshal, and seizing agency; shall specify the reason for denial.
(k) *Requests for reconsideration*: must be filed within ten days of notice of denial of petition; must be based upon new or additional evidence; and such request must be ruled upon by a different official.
(l) *Restoration of proceeds from sale*: if petition comes after sale due to lack of notice, it must be submitted within ninety days of sale.

9.5 Criteria governing administrative and judicial remission and mitigation
(a) *Remission*: may be granted only if petitioner establishes valid, good faith, and legally cognizable interest in the seized property as owner or lienholder; if owner, must be "innocent owner;" petitioner has burden of proof and must overcome presumption that forfeiture was valid.
(b) *Mitigation*: even if remission is not justified, ruling official may find that some relief should be granted to avoid extreme hardship; mitigation may consist of monetary or other condition on petitioner's continued use of the property; such monetary amount must be paid within twenty days of receipt of the decision.

9.6 Special rules for specific petitioners
(a) *General creditors*: Unsecured creditors do not qualify for remission or mitigation as such; would have to meet other requirements to qualify as petitioner.
(b) *Rival claimants*: Owners will generally prevail over lienholders, where both petitions are found meritorious.
(c) *Voluntary bailments*: Petitioners who informally allowed use of their property without charge are generally entitled to remission.
(d) *Lessors*: Commercial lessors must satisfy "innocent owner" requirements to prevail.
(e) *Straw owners*: Petitioners who received property to help prior owner circumvent forfeiture will lose.
(f) *Judgment creditors*: Creditors' liens must predate forfeiture, be valid under state law, and have been recorded without knowledge of the acts giving rise to the forfeiture; they only prevail to the extent of their judgment, not the full value of the property.

9.7 Terms and conditions of remission and mitigation
(a) *Owners*: describes factors determining whether the property or monetary equivalents are remitted, calculation of remitted amounts, treatment of government costs, and potential imposition of other conditions.
(b) *Lienholders*: describes the calculation and processing of remission for lienholders, either by returning the property or by satisfying the amount of the lien from sale proceeds, which may be subject to various conditions.

9.8 Remission procedures for victims

(a) *Remission procedures for victims*: this section only applies where statute explicitly authorizes remission to victims of forfeited property in which they did not have pre-forfeiture ownership or other interest. Same general procedures for filing claims apply.

(b) *Qualification to file*: must establish pecuniary loss directly caused by the illegal acts committed as part of the criminal offense; victim did not knowingly aid in the offense; no prior compensation for the loss; and no other potential source of recovery.

(c) *Pecuniary loss*: limited to fair market value as of the date of the loss.

(d) *Torts*: remission may not be based upon loss from torts related to the offense, unless the tort constitutes the illegal activity; no remission for consequential damages.

(e) *Denial of petition:* may be denied if pecuniary loss is difficult to calculate, or so small as to be impractical to administer.

(f) *Pro rata basis*: multiple victim petitioners should generally be treated pro rata, with some consideration for financial condition or particularized relationship to the offense.

(g) *Reimbursement*: recipient of remission must reimburse government to extent victim later receives compensation.

(h) *Claims of financial institution regulatory agencies:* claims of financial institution regulatory agencies generally take priority over victim remission petitions.

(i) *Amount of remission:* amount of victim remission limited to victim's share of net proceeds of the related forfeiture, after deducting government expenses and valid third-party claims.

9.9 Miscellaneous provisions

(a) *Priority of payment:* government costs to be paid first, then owners, lienholders, federal financial institution regulatory agencies, and lastly victims.

(b) *Sale or disposition of property prior to ruling*: if property was already sold, remission relief would be in monetary amount, distributed first to the government for forfeiture and sale expenses, second to successful remission petitioner, third to Assets Forfeiture Fund for any other costs, fourth to victims to the extent of their loss, and finally, any remaining balance to Assets Forfeiture Fund.

(c) *Trustees and other assistants:* authorizes use of trustees or contractors to process petitions.

(d) *Other agencies of the United States:* other agencies may petition for remission based upon cognizable interest in the property; same general rules apply.

(e) *Financial institution regulatory agencies:* such agencies may file simple request for transfer of property under specific statutory authorization.

(f) *Transfers to foreign governments:* remission may be denied to petitioners other than owners or lienholders, so that forfeited property can be transferred to a foreign government.

(g) *Filing by attorneys:* petitioners may be represented by counsel; petition must include signed, sworn statement of petitioner to key elements and authority of counsel to represent petitioner.

(h) *Consolidated petitions:* petition may be filed by one petitioner on behalf of multiple petitioners based upon similar underlying facts; written authority for lead petitioner is required from each represented petitioner; may be consolidated for consideration; and insurers, administrators of employee benefit plans, and similar representatives may file petitions on behalf of members of the group, but any remission payments go directly to the individual petitioner, not the class representative, unless the intermediary is expressly authorized to disburse the funds or property.

Appendix C

Brief Summaries of Major Cases Involving Both Forfeiture Proceedings and Insolvency Proceedings

1. Bernard Madoff (New York)

Bernard Madoff operated Bernard L. Madoff Investment Securities LLC (BLMIS), a stock brokerage and other businesses that were publicly revealed to be a massive Ponzi scheme in December 2008, when Madoff was arrested. The scheme had operated undetected for three decades, defrauding investors of approximately $18–20 billion. Although the brokerage received funds from investors for the purchase of securities, in fact Madoff never purchased securities or invested the funds. He created fictitious paper account statements and trading records that listed purported securities transactions. In classic Ponzi-scheme fashion, early investors received returns paid from later investors' funds. He particularly targeted his own Jewish community, with many Jewish nonprofit organizations suffering losses due to the fraud.

The litigation commenced with the filing of a complaint by the SEC against BLMIS and Madoff alleging securities fraud, and an action by the Securities Investor Protection Corporation (SIPC) under the Securities Investor Protection Act (SIPA) to shut down and liquidate the brokerage based on BLMIS's inability to meet its obligations to securities customers as they came due. The SEC agreed to consolidate its case with the SIPA action and to have both of them removed to the bankruptcy court for administration.

An involuntary bankruptcy case was filed against Madoff personally. It was substantively consolidated with the SIPA liquidation. *See generally* Consent Order Substantively Consolidating the Estate of Bernard L. Madoff into the SIPA Proceeding of Bernard L. Madoff Investment Securities LLC and Expressly Preserving All Rights, Claims and Powers of Both Estates, Sec. Inv'r Prot. Corp. v. Bernard L. Madoff Inv. Sec. LLC (*In re Madoff*), No. 08-1789-smb (Bankr. S.D.N.Y. June 10, 2009), ECF No. 252.

Madoff pled guilty to eleven counts of securities fraud, mail fraud, and money laundering, admitting that he had operated a Ponzi scheme through the investment advisory side of BLMIS, but he otherwise provided no cooperation with the trustee. He was sentenced to 150 years in prison and agreed to forfeit all of his assets, estimated at $170 million in assets. The government agreed to allow his wife to retain $2.5 million, but the plea deal allowed the SIPA trustee to pursue Ruth Madoff for additional recoveries.

The government and the trustee initiated clawback actions against investors who had received payments from BLMIS over the years. The goal was to equalize the distributions among the customers. Among the noteworthy clawback actions and rulings:

- *Clawback/forfeiture action against Ruth Madoff*: In July 2009, the SIPA trustee sued Ruth Madoff to recover fraudulent transfers made to her during the long-running fraud scheme. Picard v. Madoff, No. 09-01391-smb (Bankr. S.D.N.Y. filed July 29, 2009). She ultimately settled by agreeing to turn over another $85 million in assets.
- *Clawback/forfeiture action against Picower*: In December 2010, the trustee settled with Madoff's leading investor/feeder source who invested through many different accounts on behalf of a variety of individual investors. The trustee sought recovery of $7.2 billion in payments that had been made to Picower over the years. In aid of the clawback action, the government filed a civil forfeiture action against Picower's funds on deposit at JPMorgan Chase. United States v. $7,206,157,717 on Deposit at JPMorgan Chase Bank, N.A., No. 1:10-cv-09398-TPG (S.D.N.Y. filed Dec. 17, 2010) (judgment entered May 24, 2011). The parties settled for the return of $5 billion to the estate.

SEC case:	S.E.C. v. Madoff, No. 1:08-cv-10791-LLS (S.D.N.Y. filed Dec. 11, 2008) (administratively closed March 17, 2015) (consolidated with the SIPA case).
SIPA/bankruptcy case:	Sec. Inv'r Prot. Corp. v. Bernard L. Madoff Inv. Sec. LLC (*In re* Madoff), No. 08-1789-smb (Bankr. S.D.N.Y. filed Dec. 11, 2008).
Bankruptcy cases:	*In re* Madoff, No. 09-11893-smb (Bankr. S.D.N.Y. filed Apr. 13, 2009).
	In re Madoff Sec. Int'l Ltd., No. 09-12998-smb (Bankr. S.D.N.Y. filed Apr. 14, 2009) (foreign proceeding transferred from S.D. Fla.; foreign representative recognized).
Criminal case:	United States v. Madoff, No. 1:09-cr-00213-DC (S.D.N.Y. filed Mar. 10, 2009) (preliminary order of forfeiture entered June 29, 2009; judgment entered June 29, 2009).
	United States v. Madoff, No. 1:08-mj-02735-UA (S.D.N.Y. filed Dec. 11, 2008) (terminated Mar. 10, 2009).
Civil forfeiture case:	United States v. $7,206,157,717 on Deposit at JPMorgan Chase Bank, N.A., No. 1:10-cv-09398-TPG (S.D.N.Y. filed Dec. 17, 2010) (judgment entered May 24, 2011) (Picower funds).

Reported/written decisions:

Sec. Inv'r Prot. Corp. v. Bernard L. Madoff Inv. Sec. LLC (*In re* Bernard L. Madoff Inv. Sec. LLC), 424 B.R. 122 (Bankr. S.D.N.Y. 2010) (bankruptcy court had jurisdiction to issue injunction against assertion of derivative claims to protect proper administration of the case).

In re Bernard L. Madoff Inv. Sec. LLC, 654 F.3d 229, 231–33 (2d Cir. 2011), *cert. dismissed*, 132 S.Ct. 2712, *cert. denied*, 133 S.Ct. 24, and 133 S.Ct. 25 (2012) ("Net Equity Decision") (approving "Net Investment Method" to determine a customer's net equity).

Sec. Inv'r Prot. Corp. v. 2427 Parent Corp. (*In re* Bernard L. Madoff Inv. Sec. LLC), 779 F.3d 74 (2d Cir. 2015) (SIPA does not permit interest adjustments to "net equity" claims for return of customer property).

Sec. Inv'r Prot. Corp. v. Bernard L. Madoff Inv. Sec. LLC (*In re* Bernard L. Madoff Inv. Sec. LLC), 429 B.R. 423 (Bankr. S.D.N.Y. 2010).

Order Pursuant to Section 105(a) of the Bankruptcy Code and Rules 2002 and 9019 of the Federal Rules of Bankruptcy Procedure Approving an Agreement by and Among the Trustee and the Picower BLMIS Account Holders and Issuing a Permanent Injunction, Picard v. Picower (*In re* Bernard L. Madoff Inv. Sec. LLC), No. 09-01197-smb (Bankr. S.D.N.Y. Jan. 13, 2011), ECF No. 43.

Secondary sources:

The Madoff Recovery Initiative, http://www.madofftrustee.com (last visited March 29, 2018) (the official website of the BLMIS trustee, Irving Picard).

Bernard L. Madoff Investment Securities LLC, Sec. Inv. Prot. Corp., http://www.sipc.org/cases-and-claims/open-cases/bernard-l-madoff-investment-securities-llc (last visited March 29, 2018) (SIPC's official website).

United States v. Bernard Madoff and Related Cases, U.S. Attorneys Office for the S.D.N.Y. (Aug. 21, 2015), *available at* http://www.justice.gov/usao/nys/vw_cases/madoff.html.

2. Adelphia/Rigas (Pennsylvania)

John Rigas founded Adelphia Communications in 1952 as a local, small-town operation in Pennsylvania. By 2002, Adelphia had become one of the largest cable companies in the country.

The Rigas fraud was old-fashioned looting of a company by its founding family, with an estimated $174 million having been siphoned off into the family's coffers. The fraud involved hiding $2.3 billion in liabilities in off-balance-sheet affiliates, filing false financial statements and other reports to the SEC, falsifying operations statistics, and self-dealing. Among other things, the Rigases had received the proceeds from $3 billion in loans for which Adelphia was liable.

The fraud was disclosed in March 2002, leading quickly to the May resignation of all family members from their management positions, a June Chapter 11 bankruptcy filing for Adelphia itself, and followed by the July filings of both an SEC civil action against both the company and its officers, and a criminal complaint of the family management members and other officers.

Both the SEC civil action and the criminal action sought forfeiture from the individual defendants of all of their ill-gotten gains, including all compensation and severance. The government seized many businesses and assets of the Rigases but did not attempt to seize control of Adelphia itself, allowing the remaining board members and management to run the company.

- *Criminal cases*: Defiant to the end, the Rigas family members did not plead guilty. Patriarch John Rigas and his son Timothy were convicted after trial on more than fifteen counts of conspiracy, bank fraud, and defrauding investors. They unsuccessfully appealed their convictions. Ultimately, eighty-two-year-old John was sentenced to twelve years in prison. Timothy was sentenced to seventeen years. United States v. Rigas, No. 02-cr-1236-LBS, 2008 WL 2544654, at *7 (S.D.N.Y. June 24, 2008).

- *Chapter 11 case*: During the pendency of the criminal proceedings, Adelphia's assets and businesses were managed under the auspices of the bankruptcy court, with some assets being sold along the way, but the main cable system business awaiting resolution with the SEC and the USAO.
- *Settlement among Adelphia, SEC, and DOJ*: They finally settled in April 2005, with the SEC agreeing to a Non-Prosecution Agreement as to Adelphia, which had originally been named in the suits. Under the terms of the agreement, the Rigases agreed to forfeit in excess of $1.5 billion, including their ownership interests in certain cable properties that they had kept separate from Adelphia itself. Upon the forfeiture, Adelphia obtained title to those properties and agreed to pay $715 million into a victim compensation fund as part of its emergence from Chapter 11. By resolving the ownership disputes, this settlement cleared the way for Adelphia to sell its cable systems to Time Warner and Comcast.

Bankruptcy case: *In re* Adelphia Commc'ns Corp., No. 02–41729-SHL (Bankr. S.D.N.Y. filed June 25, 2002) (plan confirmed Jan. 5, 2007).

SEC cases: SEC v. Adelphia Commc'ns Corp., No. 1:02-cv-05776-PKC (S.D.N.Y. filed July 24, 2002) (judgment entered Nov. 22, 2006).

SEC v. Deloitte & Touche LLP, No. 1:05-cv-04119-PKC (S.D.N.Y. filed April 26, 2005) (consent judgment entered May 2, 2005) (Deloitte & Touche LLP settled charges arising from its alleged failed 2000 audit of Adelphia by agreeing to pay $50 million to be paid into the victim compensation fund).

Criminal case: United States v. Rigas, No. 1:02-cr-01236-KMW-1 (S.D.N.Y. filed Sept. 23, 2002).

Criminal tax evasion case: United States v. Rigas, No. 4:05-cr-00402-JEJ-WIA-1 (M.D. Pa. Oct. 6, 2005) (dismissal order entered Jan. 26, 2012) (sought $300 million in unpaid taxes on the $1.9 billion in assets and income diverted from Adelphia to the Rigas family).

Class action: Ruskin v. Adelphia Corp., No. 2:02-cv-01781 (E.D. Pa. April 2, 2002) (terminated Aug. 7, 2003).

Reported/written decisions:

Adelphia Commc'ns Corp. v. The America Channel, LLC (*In re* Adelphia Commc'ns Corp.), No. 06-01528, 2006 WL 1529357 (Bankr. S.D.N.Y. June 5, 2006).

United States v. Rigas, 490 F.3d 208 (2d Cir. 2005) (affirming criminal fraud conviction).

United States v. Rigas, No. 02-cr-1236-LBS, 2008 WL 2544654, at *7 (S.D.N.Y. June 24, 2008) (sentencing order on fraud conviction).

United States v. Rigas, 584 F.3d 594 (3d Cir. 2009) (affirming order denying motion to dismiss tax evasion prosecution on grounds of double jeopardy, but remanding to determine whether within scope of settlement agreement with government).

Secondary sources:

Litigation Release No. 17627, Accounting and Auditing Enforcement Release No. 1599, SEC, July 24, 2002, http://www.sec.gov/litigation/litreleases/lr17627.htm.

Press Release, *SEC Charges Deloitte & Touche for Adelphia Audit*, SEC, April 26, 2005, https://www.sec.gov/news/press/2005-65.htm.

Press Release, *SEC and U.S. Attorney Settle Massive Financial Fraud Case Against Adelphia and Rigas Family for $715 Million*, SEC, April 25, 2005, https://www.sec.gov/news/press/2005-63.htm.

3. Petters/Lancelot (Minnesota)

In 2008, Thomas Petters was indicted on multiple felony counts arising from his operation of a multiyear, massive Ponzi scheme. A parallel civil proceeding followed almost immediately to place his businesses and assets under federal receivership. Multiple bankruptcy filings resulted for the various Petters entities, although not Petters personally, who remained subject to the receivership. Hundreds of clawback cases were filed both in the bankruptcy court and the district court by the receiver and trustee, seeking to recover hundreds of millions in assets.

Petters was convicted in 2009 on twenty counts of fraud, conspiracy, and money laundering, and was sentenced to fifty years in prison. A preliminary order of forfeiture was issued for Petters's personal assets and all substitute assets traceable to the fraud. A personal money judgment was entered against Petters in the amount of $3.5 billion. Restitution was not ordered, due to the complexity of the problems and to avoid delay in sentencing. Instead, the United States was authorized to proceed through the remission process under 21 U.S.C. § 853(j) (2017) and 28 C.F.R. §§ 9.1–9.9 (2017). United States v. Petters, No. 0:08-cr-00364-RHK-AJB (D. Minn. June 3, 2010), Doc. No. 459.

As part of the fallout from the Petters Ponzi scheme, the Lancelot and Colossus hedge funds managed by Gregg Bell also entered bankruptcy, having invested $1.4 million of their $1.7 million in assets in the Petters scheme. Gregg Bell tried to conceal the losses from his own investors by manipulation of accounts, which also earned him a criminal conviction on one count of mail fraud, a six-year prison sentence, as well as a criminal forfeiture order and parallel civil forfeiture proceedings by the SEC.

- *Coordination agreement*: Two years into the combined Petters proceedings, a coordination agreement was jointly approved by the bankruptcy court and the district court. It called for the United States to forego criminal forfeiture and restitution in favor of victim compensation through the process of marshaling assets and making distributions in the receivership and bankruptcy cases.

- *Federal receivership*: In October 2008, Petters individually, Petters Company, Inc. ("PCI"), and Petters Group Worldwide LLC ("Group") were placed into receivership by the United States, in connection with the pending criminal proceeding. 18 U.S.C. § 1345 (2017); Fed. R. Civ. P. 66. Petters himself did not file a bankruptcy case and remained subject to the receivership. The receivership sold Petters's assets while the criminal proceedings were pending, rather than waiting to turn them over to the government for liquidation.
- *Bankruptcy cases*: Shortly thereafter, in late 2008, the federal receiver for the corporate entities filed involuntary petitions for several key Petters entities, PCI, Group, and Petters Consumer Brands, LLC ("Brands"), having concluded that they were insolvent. The receiver was then appointed as the bankruptcy trustee for PCI and Group.

    Subsequently, Polaroid Holdings Co. ("Polaroid"), which Petters had acquired in 2005 and folded it into Brands, and its affiliates filed Chapter 7 bankruptcy cases. The Polaroid cases were administered separately by the same bankruptcy judge but a different bankruptcy trustee.

    In 2009, another Petters company, Petters Capital, also filed a Chapter 7 bankruptcy. That case was administered by a different bankruptcy judge and yet another bankruptcy trustee.
- *"Clawback" actions*: In 2010, the trustee filed more than 200 clawback adversary proceedings in bankruptcy court, seeking to recover Ponzi scheme proceeds and other assets transferred to third parties. The bankruptcy court retained jurisdiction to conduct pretrial proceedings for all of the adversary proceedings, which were to be transferred to the district court for trial, if necessary.
- *Actions against JP Morgan*: The receiver/trustee commenced a fraudulent transfer action in district court (for the receivership) and adversary proceedings in the bankruptcy court (for the bankruptcy estates) against JPMorgan Chase and certain related parties. These actions arose out of intermingled banking and other relationships between the Petters entities and JPMorgan: (i) $426 million paid to JPMorgan as Polaroid's owner when Petters acquired that company in 2005; (ii) $25 million seized from Petters's personal investment accounts at JPMorgan that had been pledged as collateral for a loan to Group; and (iii) certain other amounts claimed to have been preferential payments.

Criminal cases: United States v. Petters, No. 0:08-cr-00364-RHK-AJB (D. Minn. filed Dec. 1, 2008) (judgment entered Sept. 29, 2010).
United States v. Jackson, No. 0:09-cr-00273-JNE-JSM (D. Minn. filed Sept. 23, 2009) (judgment entered July 9, 2010).

Receivership case: United States v. Petters, No. 0:08-cv-05348-ADM-TNL (D. Minn. filed Oct. 2, 2008).

Bankruptcy cases: *In re* Petters Co., No. 08-bk-45257 (Bankr. D. Minn. filed Oct. 11, 2008) (plan confirmed Apr. 15, 2016) (jointly administered with *In re* Petters Group Worldwide, No. 08-bk-45258) (Bankr. D. Minn. filed Oct 11, 2008).
In re Polaroid Corp., No. 08-bk-46617 (Bankr. D. Minn. filed Dec. 18, 2008).

	In re Lancelot Inv'r Fund, LP, No. 08-bk-28225 (Bankr. N.D. Ill. filed Oct. 20, 2008).
SEC case:	SEC v. Petters, No. 0:09-cv-1750-ADM-BRT (D. Minn. filed July 8, 2009) (Bell is also named as a defendant) (temporarily stayed pending resolution of the criminal cases).

Reported/written decisions:

Kelley v. JPMorgan Chase & Co., 464 B.R. 854 (D. Minn. 2011) (denying defendants' motion to withdraw reference of bankruptcy clawback actions for joint proceedings with related receivership clawback action pending before the district court; specific transfers did not involve same facts).

Kelley v. Hofer (*In re* Petters Co.), 440 B.R. 805 (Bankr. D. Minn. 2010) (denying motion to transfer other clawback actions to district court as premature).

United States v. Petters, No. 08-cr-364 (RHK/AJB), 2010 WL 1254353 (D. Minn. 2010) (granting the government's motion for preliminary order of forfeiture after Petters' conviction for fraud, conspiracy, and money laundering).

United States v. Petters, 663 F.3d 375 (8th Cir. 2011), *cert. denied*, 132 S.Ct. 2417 (2012) (affirming conviction and sentence).

Memorandum Opinion and Order, SEC v. Petters, No. 0:09-cv-01750-ADM-BRT (D. Minn. Oct. 20, 2009), ECF No. 112.

Secondary sources:

Carey Spivak, *Lawsuit Over Ponzi Scheme Seeks $1 Billion From M&I*, Journal Sentinel (Apr. 1, 2012), *available at* www.jsonline.com/business/lawsuit-over- ponzi-scheme-seeks-1-billion-from-mi-ki4q25j-145716085.html (discussing suit against Petters's former lender).

Litigation Release No. 21245, Hedge Fund Manager Greg Bell, Previously Sued by SEC for Fraud, Pleads Guilty to Wire Fraud, SEC, Oct. 9, 2009, https://www.sec.gov/litigation/litreleases/2009/lr21245.htm.

4. Mark Dreier (New York)

Mark Dreier was the sole equity partner of the 200-lawyer firm of Dreier LLP. He committed extensive fraud against his clients by selling them phony promissory notes over a five-year period. In December 2008, the district court granted the United States application for a pre-indictment restraining order, to which Dreier later consented, to allow the US Marshals to take custody of artworks and other assets. Dreier was ultimately charged with eight counts of securities fraud, wire fraud, and money laundering, to which he pled guilty. He was sentenced to forfeit $747 million as proceeds and certain other specific properties but not the seized artworks.

- *Clawback action against GSO*: GSO, an investment manager for some purchasers of Dreier's notes, transferred over $100 million to Dreier accounts and had received various payments from Dreier LLP. GSO agreed to settle clawback claims for $13 million.

- *Coordination agreement*: In December 2009, the US Attorney's Office and the Chapter 11 trustee entered into a coordination agreement that divided the assets as follows:
  (i) The Chapter 11 trustee would receive the seized artworks and would have the exclusive right to pursue fraudulent transfer actions against designated persons for benefit of the bankruptcy estate;
  (ii) The US government would have sole right to the forfeiture of the specific properties enumerated in the forfeiture order; and
  (iii) The United States reserved the right to file a claim in the Chapter 11 case and to pursue the potential fraudulent transfer targets if they turned out to have received any criminal proceeds.

Criminal case: United States v. Dreier, No. 1:09-cr-00085-JSR (S.D.N.Y. filed Jan. 29, 2009) (judgment entered July 17, 2009).

Bankruptcy case: In re Dreier, LLP, No. 08-15051-smb (Bankr. S.D.N.Y. filed Dec. 16, 2008).

Reported/written decisions:

United States v. Dreier, 682 F. Supp. 2d 417 (S.D.N.Y. 2010) (approving coordination agreement).

In re Dreier LLP, 429 B.R. 112 (Bankr. S.D.N.Y. 2010) (bankruptcy court had jurisdiction to permanently enjoin derivative clawback actions as part of a settlement that included an interlocking agreement with the US government to forfeit money, but the requested injunction was not sufficiently limited or specific).

Gardi v. Gowan (In re Dreier LLP), Nos. 10 Civ. 4758(DAB) & 10 Civ. 5669(DAB), 2010 WL 3835179, at *4–5 (S.D.N.Y. Sept. 10 2010) (affirming subsequent grant of narrower injunction).

Gowan v. The Patriot Group, LLC (In re Dreier LLP), 452 B.R. 391 (Bankr. S.D.N.Y. 2011) (denying motions to dismiss; criminal guilty plea is sufficient basis for fraudulent transfer complaint).

5. Rothstein (Florida)

Like *Dreier*, the Rothstein case involved a Ponzi scheme run by a criminal defendant through a legitimate law firm, Rothstein Rosenfeldt Adler, P.A., of which Scott Rothstein was the 50 percent owner. Before the scandal hit, the firm had seventy lawyers and generated $11–12 million annual revenues from legitimate law firm services.

The other owner of the firm apparently discovered his partner's malfeasance. In early November 2009, Stuart Rosenfeldt filed a state court receivership action to dissolve the firm. This triggered an involuntary Chapter 7 bankruptcy petition by creditors filed on November 10, to which the firm assented on November 25. A trustee was immediately appointed.

A few days later, on December 1, 2009, Rothstein was formally charged with five counts of RICO, money laundering, and mail and wire fraud offenses. His scheme involved inducing investors to purchase purported settlement agreements, falsely soliciting bridge loans on behalf of purported firm clients, and falsely informing a firm client that a bond was required to secure a nonexistent judgment. On January 27, 2010, Rothstein pled guilty. He was sentenced to fifty years in prison and stipulated to the forfeiture of all of his assets, including many assets as to which the law firm held legal title.

This case is notable for the hotly contested nature of the relationship between the bankruptcy trustee and the US Attorney's Office regarding the government's seizure of bank accounts and other assets to which the law firm held title. The government was determined to have overreached by trying to retain not only the defendant's shareholder interest in the assets but also the firm's interest that came from sources other than the defendant's criminal activity.

- *Seizure of law firm assets*: In connection with the criminal case, the United States seized twelve law firm bank accounts and other real and personal property assets. The bank accounts included a payroll account, two operating accounts, a merchant account, and eight IOTA trust accounts. The government took the position that it could forfeit property owned by the law firm—without establishing that the defendant had a legal interest in the assets as to which the firm held title—on the basis that the assets constituted "crime proceeds."
- *Trustee's efforts to intervene in the criminal case*: The trustee moved to modify the protective/seizure order. The district court held that he was statutorily barred from intervening in the criminal case and that any estate interest could be protected in subsequent ancillary proceedings.
- *Trustee's efforts to recover assets in ancillary proceedings*: The trustee was allowed to participate in post-conviction proceedings regarding the ownership and interests in the seized assets. However, the court sharply limited the amount of discovery he was allowed to conduct, allowing certain discovery but only as to the twelve seized bank accounts. The court held that the trustee had the burden of proof to establish that the funds on deposit were from legitimate sources, not criminal proceeds, and that the trustee had met that burden with respect to 80 percent of the funds. However, the court ordered that the client trust funds be refunded directly to the client beneficiaries instead of the trustee.
- *Clawback proceedings*: As in the other fraud cases, the trustee sought to recover fraudulent transfers from early investors who received payments from funds provided by new investors.

Receivership case: Rosenfeldt v. Rothstein, No. CACE09059301 (Sup. Ct. Fla. Broward filed Nov. 2, 2009) (receivership action by Rosenfeldt to dissolve law firm in light of malfeasance by Rothstein) (stayed by bankruptcy filing).

Bankruptcy case: In re Rothstein Rosenfelt Adler, PA, No. 09-34791- RBR (Bankr. S.D. Fla. filed Nov. 25, 2009) (plan confirmed July 17, 2013) (involuntary bankruptcy).

Criminal case: United States v. Rothstein, No. 0:09-cr-60331-JIC (S.D. Fla. filed Dec. 1, 2009) (judgment entered June 9, 2010).

Reported/written decisions:

United States v. Rothstein, No. 09-60331-CR, 2010 WL 2730749, at *1 (S.D. Fla. July 9, 2010) (holding that the Chapter 11 Trustee has standing to seek to recover forfeited property in which he has alleged a vested interest), *vacated and remanded*, United States v. Rothstein (*In re* Rothstein, Rosenfeldt, Adler, P.A.), 717 F.3d 1205 (11th Cir. 2013).

United States v. Rothstein, No. 09-60331-CR, 2010 WL 4064809 (S.D. Fla. Oct. 14, 2010).

First Final Order of Forfeiture, United States v. Rothstein, No. 0:09-cr-60331-JIC (S.D. Fla. Feb. 1, 2011), ECF No. 708.

Opinion and Order, Stettin v. United States, No. 0:12-cv-62193-RSR (S.D. Fla. Aug. 6, 2013), ECF No. 29 (affirming bankruptcy court's dismissal of fraudulent transfer complaint; trustee could not sue the government on a fraudulent transfer claim based on its seizure of law firm assets; sole remedy lay in ancillary proceedings in the criminal forfeiture case).

United States v. Rothstein (*In re* Rothstein, Rosenfeldt, Adler, P.A.), 717 F.3d 1205 (11th Cir. 2013) (vacating forfeiture of firm's bank accounts; district court should have applied the applicable substitute-property provisions of criminal-forfeiture law; in pursuing substitute assets, the United States could only reach interests held individually by Rothstein, such as his shareholder's interest in firm and (indirectly) its bank accounts; court lacks in rem jurisdiction over Rothstein's share of firm's assets, due to the United States' election to proceed in personam, and cannot directly award Rothstein's share of firm assets to the government).

Secondary sources:

Jordan D. Maglich, *While Rothstein Victims Wait, Appellate Court Hears Argument Over Entitlement To Forfeited Assets*, LexisNexis Legal Newsroom, Jan. 10, 2013, https://www.lexisnexis.com/legalnewsroom/securities/b/securities/posts/while-rothstein-victims-wait-appellate-court-hears-argument-over-entitlement-to-forfeited-assets.

Caitlin F. Saladrigas, *Corporate Criminal Liability: Lessons from the Rothstein Debacle*, 66 U. Miami. L. Rev. 435 (2012).

6. Deepal Wannakuwatte (California)

Sacramento businessman and professional tennis team owner Deepal Wannakuwatte defrauded investors of more than $200 million, with a net loss estimated at over $100 million. He falsely represented that his companies held valuable government contracts to supply gloves to the Veterans' Administration and that his businesses generated in excess of $100 million in annual revenues, when in fact they only generated $25,000. In typical Ponzi scheme fashion, he paid early investors out of new investors' money. His arrest, however, actually stemmed from a false financial statement that he provided to a local bank in arranging for a multimillion loan.

Arrested February 23, 2014, Wannakuwatte pled guilty to multiple counts of fraud. On November 13, 2014, he was sentenced to twenty years in prison and agreed to forfeit his assets, having a value of approximately $3.5 million. Final orders of forfeiture were entered on January 13, 2014, forfeiting all of his assets. Final Order of Forfeiture Regarding Real Property at 2120 22nd Avenue, Sacramento, CA, United States v. Wannakuwatte, No. 2:14-cr-00067-TLN (E.D. Cal. Jan. 13, 2015), ECF No. 91; Final Order of Forfeiture Regarding Personal Property, United States v. Wannakuwatte, No. 2:14-cr-00067-TLN (E.D. Cal. Jan. 13, 2015), ECF No. 92.

Civil lawsuit:	Gen. Elec. Capital Corp. v. RelyAid Glob. Healthcare, Inc., 2:13-cv-01683-JAM-AC (E.D. Cal. filed Aug. 15, 2013) (stipulated judgment entered Mar. 26, 2014) (collection action by secured creditor to collect $4.6 million defaulted loan; writ of possession issues for corporate aircraft collateral).
Criminal case:	United States v. Wannakuwatte, No. 2:14-cr-00067-TLN (E.D. Cal. filed Mar. 13, 2014) (judgment entered Nov. 17, 2014).
Bankruptcy case:	In re Wannakuwatte, No. 14-25816 (Bankr. E.D. Cal. filed May 30, 2014).

Secondary sources:

Press Release, *Sacramento Businessman Indicted for Bank Fraud*, U.S. Attorney's Office, East District of California (Apr. 8, 2015), *available at* http://www.justice.gov/usao-edca/pr/sacramento-businessman-indicted-bank-fraud.

7. Monroe Beachy (Ohio)

For nearly twenty years, Monroe Beachy ran a Ponzi scheme in which he represented to investors that money deposited with his investment company, A&M Investments, would be safe and would secure a positive rate of return. He defrauded nearly 2,700 people, mostly Amish, out of $16.8 million but continued to live the modest Amish lifestyle himself. At age 78, he pled guilty to one count of mail fraud and was sentenced to 6 1/2 years in prison. He stipulated to restitution of $16.8 million.

The trustee pursued the usual clawback actions against investors that had received distributions, recovering nearly $900,000 from approximately 160 investors, in addition to more than $16 million in assets liquidated by the trustee.

The SEC civil complaint was immediately resolved by stipulation to a consent judgment enjoining Beachy from violating the securities laws. No civil penalty was imposed. Final Judgment as to Defendant Monroe L. Beachy, SEC v. Beachy, No. 5:11-cv-00320-SL (N.D. Ohio Feb. 18, 2011), ECF No. 4.

Criminal case:	United States v. Beachy, 11-cr-00422 (N.D. Ohio, filed Sept. 14, 2011) (plea entered Mar. 15, 2012; sentence entered June 15, 2012).
SEC case:	SEC v. Beachy, No. 5:11-cv-00320-SL (N.D. Ohio filed Feb. 15, 2011) (terminated by consent judgment Feb. 18, 2011).
Bankruptcy case:	In re Beachy, No. 10-62857-rk (Bankr. N.D. Ohio filed June 30, 2010) (Final Decree entered Feb. 29, 2016).

Secondary sources:

Press Release, *Monroe Beachy Sentenced to Over Six Years in Prison for Defrauding Nearly 2,700 People and Businesses out of $16.8 Million*, Fed. Bureau of Investigation, Cleveland Division (June 13, 2012), *available at* https://www.fbi.gov/cleveland/press-releases/2012/

monroe-beachy-sentenced-to-over-six-years-in-prison-for-defrauding-nearly-2-700-people-and-businesses-out-of-16.8-million.

Associated Press, *Ohio Man Admits to Swindling Fellow Amish of Millions*, The New York Times (Mar. 15, 2012), *available at* https://www.nytimes.com/2012/03/16/business/amish-man-admits-to-a-17-million-fraud.html (discussing the fraud conviction and bankruptcy of Monroe Beachy, age 77).

8. Lydia Cladek (Florida)

Formed in 1998, Lydia Cladek, Inc. ("LCI") was in the business of purchasing high-interest (up to 29 percent) automobile installment finance contracts from multiple used car dealers in the southeastern United States at a discounted price. LCI then serviced the notes, repossessing and liquidating the cars if necessary. To finance the purchases of the car notes, Cladek or her agents solicited private investments from individuals in the form of one- to two-year loans to LCI to be secured by the car notes purchased by LCI. LCI guaranteed a rate of return of 15–20 percent. Whatever its original design, the business operations failed to generate enough car notes to collateralize the investor notes. Cladek falsified the existence of the car loan collateral, fraudulently assigned the same car note as collateral for multiple investor notes, and generally devolved into a Ponzi scheme, paying old investors with money from new ones. She was alleged to have defrauded more than 1,000 investors of more than $100 million.

The FBI commenced an investigation in late 2009, culminating in a well-publicized raid on LCI's offices and Cladek's home in March 2010, which seized records and other assets.

Bankruptcy filings: An involuntary Chapter 11 case against the corporation was filed in April 2010 by a large group of holders of $4.3 million in matured promissory notes, mostly ranging from $25,000 to $800,000 in amount, which was consolidated with a voluntary case filed by LCI several days later. Cladek was removed as CEO, and a Chapter 11 trustee was appointed.

- *Fraudulent transfer action vs. Cladek*: In May 2010, just weeks after the petitions were filed, the trustee sued Cladek individually, together with various entities that she allegedly owned and controlled. The adversary complaint sought to recover fraudulent transfers of assets diverted from the corporation to Cladek's entities. Cladek did not bother to contest the adversary, and a default judgment was entered against her in September 2010, granting the trustee title to twelve pieces of real property, a $12 million damages judgment, and a constructive trust imposed on all of Cladek's other assets to recover assets transferred from LCI to Cladek.
- *Clawback actions*: Numerous fraudulent transfer actions were instituted against early investors to recover amounts they had been paid by LCI.
- *Plan*: In February 2011, a plan of reorganization was confirmed, establishing a litigation trust to pursue claims for the creditors. The final distribution was made in February 2015.

Civil forfeiture complaint: Meanwhile, within one week after the bankruptcy filings, the United States filed a civil forfeiture complaint in rem against LCI, Cladek, and various entities to which she had transferred assets from LCI, alleging that Cladek and her various entities (other than LCI) should be consolidated and treated as one.

Criminal indictment and conviction: In November 2010, Lydia Cladek individually was indicted on charges of wire fraud and mail fraud. The indictment sought forfeiture of $113 million, certain real property, vehicles, artwork, jewelry, and other items. In January 2012, she was convicted on all fourteen counts after a jury trial.

Bankruptcy case: *In re* Lydia Cladek, Inc., No. 3:10-bk-02805-PMG (Bankr. M.D. Fla. filed Apr. 2, 2010) (Final Decree entered June 30, 2015).

Forfeiture case: United States v. Real Property Located at 1061 SW Alaska Way, Greenville, Madison County, Florida, No. 3:10-cv-00297-HLA-JBT (M.D. Fla. filed April 8, 2010) (dismissed May 6, 2011).

Criminal case: United States v. Cladek, No. 3:10-cr-00277-TJC (M.D. Fla. filed Nov. 19, 2010) (judgment entered Dec. 19, 2012).

Secondary sources:

Jennifer Edwards, *Cladek's Victims Now Facing Lawsuits*, St. Augustine Record (Jan. 29, 2012), *available at* http://www.staugustine.com/article/20120129/NEWS/301299941 (noting Lydia Cladek's fraud conviction).

Richard Prior, *Judge Rules That Reorganization Will Benefit Cladek Victims Most*, Fla. Times-Union (Feb. 2, 2011), *available at* http://www.jacksonville.com/article/20110202/NEWS/801258029 (discussing fraud indictment and bankruptcy of Lydia Cladek).

9. Samantha Delay-Wilson (Anchorage, Alaska)

From 1996 through 2009, Anchorage resident Samantha Delay-Wilson operated two investment companies through which she defrauded fourteen investors out of more than $7.4 million by falsely promising high rates of returns on investments in a global investment fund, European sub-prime loans, and an investment banking service company. In fact, she used the investors' money for her personal expenses and to repay earlier investors, in classic Ponzi scheme style. She also provided false financial statements to banks to obtain loans and false statements in her bankruptcy case regarding her assets.

In June 2010, one of Delay-Wilson's creditors filed an involuntary Chapter 7 bankruptcy petition against her. She failed in her efforts to get the case dismissed or converted to a Chapter 11 case. Facing sanctions, she finally filed her schedules in October. The trustee took over the operations and income of three IHOP restaurants owned indirectly by the debtor, auctioned them off for about $1.2 million, and also sold her artwork, jewelry, coin collection, and other personal property, from which little was realized.

In February 2011, Delay-Wilson was indicted on twenty-six counts of securities fraud, wire fraud, mail fraud, money laundering, bankruptcy fraud, and bank fraud, to which she ultimately pled guilty. On June 15, 2012, she was sentenced to eighty-four months in prison, to be served consecutively with the more than five-year sentence she also received on state fraud and check kiting counts. The state sentence was "lenient" because she had testified for the prosecution in a murder case. She had previously been convicted in 1999 of stealing disability checks and other funds totaling $500,000 from two people, for which she had been sentenced to seven months based on that judge's assessment that he did not think she would get into trouble with the law again.

Bankruptcy case: *In re* Delay-Wilson, No. 10-00478 (Bankr. D. Alaska filed June 7, 2010) (Final Decree entered Oct. 20, 2014) (discharge denied).

Criminal cases: United States v. Delay-Wilson, No. 3:11-cr-00011-HRH (D. Alaska filed Feb. 17, 2011) (judgment entered June 18, 2012).

Secondary sources:

Casey Grove, *Ponzi Scheme Defendant Gets 5 Years For Theft*, Anchorage Daily News (Apr. 28, 2012), *available at* https://www.adn.com/alaska-news/article/ponzi-scheme-defendant-gets-5-years-theft/2012/04/28/ (updated Sept. 27, 2016) (discussing the five-year state law theft sentence of Anchorage resident Samantha Delay-Wilson, age 65, who awaits sentencing on federal fraud charges).

Press Release, *Anchorage Woman Indicted by Federal Grand Jury for Fraud*, Fed. Bureau of Investigation, Anchorage Division (Feb. 18, 2011), *available at* https://www.fbi.gov/anchorage/press-releases/2011/anchorage-woman-indicted-by-federal-grand-jury-for-fraud.

Press Release, *Anchorage Woman Sentenced to 7 Years in Prison for Running Ponzi Scheme*, U.S. Attorney's Office, Alaska (June 15, 2012), *available at* http://www.justice.gov/archive/usao/ak/news/2012/June_2012/Samantha%20Delay-Wilson.html.

Casey Grove, *Woman Accused of Stealing Checks*, Anchorage Daily News (Jan. 22, 2009), *available at* http://www.adn.com/article/20090122/woman-accused-stealing-checks (updated Sept. 29, 2016).

10. Nick Cosmo/Agape (Long Island, NY)

Cosmo was arrested in January 2009 on mail fraud charges arising out of a Ponzi scheme he conducted through his company Agape World Inc., which claimed to make its money through commercial bridge lending. Approximately 5,000 individuals invested approximately $400 million through Cosmo and Agape, with net losses estimated at $179 million. Cosmo made only about $10 million in actual loans. He lost the rest through high-risk futures trading, personal expenditures, and siphoning off to employees who had criminal records.

- *Bankruptcy case:* An involuntary Chapter 7 bankruptcy case was filed against Agape World on February 5, 2009, and a trustee was immediately appointed. During the first 6–8 months of the case, the trustee noticed more than 100 Fed. R. Bankr. P. 2004 examinations to trace assets and unravel the complex Ponzi scheme. He then launched a variety of campaigns to recover assets for distribution. Along the way, he stipulated with the Commodity Futures Trading Commission to entry of an injunction barring Agape World from any further futures trading. Motion Pursuant to Federal Rule of Bankruptcy Procedure 9019 for an Order (I) Approving the Settlement of an Action Pending in the United States District Court for the Eastern District of New York and (II) Authorizing the Trustee to Execute the Consent Order of Permanent Injunction and Other Ancillary Relief Against Agape World, Inc. and Agape Merchant Advance LLC, *In re* Agape World, Inc., No. 8-09-70660-ast (Bankr. E.D.N.Y. Dec. 7, 2012), ECF No. 3881.

- *Fraudulent transfer actions v. fellow participants*: The bankruptcy trustee quickly brought suits against brokers, agents, and other participants in the Ponzi scheme to recover commissions and other money they received from the debtors, and to freeze their assets. *See, e.g.*, Silverman v. Hugh Arias, Inc. (*In re* Agape World, Inc.), No. 8-09-08206-dte (Bankr. E.D.N.Y. filed May 22, 2009) (judgment entered June 9, 2011); Silverman v. Cyrek Inc., Keryc (*In re* Agape World, Inc.), No. 8-09-08444-dte (Bankr. E.D.N.Y. filed Oct. 1, 2009) (order approving settlement entered June 7, 2010).
- *Fraudulent transfer actions against recipients of transferred funds*: The trustee also sought to recover assets that Agape World transferred to various entities on purported loans and unauthorized transfers. *See, e.g.*, Silverman v. Zdanio Plumbing & Heating, Inc. (*In re* Agape World, Inc.), No. 8-09-08486-dte (Bankr. E.D.N.Y. filed Oct. 14, 2009) (judgment entered Apr. 27, 2010).
- *Preference actions*: The trustee filed hundreds of preference actions to recover payments on antecedent debts that were made within 90 days before the bankruptcy filing.
- *Clawback actions v. investors*: The trustee sued investors to recover net transfers, i.e., the amounts repaid in excess of the original investments. *See, e.g.*, Silverman v. Meyers (*In re* Agape World, Inc.), No. 8-10-08748-dte (Bankr. E.D.N.Y. filed Nov. 5, 2010) (dismissal entered Nov. 12, 2012).
- *Criminal case*: In October 2010, nearly two years after his arrest, Cosmo pled guilty to one count of wire fraud, out of the thirty-two original counts. In October 2011, he was sentenced to twenty-five years in prison and was ordered to pay restitution in an amount in excess of $179 million. Like Delay-Wilson, Cosmo had previously been convicted of felony fraud (in 1999), for which he served twenty-one months in prison.
- *Criminal and SEC fraud cases against other participants*: Four former account representatives of Agape World were also indicted in April 2012 for their participation in the Ponzi scheme over a six-year period. In addition, the SEC brought securities fraud charges against fourteen Agape sales agents for false statements to investors on transactions for which the agents earned more than $52 million in commissions.

Bankruptcy case: *In re* Agape World, Inc., No. 8-09-bk-70660-ast (Bankr. E.D.N.Y. filed Feb. 5, 2009) (substantively consolidated with five other entities by stipulation).

Criminal cases: United States v. Cosmo, No. 2:09-mj-0066-ETB (E.D.N.Y. filed Jan. 29, 2009) (arrest in support of search warrant).

	United States v. Cosmo, No. 2:09-cr-00255-DRH-ETB (E.D.N.Y. filed Apr. 23, 2009) (judgment entered Oct. 17, 2011).
	United States v. Keryc, No. 2:12-mj-00410-ETB (E.D.N.Y. filed Apr. 23, 2012) (terminated May 22, 2012).
	United States v. Ciccone, No. 2:12-cr-00357-DRH (E.D.N.Y. filed May 22, 2012) (judgment entered July 7, 2017).
CFTC complaint:	U.S. Commodity Futures Trading Comm'n v. Cosmo, No. 2:09-cv-00351-LDW-ARL (E.D.N.Y. filed Jan, 27, 2009) (order approving settlement and consent order of permanent injunction entered Feb. 5, 2013) (seeking injunctive relief and civil penalties).
SEC case:	SEC v. Arias, No. 2:12-cv-02937-DRH-SIL (E.D.N.Y. filed June 12, 2012) (against fourteen Agape sales agents).

Secondary sources:

Agape World, Inc. Bankruptcy, http://agapeworldbankruptcy.com/ (last visited March 29, 2017).

David Winzelberg, *4 Brokers in Nick Cosmo Agape World Ponzi Scheme Arrested*, Long Island Bus. News (Apr. 25, 2012), *available at* http://libn.com/2012/04/25/4-associates-of-ponzi-scheme-artist-nick-cosmo-arrested/ (noting additional arrests relating to the Cosmo/Agape fraud and bankruptcy).

Press Release, *Former Agape World Inc. Account Representatives Charge in New York with Massive Ponzi Scheme*, Fed. Bureau of Investigation, N.Y. Field Office (Apr. 25, 2012), *available at* https://www.fbi.gov/newyork/press-releases/2012/former-agape-world-inc.-account-representatives-charged-in-new-york-with-massive-ponzi-scheme (four account representatives charged).

11. Reed Slatkin (Santa Barbara)

Reed Slatkin, the co-founder of Earthlink, an early Internet company, became simultaneously embroiled in SEC enforcement proceedings, federal criminal proceedings, and a bankruptcy case administered by a trustee. In mid-2001, the SEC shut down his fifteen-year-long Ponzi scheme by filing an enforcement action in federal district court and obtaining a temporary restraining order freezing his assets. Completely hamstrung by the SEC injunction, he filed a Chapter 11 personal bankruptcy case in 2001, in which a forensic accountant was immediately appointed as Chapter 11 trustee. Criminal charges were filed in 2002.

In 2003, Slatkin pled guilty to fifteen federal criminal counts of mail fraud, wire fraud, money laundering, and obstruction of justice, and admitted losing at least $254 million of investors' money. Sentenced to fourteen years in federal prison, he was released in 2013.

SEC case: SEC v. Slatkin, No. 2:01-cv-04283-RSWL-MAN (C.D. Cal. filed May 11, 2001) (consent judgment entered June 6, 2011).
Bankruptcy case: *In re Slatkin,* Bk. Case No. ND 01-11549-RR (C.D. Cal. 2001)
Criminal case: United States v. Slatkin, No. 2:02-cr-00313-MMM (C.D. Cal. filed Mar. 26, 2002) (sentencing entered Sept. 2, 2003).

Reported/written decisions:

Santa Barbara Capital Mgmt. v. Neilson (*In re* Slatkin), 525 F. 3d 805 (9th Cir. 2008) (holding that the act of entrusting funds with the individual debtor for investment constitutes securities transactions that would ordinarily trigger the stockbroker liquidation provisions, but this Ponzi scheme operator was not in fact a stockbroker).

Appendix D

Standards and Procedures Governing Substitute Property

The DOJ Forfeiture Policy Manual provides that when it is in the interests of justice, the government may forfeit a sum of money in lieu of forfeitable property or a forfeitable partial interest in otherwise nonforfeitable property. Parties often agree to substitute money for forfeitable property in connection with a settlement. When courts order an interlocutory sale of forfeitable property, by agreement or otherwise, the net sale proceeds also typically become a substitute res. Legal authority to forfeit money in lieu of other property is found in the applicable statutes, rules, regulations, and case law.[1]

The following procedures must be followed when the government accepts and forfeits money in lieu of other property:

1. Administrative Forfeitures

19 U.S.C. § 1613(c) (2017), as incorporated by, e.g., 18 U.S.C. § 981(d) (2017), and 21 U.S.C. §§ 853(j), 881(d) (2017), permits federal seizing agencies, as a form of relief from administrative forfeiture, to accept and forfeit a sum of money in lieu of forfeitable seized property. *See also* 19 U.S.C. § 1614 (2017).

As a matter of policy and discretion, however, the DEA and FBI limit their use of this authority to cases where such substitution is determined to be in the interests of justice and in which a timely claim for the forfeitable property has been filed pursuant to 18 U.S.C. § 983(a)(2) (2017) and referred by the seizing agency to the US Attorney's Office for initiation of judicial forfeiture proceedings. After consultation with the seizing agency, the US Attorney's Office may accept a monetary amount in lieu of forfeiture of the seized property and refer the matter back to the seizing agency to effect the settlement.

2. Judicial Forfeitures

After commencing a judicial forfeiture case, with court approval, and pursuant to an appropriate order of forfeiture, the government may accept and forfeit an agreed sum of money in lieu of forfeitable property.

(A) The government must transfer money received in lieu of forfeiture to the US Marshals Service's district office or the appropriate Treasury agency in place of the asset being released.

---

1. DOJ Forfeiture Policy Manual, Ch. 3, § IX.D, at 93.

(B) Pursuant to the order of forfeiture, the US Marshals Service or the appropriate Treasury agency must deposit the forfeited money (and share it when appropriate) in the same manner as applies to other forfeited property.

(C) If the US Postal Inspection Service or the National Marine Fisheries Service is the primary federal investigative agency, the US Marshals Service must deposit the money, deduct expenses (if any) incurred with respect to the property being released, deduct the approved equitable shares attributable to other federal agencies participating in the Department of Justice Assets Forfeiture Fund, and transfer the balance by refund to the above services, as appropriate. Each service is responsible for sharing with participating state and local agencies in these cases.

Finally, an agency may accept and forfeit money in lieu of seized forfeitable property under 19 U.S.C. § 1613(c) (2017), which allows such substitution as a form of "relief" from forfeiture, and under 19 U.S.C. § 1614 (2017), which authorizes agencies to release property seized for administrative forfeiture upon payment of "the value of" such property. The substituted money is "treated in the same manner as the proceeds of sale of a forfeited item." 19 U.S.C. § 1613(c) (2017).

Appendix E

DOJ Guidelines on Minimum Net Equity Levels Prior to Forfeiture

The DOJ Forfeiture Policy Manual provides the specific guidelines which set minimum net equity levels that generally must be met before federal forfeiture actions are instituted. *See* DOJ Forfeiture Policy Manual, Ch. 1, § D.1, at 5–6.

According to the DOJ Forfeiture Policy Manual, these thresholds are also intended to encourage state and local law enforcement agencies to use state forfeiture laws. These thresholds are to be applied in direct federal and adoptive cases. In general, the minimum net equity requirements are:

Type of Property	Minimum Net Equity	Method of Calculation
Residential real property and vacant land		
• worth more than $100,000	20% of appraised value	Minimum net equity threshold for $200,000 property = $40,000
• worth less than $100,000	$20,000	
Vehicles	$5,000 in general $2,000 if used in crime	Multiple vehicles may be aggregated
Cash	$5,000 in general $1,000 if used in crime	
"Monetary Instruments"	No minimum	Does not apply to bank accounts. May be administratively forfeited without regard to value. 19 U.S.C. § 1607(a)(4)
Aircraft	$10,000	Failure to obtain log books for the aircraft drastically reduces value
Vessels	$10,000	
Other personal property	$1,000 in the aggregate	Individual items less than $1,000 should only be seized if part of a group with higher aggregate value that can be easily stored, such as jewelry

Heads of investigative agencies are permitted to establish higher thresholds for seizures made by their agencies, but if they do, AFMLS must be advised in writing of the change.

Appendix F

Summary of the US Trustees Manual— Treatment of Parallel Proceedings

1. UST Memorandum

The Office of the US Trustee has a duty to report, but does not prosecute, bankruptcy crimes. The prosecuting agency is the US Attorney's Office for the respective district. More commonly, the US Trustee becomes involved in parallel proceedings in connection with its oversight of the private trustees who are assigned to administer cases. Indeed, parallel proceedings—"where both criminal and civil investigations/cases are in progress at the same time"—are a "normal" aspect of bankruptcy cases.[1] A common example would be a case in which a Chapter 7 trustee is conducting an adversary proceeding to recover property, while the debtor is being criminally investigated for bankruptcy fraud in connection with concealment of the same asset.[2]

In 1997, at the urging of the Office of the Attorney General, a Bankruptcy Fraud and Abuse Enforcement Program within the US Trustee's office issued a volume of the US Trustee Manual addressing a broad range of issues affecting parallel proceedings (Bankruptcy Fraud Manual). The following is a brief summary of some of the key provisions.

2. Pre- and Post-Criminal Referral

The Bankruptcy Fraud Manual describes the procedures to be followed by the US Trustee and private case trustees both before and after referral of a parallel criminal proceeding to the US Attorney's Office for prosecution. Note that the policy is to encourage joint participation in the criminal and civil cases, with the caveat that caution should be exercised to avoid using the civil bankruptcy case solely to develop evidence for a criminal case[3] and to seek court permission to release grand jury information in the civil case to the bankruptcy trustee. Specifically, in a pre-referral situation:

> Prior to a formal criminal referral, the United States Attorney and/or other investigative agencies may be advised of potential criminal activity and furnished with

---

1. United States Trustee Manual, Vol. 5, Bankruptcy Fraud and Abuse Enforcement Program, at 5-13 (1997) *available at* https://www.assetsearchblog.com/wp-content/uploads/sites/197/migrated/Bankruptcy%20Fraud.pdf (Bankruptcy Fraud Manual).

For the current US Trustee Manual, *see* United States Trustee Program and Practices Manual, U.S. Dep't of Justice, *available at* https://www.justice.gov/ust/united-states-trustee-program-policy-and-practices-manual (last updated Sept. 2016) (UST Manual).

2. *Id.*

3. United States v. Unruh, 855 F.2d 1363, 1374 (9th Cir. 1987).

pleadings and summaries of hearings, etc. Normally, they should not be asked for advice nor should they give advice on the civil aspects of the case that are the function of the United States Trustee. Under no circumstances should the United States Trustee or a private trustee be asked or agree to use bankruptcy proceedings solely to develop evidence for a criminal case.[4]

After a criminal referral is made:

The United States Trustee should keep the United States Attorney advised on all relevant aspects of the civil case and, in situations where it appears the civil case may have an adverse effect on the criminal case, should normally follow the recommendation of the United States Attorney until the criminal case is concluded. If United States Trustee personnel are assisting in the criminal case and have been given access to grand jury material, they may not use that information in any way for civil purposes without district court permission. Wherever possible, different individuals should be assigned to work the criminal and civil aspects of a case.[5]

3. Information Sharing and Protective Orders

Proceedings that are authorized under the Bankruptcy Code and that are related to a pending bankruptcy case have a proper civil purpose.[6] Thus, information that a trustee or other party develops in the any related civil proceeding may be shared with prosecutors.[7] Additionally, US Trustees are required to oppose any request for a protective order seeking to deny criminal investigators, including grand juries and access to evidence developed in the civil case.[8]

4. Fifth Amendment Privilege

The Bankruptcy Code requires a debtor to submit to examination of creditors (conducted by either the US Trustee's office or the private case trustee), file numerous asset and liability disclosure statements, and make available the books and records of the business. In appropriate circumstances, the Code further provides criminal sanctions for the failure to adhere to bankruptcy requirements. Thus, an individual may be exposed to possible criminal liability either arising out of acts of misconduct disclosed by materials required to be disclosed in the bankruptcy case or arising out of improprieties engaged in through filing the case.

An individual party may assert a Fifth Amendment privilege against self-incrimination in the bankruptcy proceeding. However, a debtor who has sought the protection of the Bankruptcy Code may risk dismissal of the bankruptcy case for failure to provide relevant information about the estate under a claim of Fifth Amendment protection.[9] Nor

---

4. Bankruptcy Fraud Manual at 5-13.4.2.
5. *Id.* at 5-13.4.3.
6. *Id.* at 5-13.3.
7. SEC v. Dresser Indus., 628 F.2d 1368 (D.C. Cir. 1980, *en banc*), *cert. denied*, 449 U.S. 993 (1980).
8. Bankruptcy Fraud Manual, at 5-13.3.2.
9. *In re* Connelly, 59 B.R. 421, 448 (Bankr. N.D. Ill. 1986); Bankruptcy Fraud Manual, at 5-13.3.

can the sole officer and director of a corporate debtor refuse to answer all questions on the schedules and statement of affairs absent a specific, well-supported basis for fearing a personal criminal prosecution for his answers.[10] Additionally, the court may draw an adverse inference against the debtor or other key witnesses when the privilege is invoked and results in a refusal to testify. Nevertheless, if an active criminal investigation is pending against an individual debtor, the prosecutor and the trustee should consider whether the Fifth Amendment issues can be resolved either by deferring the submission of schedules or by agreeing that providing unsworn schedules will not be regarded as testimonial or an admission.[11]

Conversely, the problem of waiver is also prevalent by virtue of the Bankruptcy Code's broad disclosure requirements. The courts will examine the issue on a case-by-case basis to determine if a waiver has in fact occurred during the bankruptcy proceeding. Waiver is strictly construed.[12]

5. Attorney-Client Privilege

Corporate and partnership debtors: A court-appointed bankruptcy trustee may waive the attorney-client privilege of the corporate debtor for communications prior to the declaration of bankruptcy.[13] The debtor's directors do not have the right to assert the corporation's attorney-client privilege against the trustee.[14] Likewise, corporate officers cannot assert an individual attorney-client privilege to prevent disclosure of corporate communications with corporation's counsel after the corporation's privilege was waived by the trustee.[15] A Chapter 7 trustee of a limited partnership debtor has the authority to

---

10. *In re* John Lakis, Inc., 228 F. Supp. 918, 920 (S.D.N.Y. 1964) (involuntary corporate case where officer made blanket refusal to file schedules inappropriate where no criminal proceedings were pending and no specific justification offered for assertion of the Fifth Amendment). However, where criminal proceedings are, in fact, pending against individual (not corporate) debtor in involuntary case, it may be necessary to defer the filing of schedules until after prosecutor and debtor reach a plea agreement. *See, e.g., In re* McNall, No. 2:94-bk-28439-EC (Bankr. C. D. Cal. filed May 13, 1994) (discharge entered Jan. 19, 2001). Bruce McNall subsequently pled guilty to conspiracy, bank fraud, and wire fraud in connection with defrauding banks of $236 million. United States v. McNall, No. 2:94-cr-00890 (C.D. Cal. filed Jan. 14, 1994) (sentencing order entered Jan. 9, 1997); *see* James Bates and Lisa Dillman, *McNall Agrees to Plead to Fraud Charges: Kings: Prosecutors say he defrauded banks for more than $236 million. Gretzky also allegedly was deceived.*, Los Angeles Times, Nov. 15, 1994, *available at* http://articles.latimes.com/1994-11-15/sports/sp-62870_1_bank-fraud.

11. *See, e.g., In re* McNall, No. 2:94-bk-28439-EC (Bankr. C. D. Cal. filed May 13, 1994) (discharge entered Jan. 19, 2001).

12. *In re* Jacques, 115 B.R. 272, 273–74 (D. Nev. 1990) (holding that debtor had not waived his Fifth Amendment privilege by answering certain questions at a meeting of creditors, but refusing to answer other questions); Nursing Home Pension Fund v. Oracle Corp., No. C01-00988 MJJ, 2007 WL 1880381, at *12–13 (N.D. Cal. June 29, 2007) (finding no waiver where witness testified as to the drafting and signing of a sworn statement, but refused to testify as to its content); Universal Trading & Inv. Co. v. Kiritchenko, No. C-99-03073, 2007 WL 2300740, at *4–5 (N.D. Cal. August 2, 2007) (finding no waiver where the defendant answered a particular question in a deposition, but later refused to answer the same question when the deposition was re-opened).

13. Commodity Futures Trading Comm'n v. Weintraub, 471 U.S. 343, 353 (1985).

14. *Id.* at 350.

15. *In re* Bevill, Bresler & Schulman Asset Mgmt. Corp., 805 F.2d 120, 125 (3rd Cir. 1986).

waive the attorney-client privilege of the partnership in the case of a criminal bankruptcy fraud trial of a general partner.[16]

Individual debtors: Absent a Fifth Amendment claim, a trustee may be able to waive the attorney-client privilege of an individual debtor, but few reported cases exist.[17] However, the Bankruptcy Fraud Manual reports that no reported circuit court cases hold that a trustee can waive an individual debtor's attorney-client privilege where the debtor has asserted a Fifth Amendment privilege.

Bankruptcy schedules and statement of affairs: The courts have held that no attorney-client privilege attaches to bankruptcy work papers where the information has been provided to bankruptcy counsel for the purpose of assembly into a bankruptcy petition and supporting schedules. This information is intended to be disclosed on documents filed with the court and not held in confidence. Significantly, where there is no evidence that a debtor sought legal advice regarding disclosure and the debtor failed to reveal the existence of certain assets to their bankruptcy counsel, the attorney may disclose the fact of such omission without violating the attorney-client privilege. United States v. White, 970 F.2d 328, 335 (7th Cir. 1992).

6. Rule 2004 Examination

Federal Rule of Bankruptcy Procedure 2004 allows a case trustee and other parties to obtain sworn testimony and to subpoena documents from witnesses with "relevant" information.[18] Taking the 2004 examination of a key witness to help the trust identify and develop potential claims does not later prevent the same party from deposing the same witness in an adversary proceeding. A witness or party seeking to prevent a subsequent oral deposition bears a heavy burden. A 2004 examination is not a substitute for a deposition and serves a distinct purpose as a broad investigative tool facilitating inquiry into the debtor's business and financial affairs. A 2004 examination allows a broad range of questioning, whereas the use of civil depositions is somewhat narrower in scope. The bankruptcy court may retain jurisdiction to order a Rule 2004 examination even post-confirmation.[19] Of course, information obtained during a 2004 examination may be shared in parallel proceedings.

7. Stays in Bankruptcy

Either the US Attorney or a party to the bankruptcy proceeding may request a stay of the civil proceedings.[20]

---

16. United States v. Campbell, 73 F.3d 44, 47 (5th Cir. 1996).
17. Whyte v. Williams, 152 B.R. 123, 129–130 (Bankr. N.D. Tex. 1992).
18. Fed. R. Bankr. P. 2004 (b) provides in pertinent part: "The examination of an entity under this rule or of the debtor under § 343 of the Code may relate only to the acts, conduct, or property or to the liabilities and financial condition of the debtor, or to any matter which may affect the administration of the debtor's estate, or to the debtor's right to a discharge."
19. *See* Ernst & Young, LLP v. Pritchard (*In re* Daisytek, Inc.), 323 B.R. 180, 187 (N.D. Tex. 2005).
20. Bankruptcy Fraud Manual, at 5-13.3.1.

8. Double Jeopardy Regarding Petition Preparer Prosecutions

The Bankruptcy Reform Act of 1994 added a new section authorizing criminal prosecution of bankruptcy preparers who violate the provisions of title 11 or the Federal Rules of Bankruptcy Procedure. 18 U.S.C. § 156 (2017). A preparer is anyone other than the debtor's attorney or employee who prepares for compensation bankruptcy documents for filing. Preparers are also subject to civil fines pursuant to 11 U.S.C. § 110 (2017), but such fines are deemed to be remedial in nature rather than punitive. Thus, a criminal prosecution under section 156 arising out of the same conduct by the preparer who was fined under section 110 is not deemed to constitute double jeopardy.[21]

---

21. Bankruptcy Fraud Manual, at 5-13.4.1.

Appendix G

Sample Coordination Agreements and Related Orders

Dreier Coordination Agreement

http://www.theponzibook.com/coordination_agreements/dreier_coordination_agreement.pdf

Dreier Opinion

https://casetext.com/case/united-states-v-dreier-1

https://www.justice.gov/sites/default/files/usao-sdny/legacy/2015/03/25/Dreier%2C%20Marc%20Opinion%20%26%20Order.pdf

Petters Coordination Agreement

https://www.justice.gov/sites/default/files/usao-mn/legacy/2010/12/21/Coordination%20Agreement%20Final%20-%20executed.pdf

http://www.theponzibook.com/coordination_agreements/petters_coordination_agreement.pdf

Petters Order Declining Restitution

https://www.justice.gov/sites/default/files/usao-mn/legacy/2010/12/21/Declining%20to%20enter%20restitution%20order%206-3-10.pdf

For a summary of *United States v. Petters*, together with case documents, *see also* https://www.justice.gov/usao-mn/tom-petters-case

DeMiro Coordination Agreement

http://www.alloquor.com/theponzibook.com/coordination_agreements/demiro_coordination_agreement.pdf

Tri-Continental Coordination Agreement 1

http://www.alloquor.com/theponzibook.com/coordination_agreements/Tri-Continental_Exchange_Agreement_1.pdf

Tri-Continental Coordination Agreement 2

http://www.alloquor.com/theponzibook.com/coordination_agreements/Tri-Continental_Exchange_Agreement_2.pdf

Appendix H

Case Management Sample Order

UNITED STATES BANKRUPTCY COURT
FOR THE SOUTHERN DISTRICT OF NEW YORK

SECURITIES INVESTOR PROTECTION CORPORATION,
    Plaintiff-Applicant,
v.
BERNARD L. MADOFF INVESTMENT SECURITIES LLC,
    Defendant.
	Adversary Proceeding
	
	No. 08-01789-BRL

ORDER ON APPLICATION FOR AN ENTRY OF AN ORDER APPROVING FORM AND MANNER OF PUBLICATION AND MAILING OF NOTICES, SPECIFYING PROCEDURES FOR FILING, DETERMINATION, AND ADJUDICATION OF CLAIMS; AND PROVIDING OTHER RELIEF

An order having been entered on consent by the Honorable Louis L. Stanton, United States District Judge, on December 15, 2008 (the "Protective Order") (1) finding that the customers of Bernard L. Madoff Investment Securities LLC (the "Debtor") are in need of the protection afforded by the Securities Investor Protection Act, 15 U.S.C. §78aaa et seq. ("SIPA"), (2) appointing Irving H. Picard as Trustee (the "Trustee") and Baker & Hostetler LLP as counsel for the Trustee, and (3) removing the liquidation proceeding to this Court; and it appearing, as set forth in the Trustee's Application dated December 21, 2008 (the "Application"), that this Court is required by SIPA and the Bankruptcy Code to direct the giving of notice regarding, among other things, the commencement of this liquidation proceeding, the appointment of the Trustee and his counsel; the hearing on disinterestedness of the Trustee and his counsel; the meeting of creditors; and the Trustee having recommended procedures for resolution of customer claims and distributions; and it appearing that notice of the Application has been given to the Securities Investor Protection Corporation ("SIPC") and that no other notice need be given; no adverse interest having been represented, and sufficient cause appearing therefor, it is:

ORDERED, that the Application is granted; and it is further

ORDERED, that the Notice, explanatory letters, claim forms, and instructions appearing as Exhibits A, B, C, D, E, F, G and H to the Application, or substantially in that form, be, and they hereby are, authorized and approved, and shall be mailed by the Trustee to all former customers, broker-dealers, and other creditors of the Debtor, in conformance with this Order and in substantially the form appearing in those Exhibits, on or before January 9, 2008; and it is further

ORDERED, that the Trustee shall have the authority, on the advice and consent of SIPC, to amend these forms without further order of this Court; and it is further

ORDERED, that under 15 U.S.C. §78fff-2(a)(1), the Trustee be, and he hereby is, authorized and directed to cause the notice annexed as Exhibit A to the Application (the "Notice") to be published once in *The New York Times*, all editions; *The Wall Street Journal*, all editions; *The Financial Times*, all editions; *USA Today*, all editions; *Jerusalem Post*, all editions; *Ye'diot Achronot*, all editions, on or before January 9, 2008; and it is further

ORDERED, that under 15 U.S.C. §78fff-2(a)(1), the Trustee be, and he hereby is, authorized and directed to mail (a) a copy of the Notice, explanatory information, and claim form to each person who, from the books and records of the Debtor, appears to have been a customer of the Debtor with an open account during the twelve (12) month period prior to December 11, 2008, (b) a copy of the Notice, explanatory letter, and claim form to creditors other than customers, and (c) a copy of the Notice, explanatory letter and Series 300 Rules to broker-dealers, at the addresses of such customers, broker-dealers, and creditors as they appear on available books and records of the Debtor, and finding that such mailing complies with the Notice Provision; and it is further

ORDERED, that under 15 U.S.C. §78fff-2(a)(3), any claim of a customer for a net equity which is received by the Trustee after the expiration of sixty (60) days from the date of publication of the Notice need not be paid or satisfied in whole or in part out of customer property, and, to the extent such claim is satisfied from monies advanced by SIPC, it shall be satisfied in cash or securities (or both) as the Trustee may determine to be most economical to the estate; and it is further

ORDERED, that, pursuant to 15 U.S.C. §78fff-2(a)(2), all claims against the Debtor shall be filed with the Trustee; and it is further

ORDERED, that all claims against the Debtor shall be deemed properly filed only when received by the Trustee at Irving H. Picard, Esq., Trustee for Bernard L. Madoff Investment Securities LLC, Claims Processing Center, 2100 McKinney Ave., Suite 800, Dallas, TX 75201; and it is further

ORDERED, that February 4, 2009, at 10:00 a.m., at Courtroom 601 of the United States Bankruptcy Court, One Bowling Green, New York, New York, is fixed as the time and place for a hearing on the disinterestedness of the Trustee and his counsel, as required by 15 U.S.C. §78eee(b)(6)(B); and it is further

ORDERED, that objections, if any, to the appointment and retention of the Trustee or his counsel shall be in the form prescribed by the Federal Rules of Civil Procedure and shall be filed with the Court, preferably electronically (with a courtesy hard copy for Chambers) and a hard copy personally served upon Baker & Hostetler LLP, 45 Rockefeller Plaza, New York, NY 10111, Attention: David J. Sheehan, Esq. and Douglas E. Spelfogel, Esq., and the Securities Investor Protection Corporation, 805 Fifteenth Street, N.W., Suite 800, Washington, D.C. 20005-2215, Attention: Kevin Bell, on or before 12:00 noon on January 30, 2009; and it is further

ORDERED, that (a) the meeting of creditors required by Section 341(a) of the Bankruptcy Code, 11 U.S.C. §341(a), shall be held on February 20, 2009, at 10:00 a.m., at the Auditorium at the United States Bankruptcy Court, Southern District of New York, One Bowling Green, New York, New York 10004 and (b) the Trustee shall preside at such meeting of creditors for the purpose of examining the Debtor and any of its officers, directors or stockholders and conducting such other business as may properly come before such meeting; and it is further

ORDERED, that the Debtor, by any of its officers, directors, employees, agents or attorneys, shall comply with SIPA and the pertinent sections of the Bankruptcy Code, including, without limiting the generality of the foregoing, (a) by designating a person to appear and submit to examination under oath at the meeting of creditors under Section 341(a) of the Bankruptcy Code, and (b) by complying with the Debtor's duties under Section 521 of the Bankruptcy Code, 11 U.S.C. §521, i.e., (i) by timely filing the schedules of assets and liabilities, of executory contacts, of pending litigations and information about any other pertinent matters; (ii) timely filing a list of creditors, a schedule of assets and liabilities and a statement of financial affairs; (iii) cooperating with the Trustee as necessary to enable the Trustee to perform his duties; and (iv) surrendering forthwith to the Trustee all property of the Debtor's estate and any and all recorded information, including, but not limited to, books, documents, records, papers and computer; and it is further

ORDERED, that the Trustee be, and he hereby is, authorized to satisfy, within the limits provided by SIPA, those portions of any and all customer claims and accounts which agree with the Debtor's books and records, or are otherwise established to the satisfaction of the Trustee pursuant to 15 U.S.C. §78fff-2(b), provided that the Trustee believes that no reason exists for not satisfying such claims and accounts; and it is further

ORDERED, that the Trustee be, and he hereby is, authorized to satisfy such customer claims and accounts (i) by delivering to a customer entitled thereto "customer name securities," as defined in 15 U.S.C. §78*lll*(3); (ii) by satisfying a customer's "net equity" claim, as defined in 15 U.S.C. §78*lll*(11), by distributing on a ratable basis securities of the same class or series of an issue on hand *as* "customer property," as defined in 15 U.S.C. §78*lll*(4), and, if necessary, by distributing cash from such customer property or cash advanced by SIPC, or purchasing securities for customers as set forth in 15 U.S.C. §78fff-2(d) within the limits set forth in 15 U.S.C. §78fff-3(a); and/or (iii) by completing contractual commitments where required pursuant to 15 U.S.C. §78fff-2(e) and SIPC's Series 300 Rules, 17 C.F.R. §300.300 et seq., promulgated pursuant thereto; and it is further

ORDERED, that with respect to claims for "net equity," as defined in 15 U.S.C. § 78*lll*(11), the Trustee be, and he hereby is, authorized to satisfy claims out of funds made available to the Trustee by SIPC notwithstanding the fact that there has not been any showing or determination that there are sufficient funds of the Debtor available to satisfy such claims; and it is further

ORDERED, that with respect to claims relating to, or net equities based upon, securities of a class and series of an issuer which are ascertainable from the books and records of the Debtor or are otherwise established to the satisfaction of the Trustee, the Trustee be, and he hereby is, authorized to deliver securities of such class and series if and to the extent available to satisfy such claims in whole or in part, with partial deliveries to be made pro rata to the greatest extent considered practicable by the Trustee; and it is further

ORDERED, that with respect to any customer claim in which there is disagreement between such claimant and the Trustee with regard to satisfaction of a claim, the Trustee be, and he hereby is, authorized to enter into a settlement with such claimant with the approval of SIPC, and without further order of the Court, provided that any obligations incurred by the Debtor estate under the settlement are ascertainable from the books and records of the Debtor or are otherwise established to the satisfaction of the Trustee; and it is further

ORDERED, that with respect to customer claims which disagree with the Debtor's books and records and which are not resolved by settlement, the following procedures shall apply to resolve such controverted claims:

- A. The Trustee shall notify such claimant by mail of his determination that the claim is disallowed, in whole or in part, and the reason therefor, in a written form substantially conforming to Exhibit G to the Application.
- B. If the claimant desires to oppose the determination, the claimant shall be required to file with this Court, preferably electronically, and a hard copy with the Trustee a written statement setting forth in detail the basis for the opposition, together with copies of any documents in support of such opposition, within thirty (30) days of the date on which the Trustee mails his determination to the claimant. If the claimant fails to file an opposition as hereinabove required, the Trustee's determination shall be deemed approved by the Court and binding on the claimant.
- C. Following receipt by the Trustee of an opposition by a claimant, the Trustee shall obtain a date and time for a hearing before this Court on the controverted claim and shall notify the claimant in writing of the date, time, and place of such hearing.
- D. If a claimant or his counsel fails to appear at the hearing on the controverted claim, then the Trustee's determination may be deemed confirmed by this Court and binding on the claimant.

ORDERED, that the bar date for all claims is six (6) months from the date of publication of Notice and mailing that complies with the Notice Provisions ("Publication Date"), and the bar date for receiving the maximum possible protection for customer claims under SIPA is sixty (60) days from the Publication Date; and it is further

ORDERED, that under 15 U.S.C. §78fff-1(c) the Trustee shall file a progress report with this Court within six (6) months after publication of the Notice of Commencement, and shall file interim reports every six (6) months thereafter; and it is further

ORDERED, that the requirement of Local Bankruptcy Rule 9013-1(b) regarding the filing of a separate memorandum of law is waived.

Dated: December 23, 2008
    New York, New York

                                 /s/Burton R. Lifland
                                 BURTON R. LIFLAND
                                 UNITED STATES BANKRUPTCY JUDGE

Appendix I
Links to Related Materials

(i) United States Department of Justice Forfeiture Program
Asset Forfeiture Program, US Dep't of Justice, https://www.justice.gov/afp
Asset Forfeiture Policy Manual, US Dep't of Justice, https://www.justice.gov/criminal-afmls/file/839521/download
Asset Forfeiture Program, Participants and Roles, US Dep't of Justice, http://justice.gov/afp/

(ii) United States Trustee Manual
United States Trustee Program Policy and Practices Manual, US Dep't of Justice, https://www.justice.gov/ust/united-states-trustee-program-policy-and-practices-manual

(iii) Federal Judicial Center Educational Video
Asset Forfeiture and Bankruptcy Case Coordination, available at Federal Judiciary Channel (Jan. 16, 2014), https://www.youtube.com/watch?v=kQlPZLpg6HE

About the Editors and Co-Authors

Jaime L. Dodge is the Founding Director of the Institute for Complex Litigation and Mass Claims at Emory Law School.

Hon. Lisa Hill Fenning recently retired as a partner in Arnold & Porter's bankruptcy and corporate reorganization practice group, based in the Los Angeles office. From 1985 to 2000, Ms. Fenning served as a US Bankruptcy Judge for the Central District of California, and then as a mediator with JAMS. Before her appointment to the bench, she was a litigator and bankruptcy practitioner with firms in Chicago and Los Angeles. Ms. Fenning graduated from Yale Law School in 1974. A fellow of the American College of Bankruptcy, Ms. Fenning served on numerous boards, commissions, and committees, including the boards of the American Bankruptcy Institute, the National Conference of Bankruptcy Judges, and the Los Angeles Bankruptcy Forum. She chaired the board of NCBJ's Endowment for Education and the Ninth Circuit Council for the Board of Regents of the American College of Bankruptcy. As president of the National Conference of Women's Bar Associations, she urged the creation of and then became a founding member of both the ABA's Commission on Women in the Profession and the California State Bar's Committee on Women in the Law. She has authored many articles and contributed to several books on bankruptcy and related issues.

Karen M. Gebbia earned her JD, magna cum laude, from Georgetown University Law Center, where she served on the American Criminal Law Review. She practiced corporate restructuring and commercial transactions law for ten years before teaching bankruptcy, commercial transactions, and other courses as a full-time law professor for twenty years. She was founding chair of the American Bar Association's cross-sectional Working Group and Subcommittee on Asset Forfeiture and Bankruptcy, and held that position for seven years. She has frequently lectured, presented symposia and programs, and written published materials on the intersections between asset forfeiture and bankruptcy.

Jane Lyle Hord (Ghaelian) is a 2012 graduate of the University of Kentucky School of Law and member of the Kentucky Bar.

Henry C. Kevane has represented both debtors and creditors in bankruptcy matters nationwide for over thirty years. He is the managing partner of the San Francisco office of Pachulski Stang Ziehl & Jones LLP. Mr. Kevane has worked with clients from a wide variety of industries, including the debtors in the Chapter 11 cases of Deltagen, Yipes Communications and Worlds of Wonder, and the creditors' committees in the Chapter 11 cases of SeraCare Life Sciences, America West Airlines and Guy F. Atkinson Company. He has also participated in several Chapter 9 municipal bankruptcy cases, including the Mendocino Coast Health Care District, County of Orange, Adair County Hospital District (Kentucky), West Contra Costa Healthcare District and Palm Drive Health Care District. Mr. Kevane has written and lectured on numerous cross-border, intellectual property, federal asset forfeiture and municipal restructuring topics. He is an author of the book CHAPTER 9 BANKRUPTCY STRATEGIES published in 2011 by Thomson Reuters/Aspatore and also contributed to the book DEBTOR-IN POSSESSION FINANCING: FUNDING A CHAPTER 11 CASE published in 2012 by the American Bankruptcy Institute. In 2015, he was inducted as a Fellow in the American College of Bankruptcy. He is a past chair of two committees of the State Bar of California, the Insolvency Law Committee of the Business Law Section (1995–1999) and the Committee on Federal Courts (1996–2001). Mr. Kevane is a graduate of Brown University and Southwestern Law School. He is a member of the Board of Directors and the Treasurer of the Ocean Avenue Association, a California public benefit corporation.

Mark E. Leipold is chair of Gould & Ratner LLP's Corporate Practice. Mark Leipold leverages his extensive experience in distressed businesses and insolvency to advise on mergers and acquisitions, with specific expertise in distressed and value-added transactions and debt purchases, corporate restructuring, and secured lending transactions. He has taught secured transactions at DePaul University College of Law and co-taught In the Real Estate master's degree program on real estate and bankruptcy at John Marshall Law School. Mark is an active member of the Business Bankruptcy Committee of the American Bar Association's Business Section. Currently, he co-chairs the Trustee and Examiner Subcommittee.

Miriam Weismann, JD, LLM, is a Professor of Business Law and Tax at Florida International University. She practiced law for almost 30 years and was appointed by the President as the United States Attorney for the Southern District of Illinois. Her most recent book is *Money Laundering: Legislation, Regulation and Enforcement*.

Sarah N. Welling is the William L. Matthews, Jr. Professor of Law and an Ashland-Spears Distinguished Research Professor of Law at the University of Kentucky, where she teaches Criminal Law, Federal Criminal Law, and Criminal Procedure. Her scholarship focuses on federal criminal law, particularly money laundering. Her most recent books include Wright & Welling, *Federal Practice and Procedure* (formerly known as Wright & Miller), Volumes 3 and 3A (4th ed. 2010), and *Federal Criminal Law and Related Actions: Crimes, RICO, Forfeiture and the False Claims Act*, a two-volume co-authored treatise. Professor Welling is a member of the American Law Institute and a Fellow of the American Bar Association. She holds a BA, cum laude, from the University of Wisconsin, and a JD, with high distinction, from the University of Kentucky.

Adam S. Zimmerman is a Professor of Law and Gerald Rosen Fellow at Loyola Law School in Los Angeles, where he teaches Tort Law, Administrative Law, Mass Tort Law, and Complex Litigation. His scholarship explores the way class action attorneys, regulatory agencies and criminal prosecutors provide justice to large groups of people through overlapping systems of tort law, administrative law and criminal law. Professor Zimmerman holds a BA from University of the California, Berkeley, and a JD from Georgetown University Law Center.